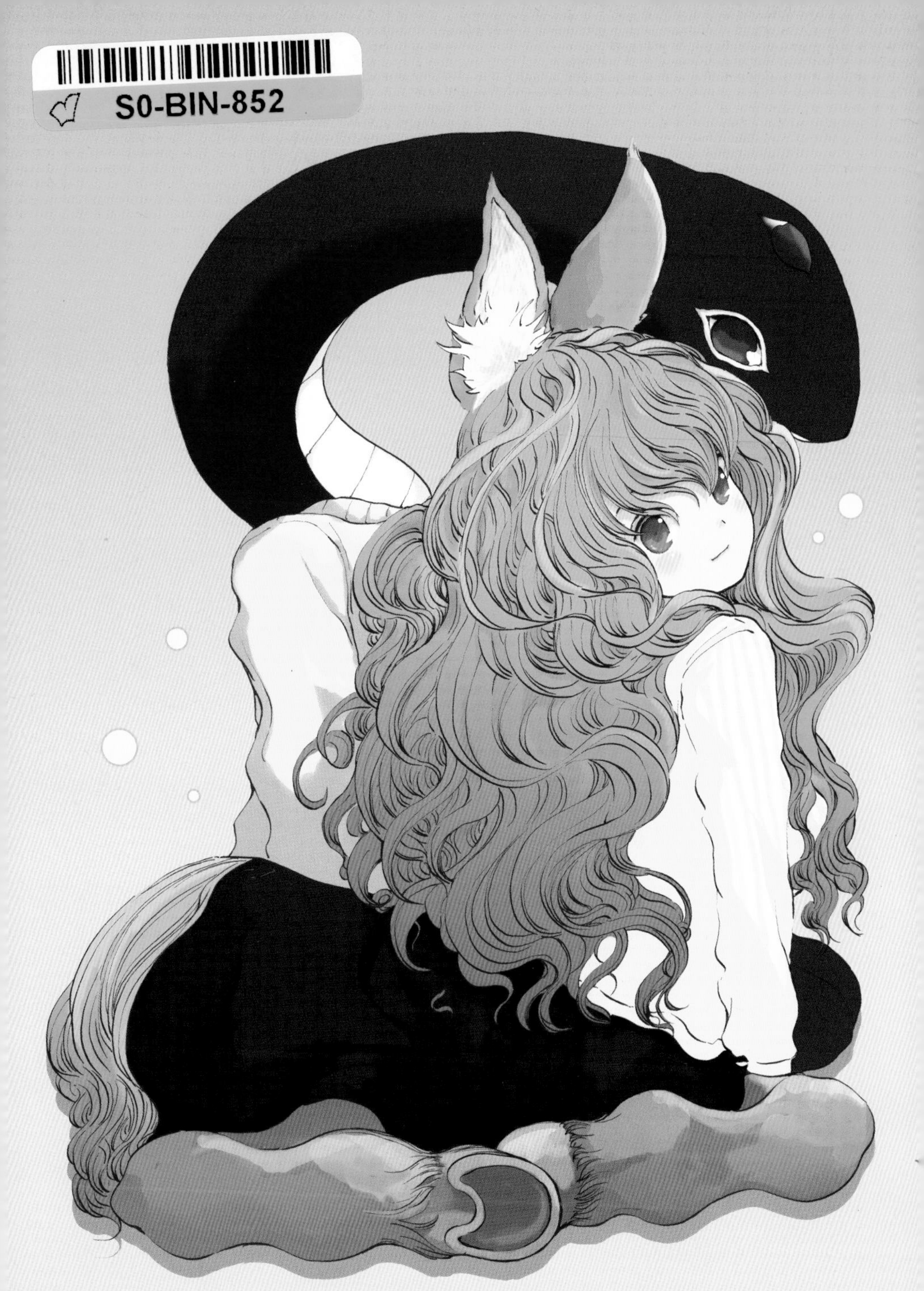

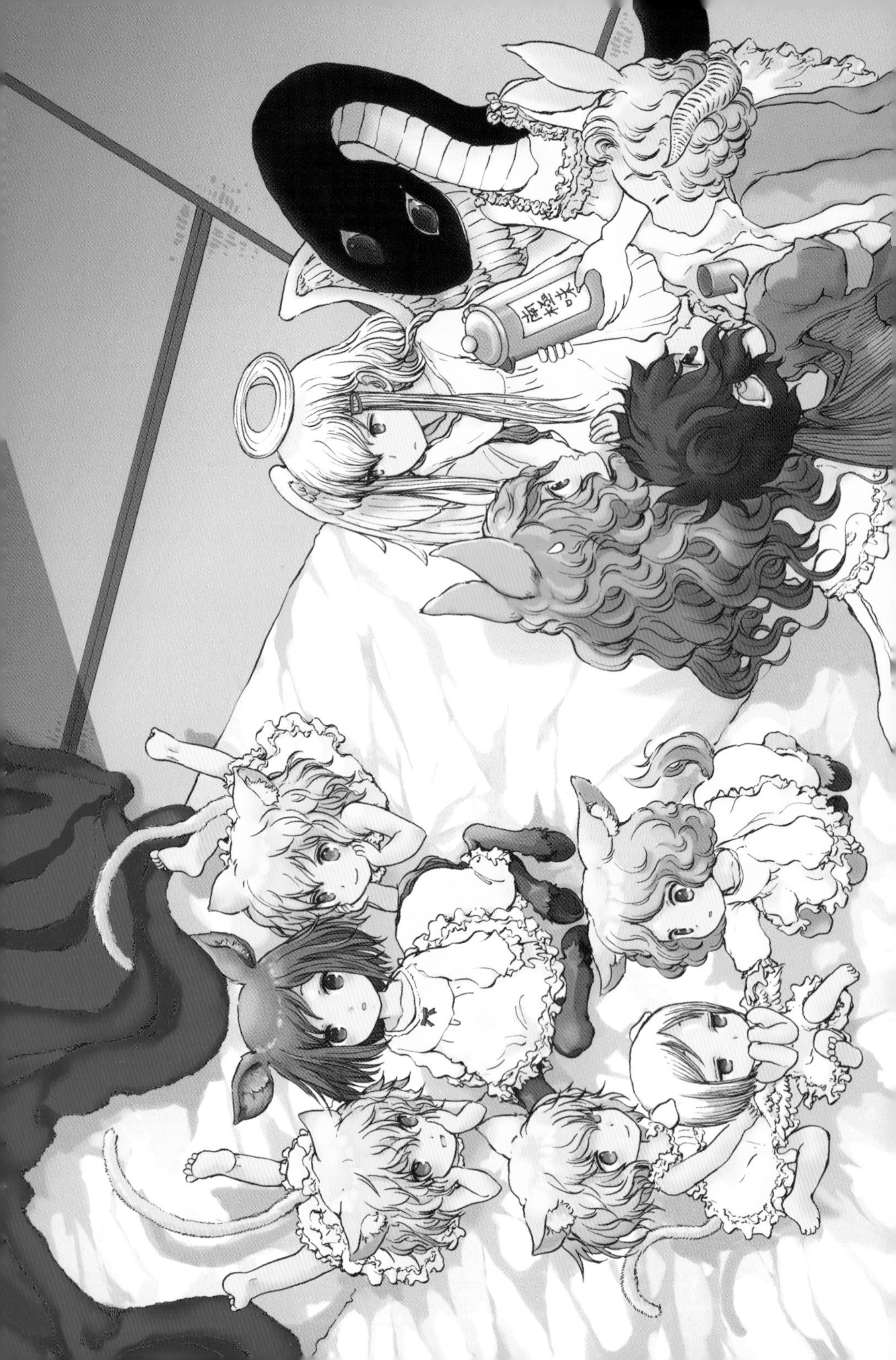

...as the Syrian military continues to strengthen its offensive...

SPLASH

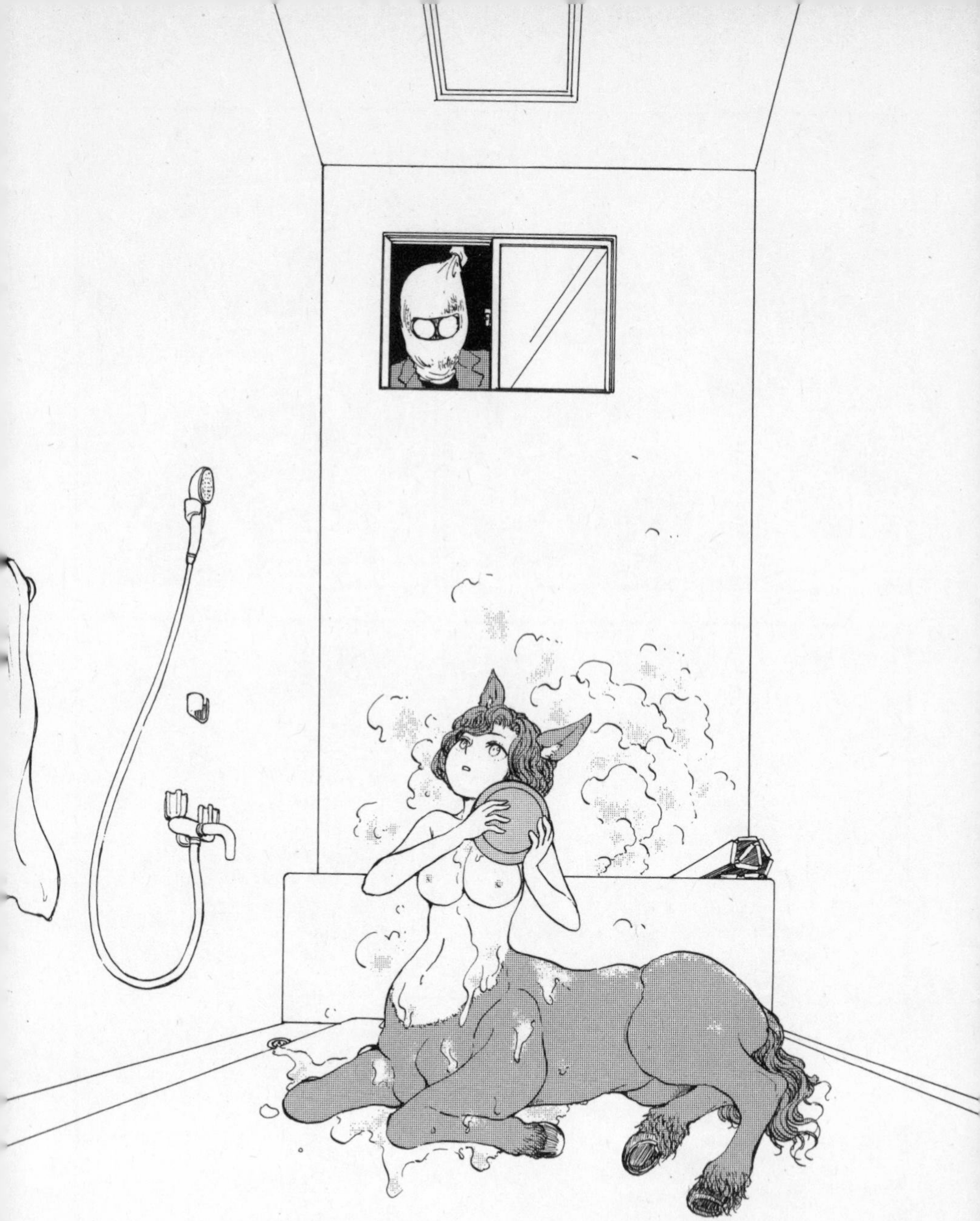

CHAPTER 30

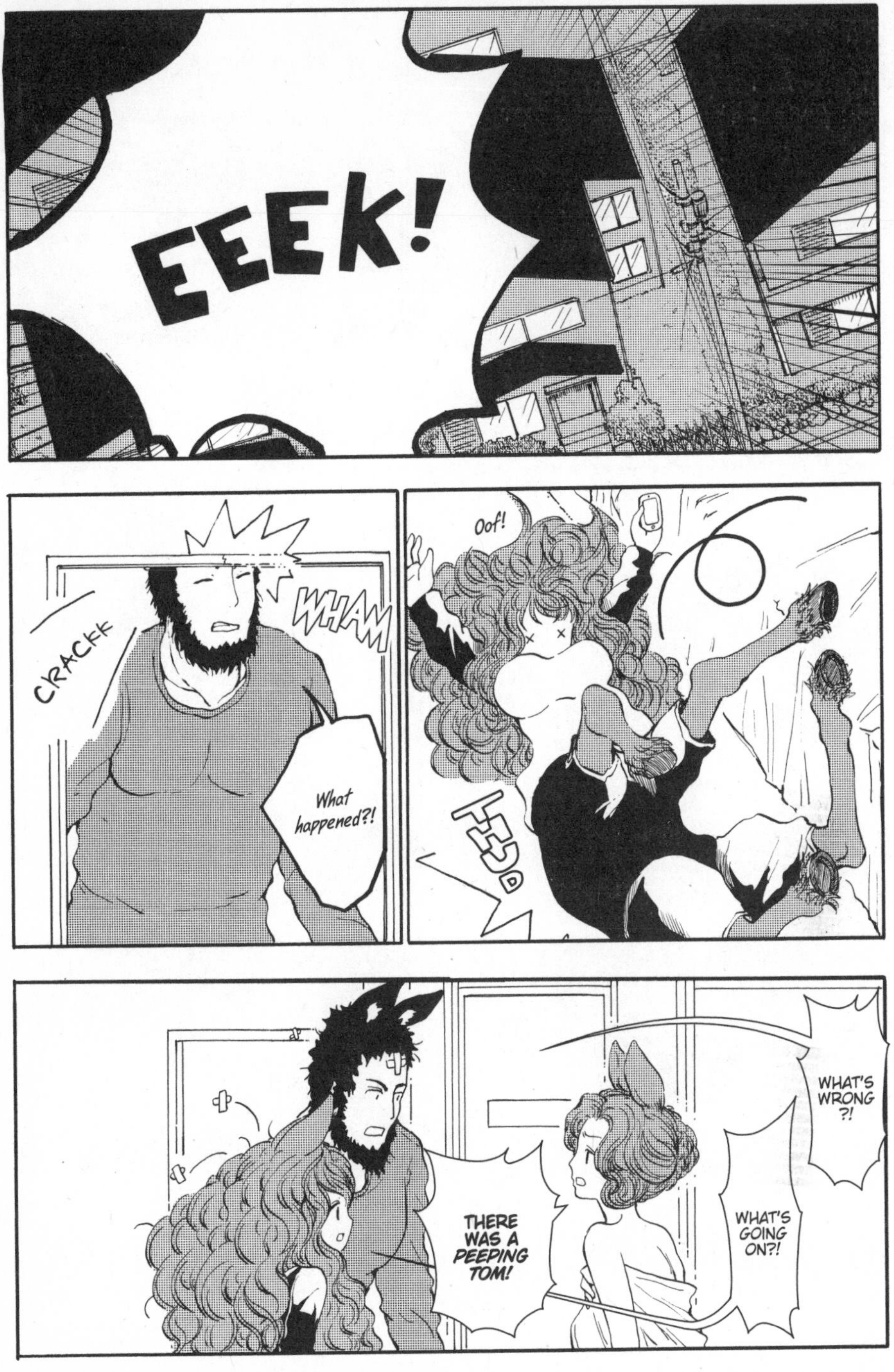
EEEK!
Oof!
THUD
WHAM
CRACKK
What happened?!
WHAT'S WRONG?!
WHAT'S GOING ON?!
THERE WAS A PEEPING TOM!

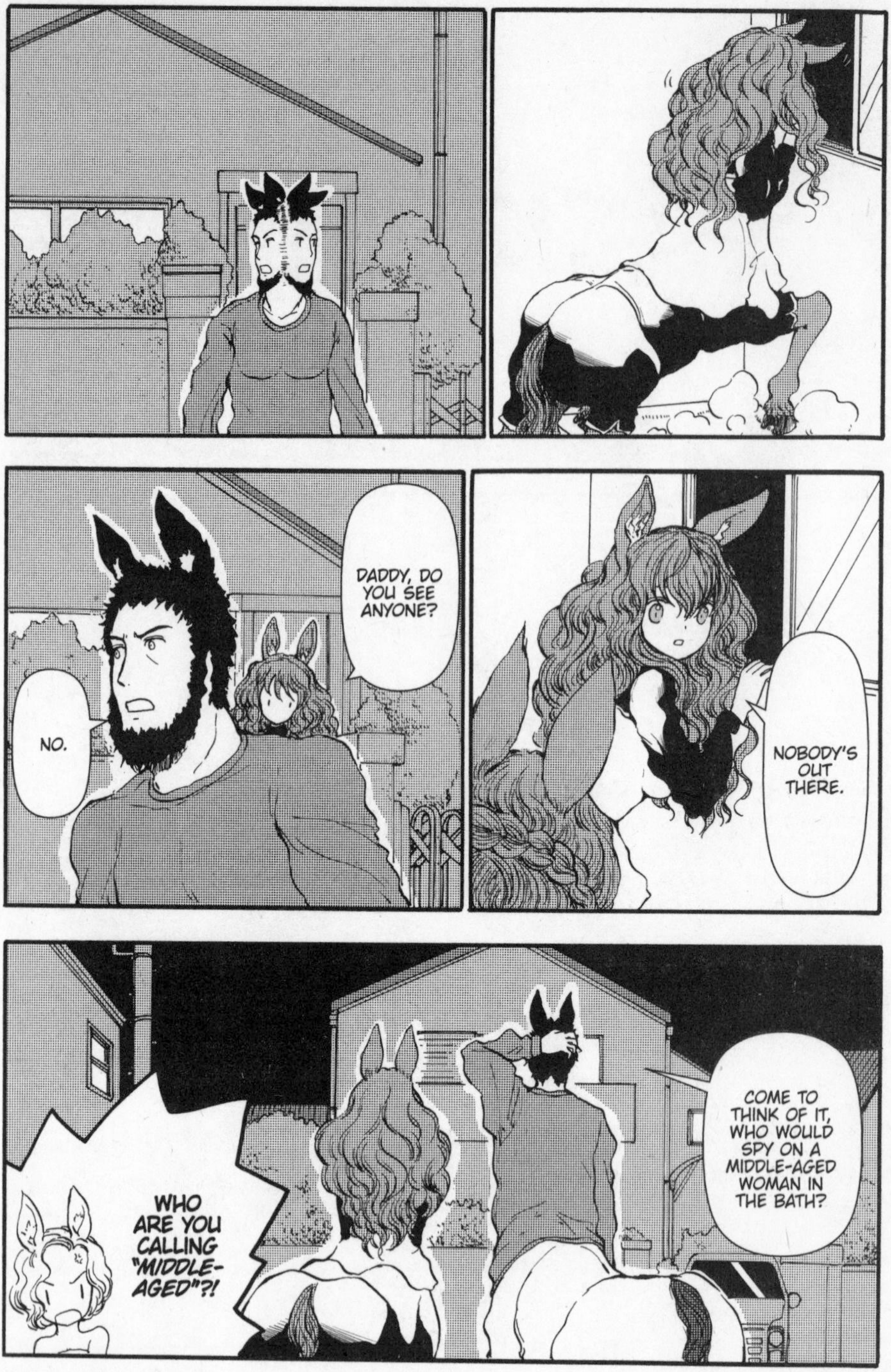
DADDY, DO YOU SEE ANYONE?
NO.
NOBODY'S OUT THERE.
COME TO THINK OF IT, WHO WOULD SPY ON A MIDDLE-AGED WOMAN IN THE BATH?
WHO ARE YOU CALLING "MIDDLE-AGED"?!

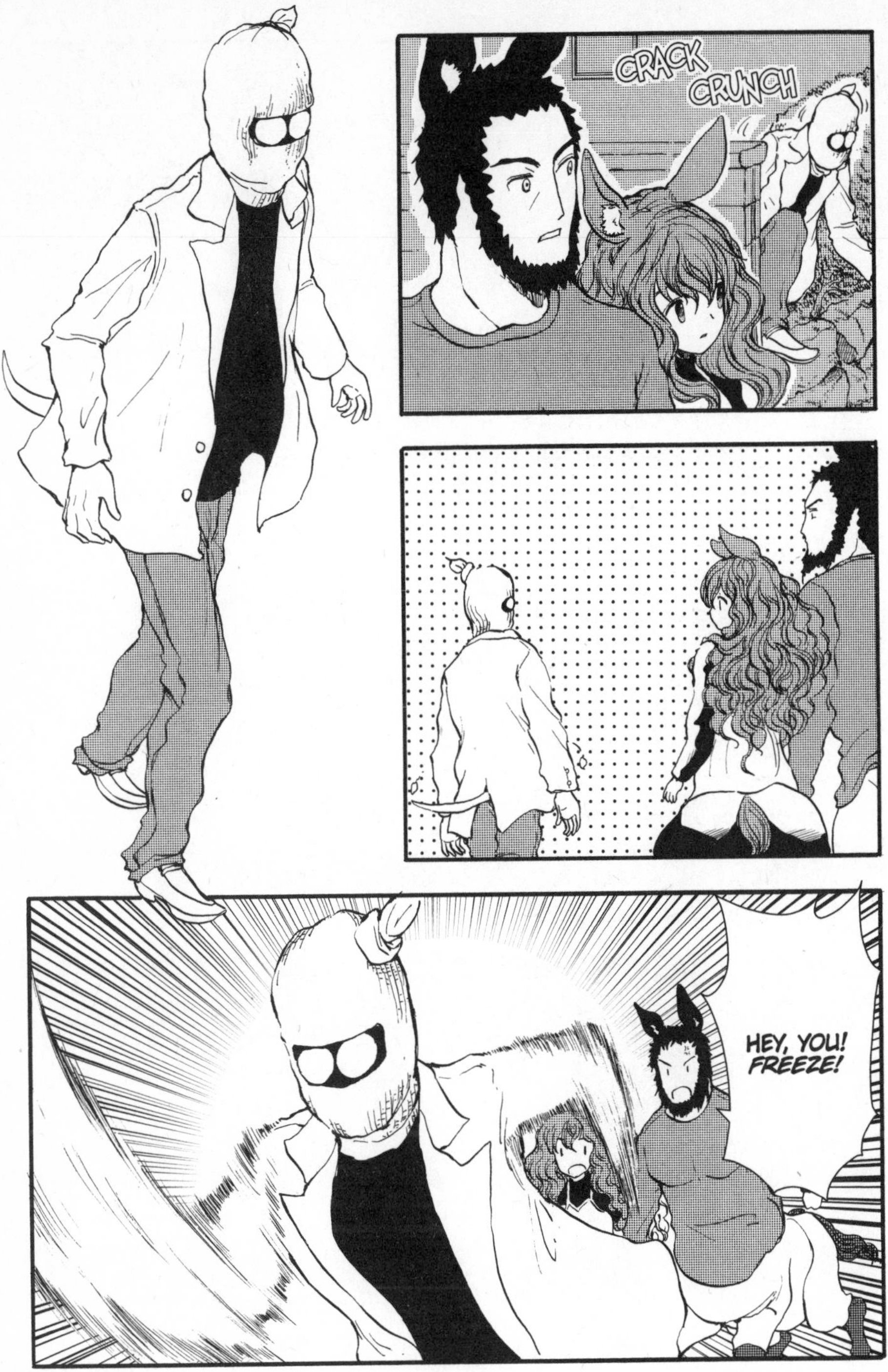
CRACK
CRUNCH
HEY, YOU! FREEZE!

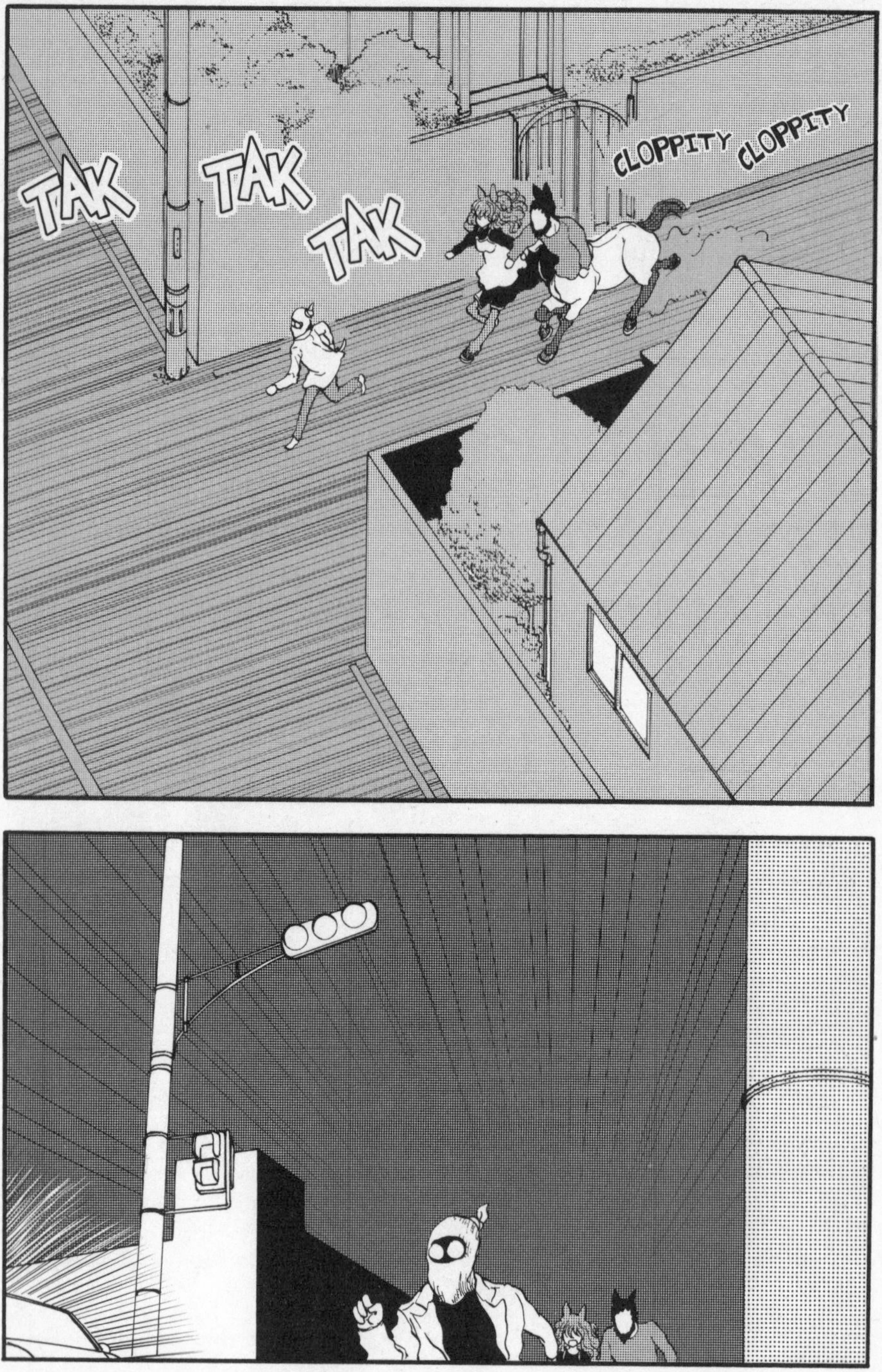
CLOPPITY CLOPPITY
TAK TAK
TAK

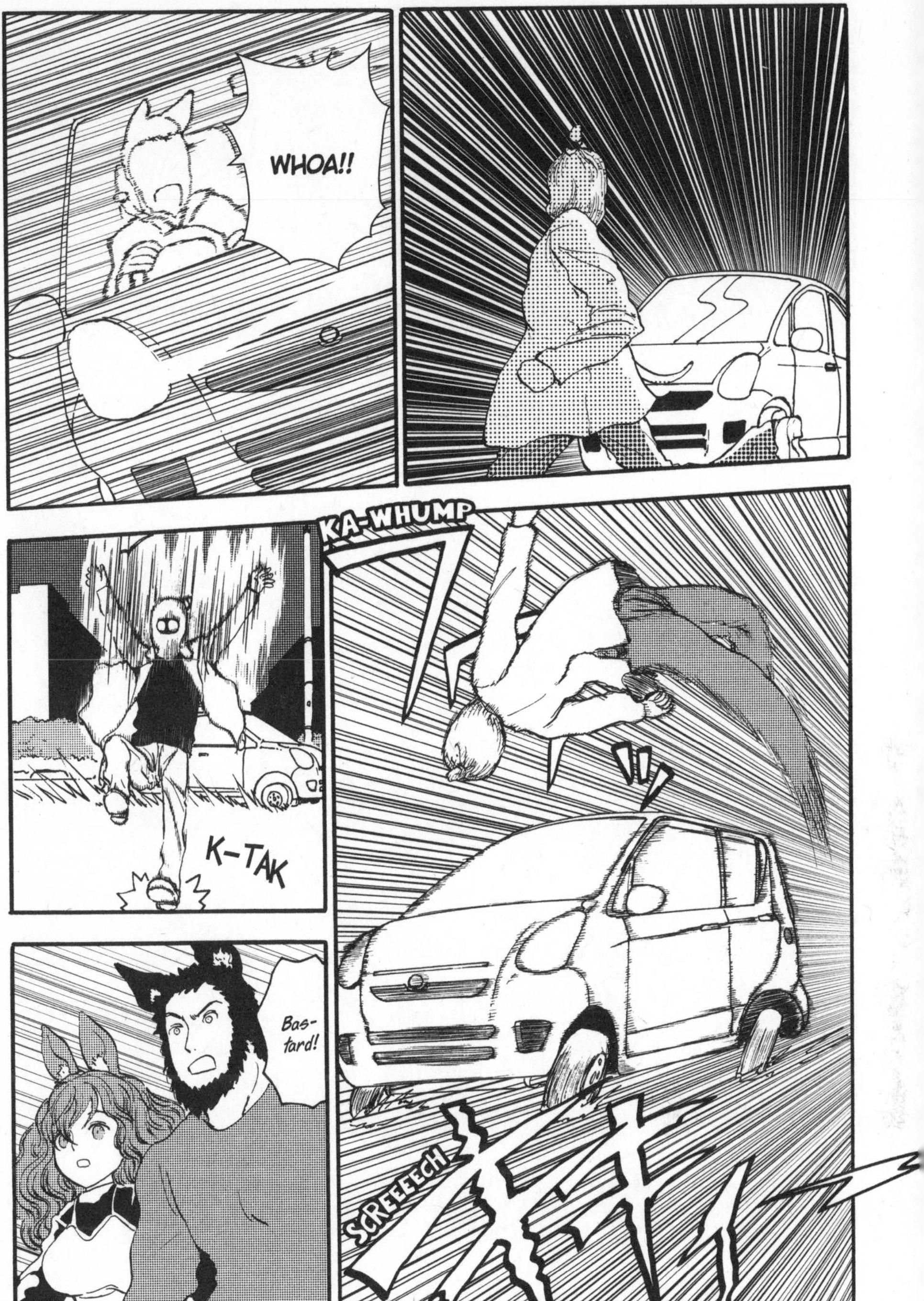
WHOA!!
KA-WHUMP
SCREEEECH
K-TAK
Bas-
tard!

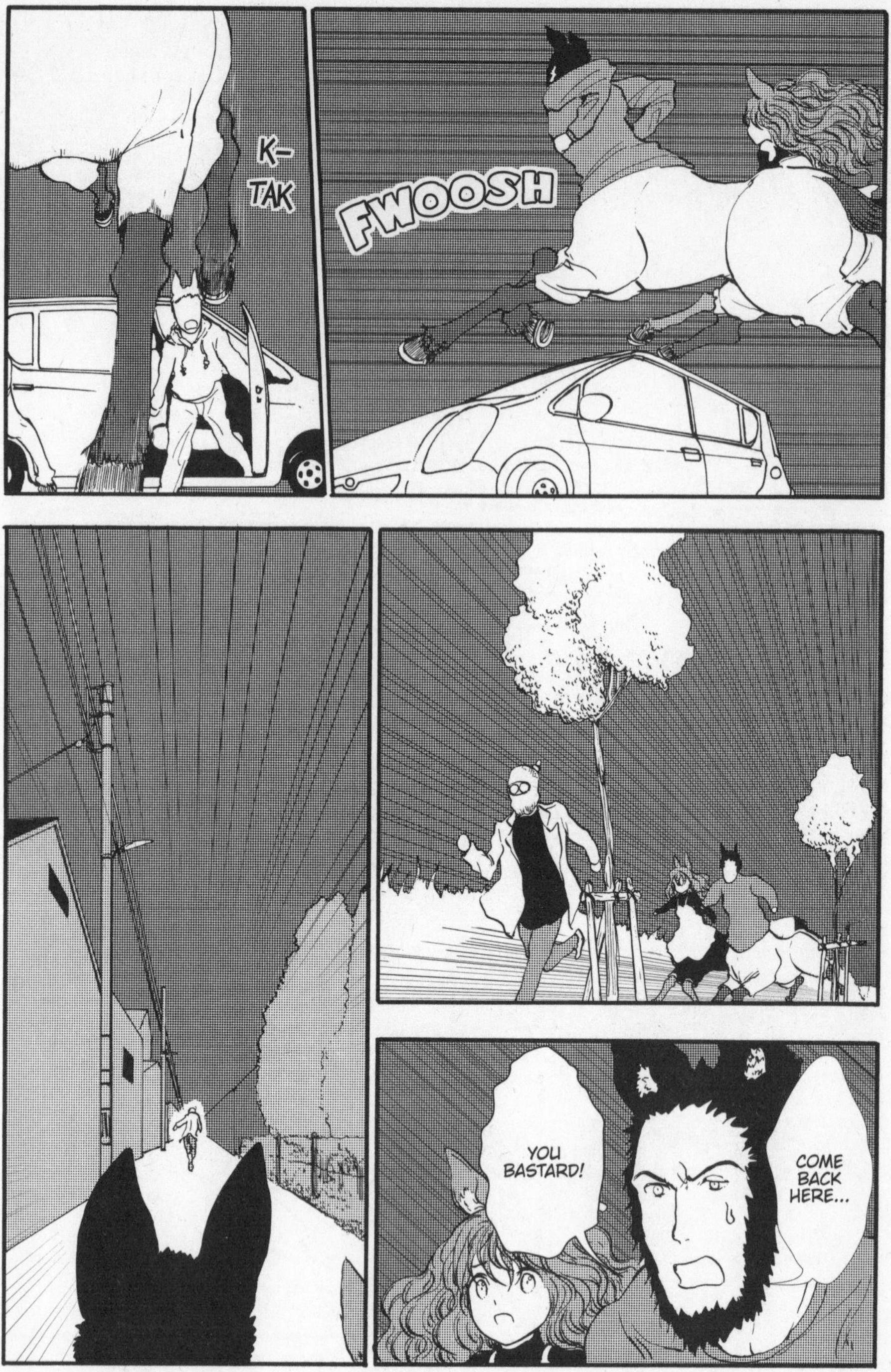
FWOOSH
K-
TAK
COME BACK HERE...
YOU BASTARD!

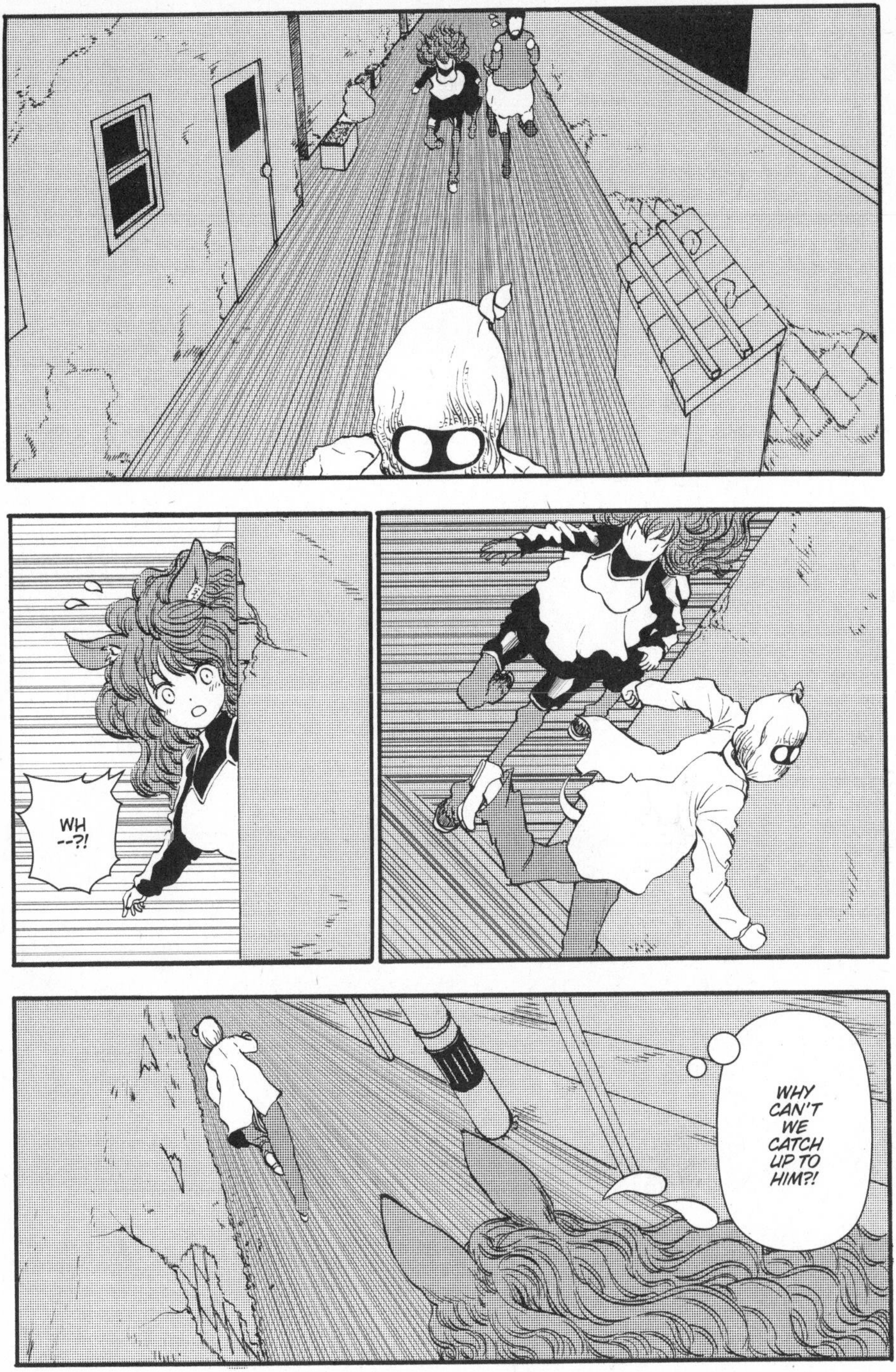
WH--?!
WHY CAN'T WE CATCH UP TO HIM?!

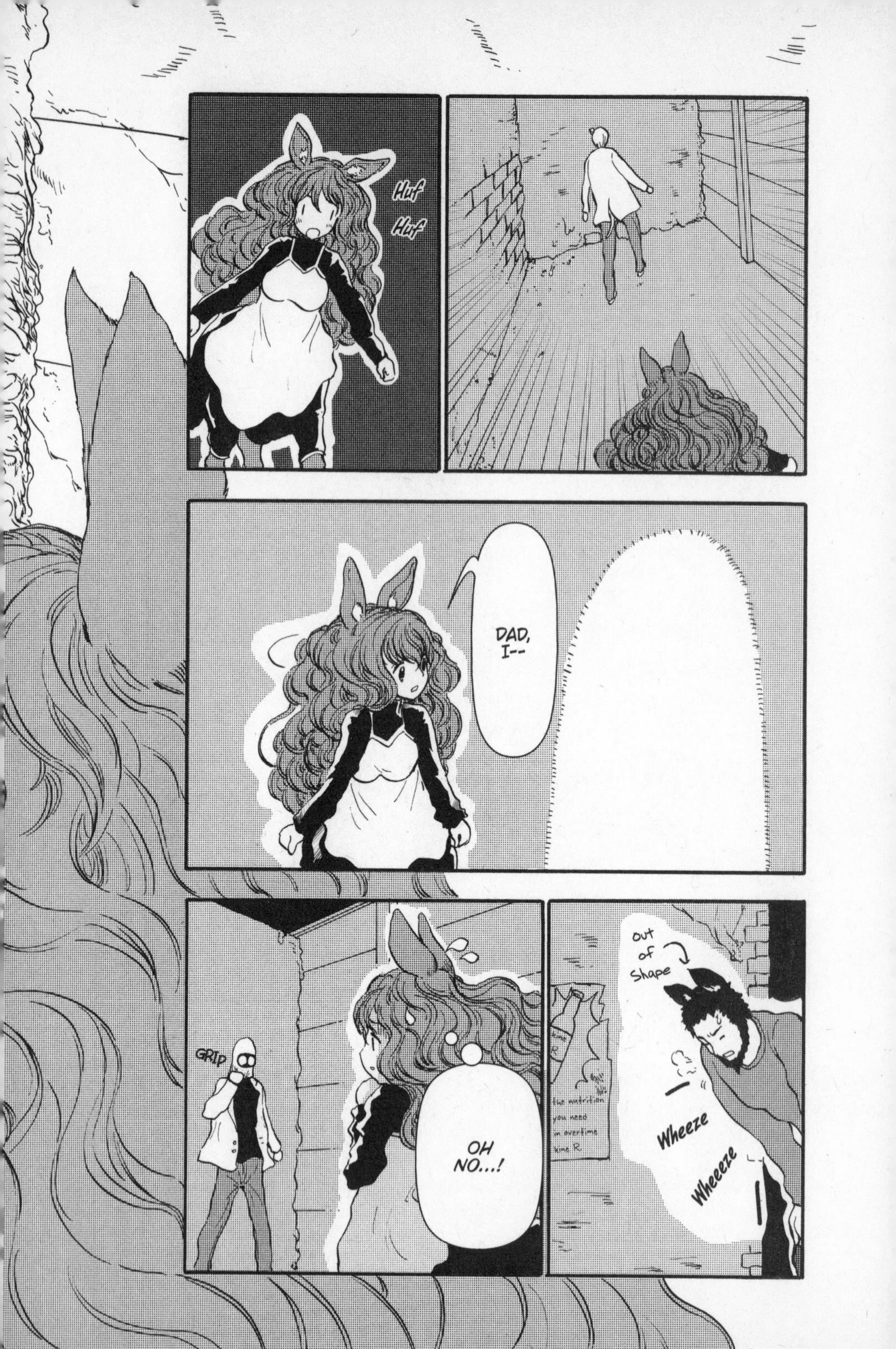
Huf
Huf
DAD, I--
Out of Shape
Wheeze
Wheeeze
OH NO...!
GRIP

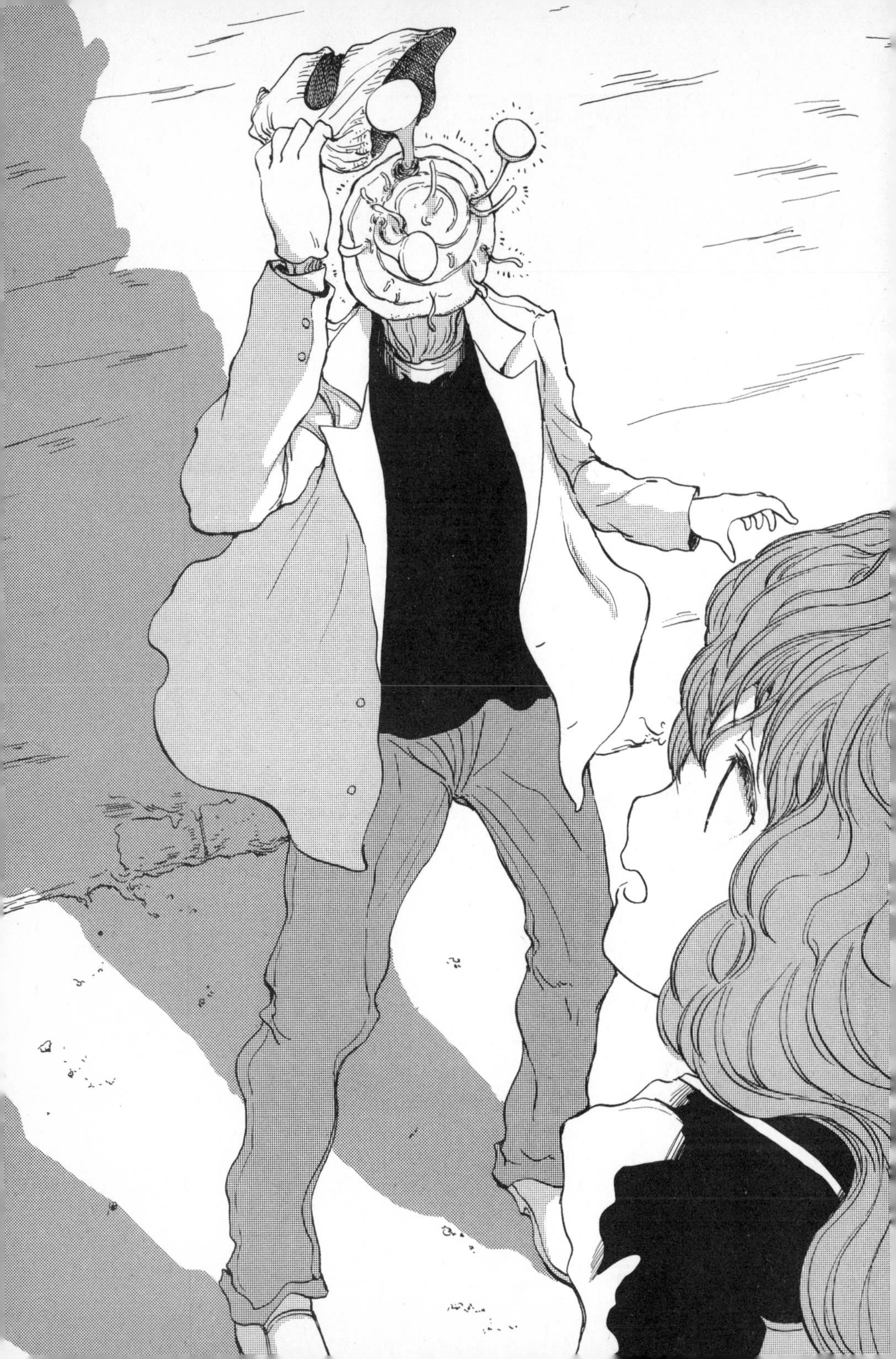

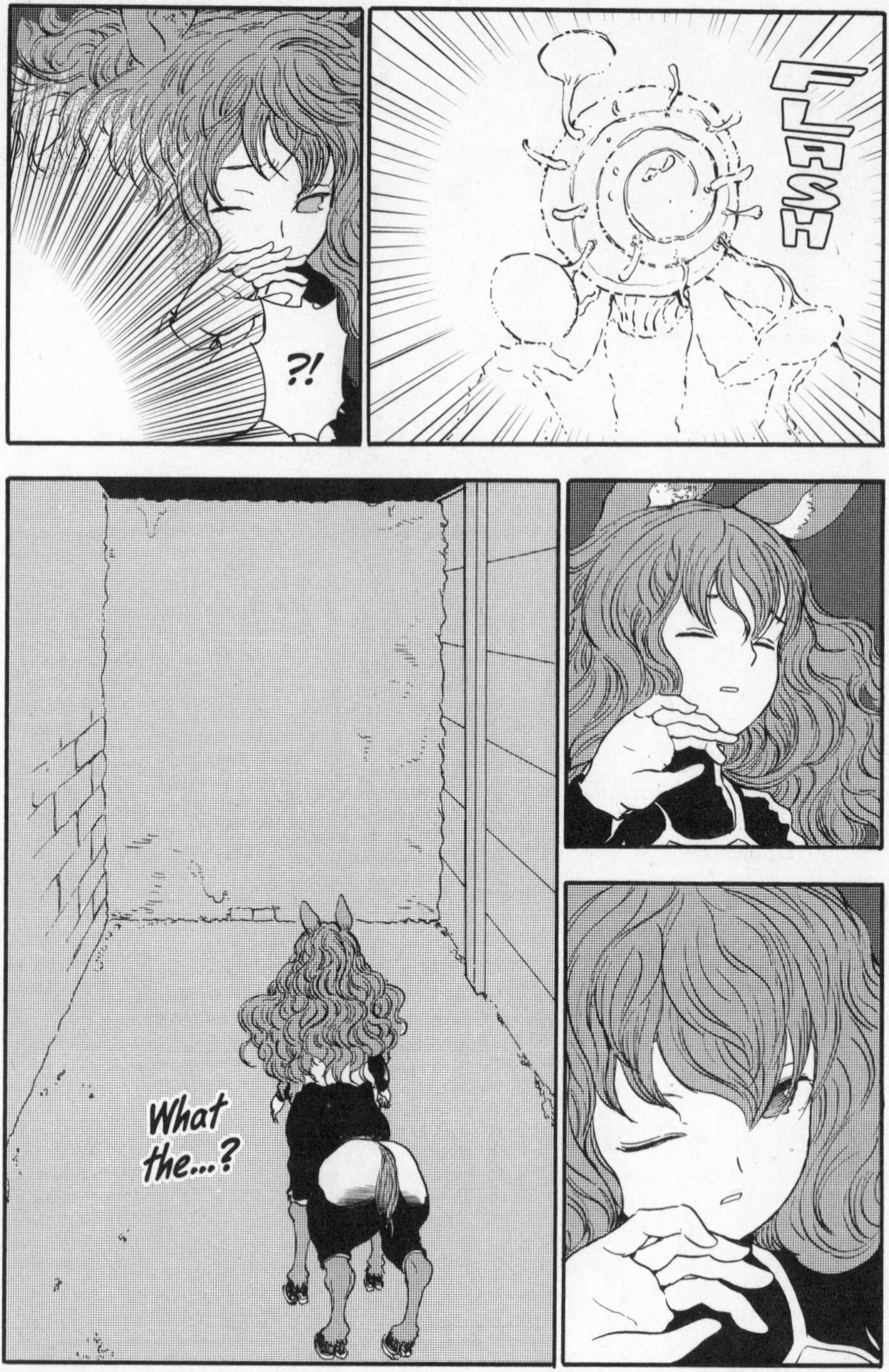
FLASH
?!
What the...?

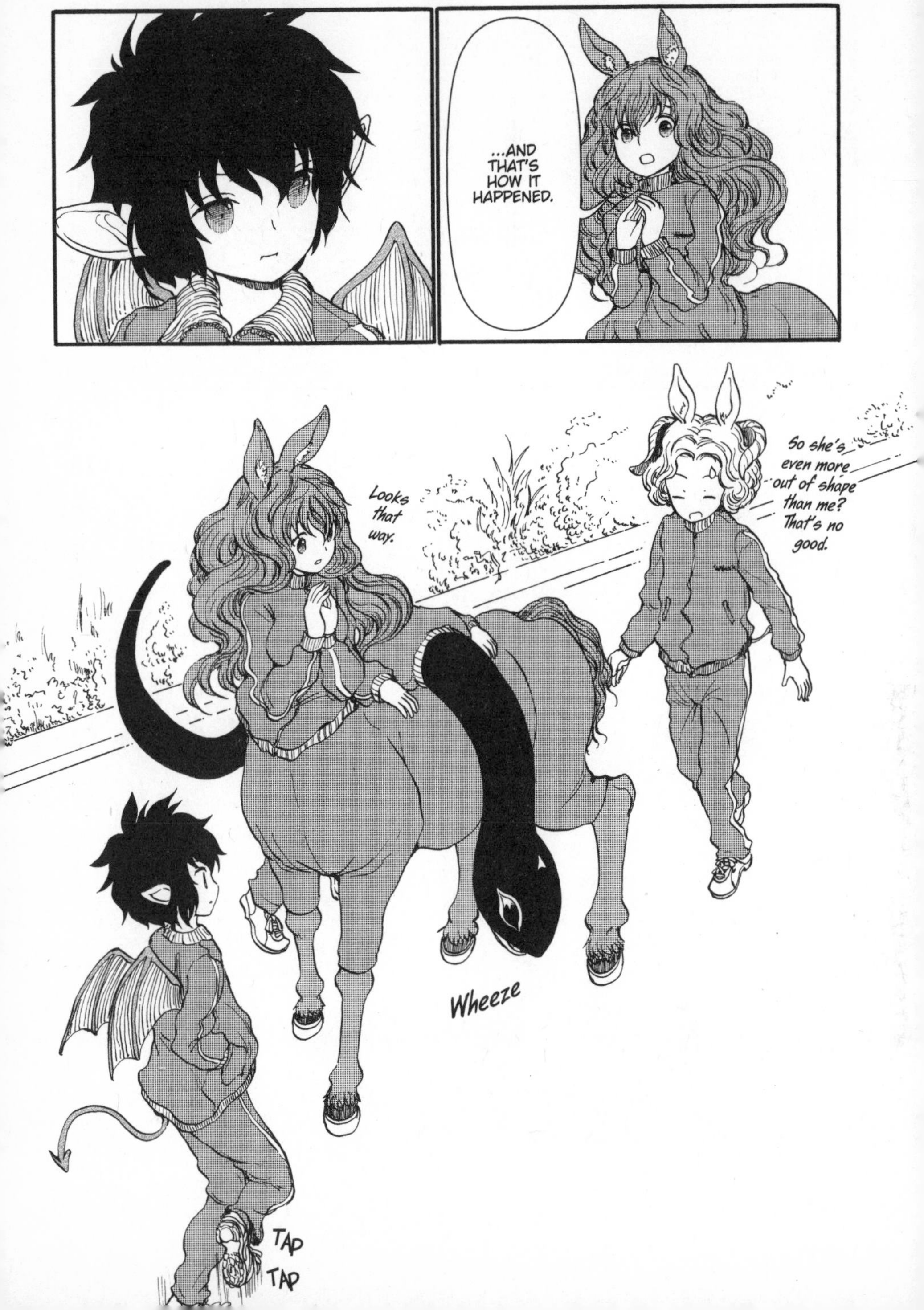
...AND THAT'S HOW IT HAPPENED.
So she's even more out of shape than me? That's no good.
Looks that way.
Wheeze
TAP TAP

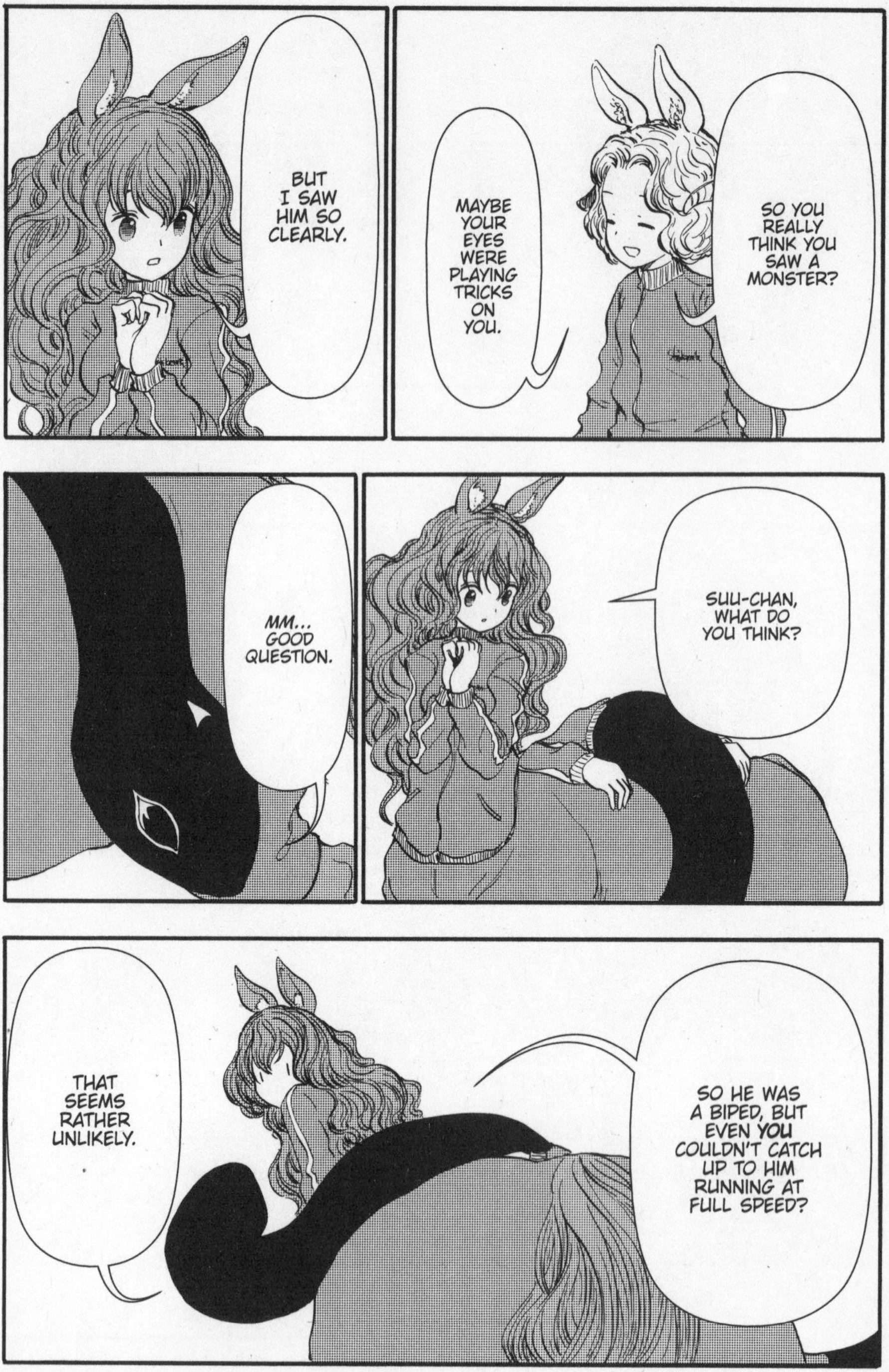
SO YOU REALLY THINK YOU SAW A MONSTER?
MAYBE YOUR EYES WERE PLAYING TRICKS ON YOU.
BUT I SAW HIM SO CLEARLY.
SUU-CHAN, WHAT DO YOU THINK?
MM... GOOD QUESTION.
SO HE WAS A BIPED, BUT EVEN **YOU** COULDN'T CATCH UP TO HIM RUNNING AT FULL SPEED?
THAT SEEMS RATHER UNLIKELY.

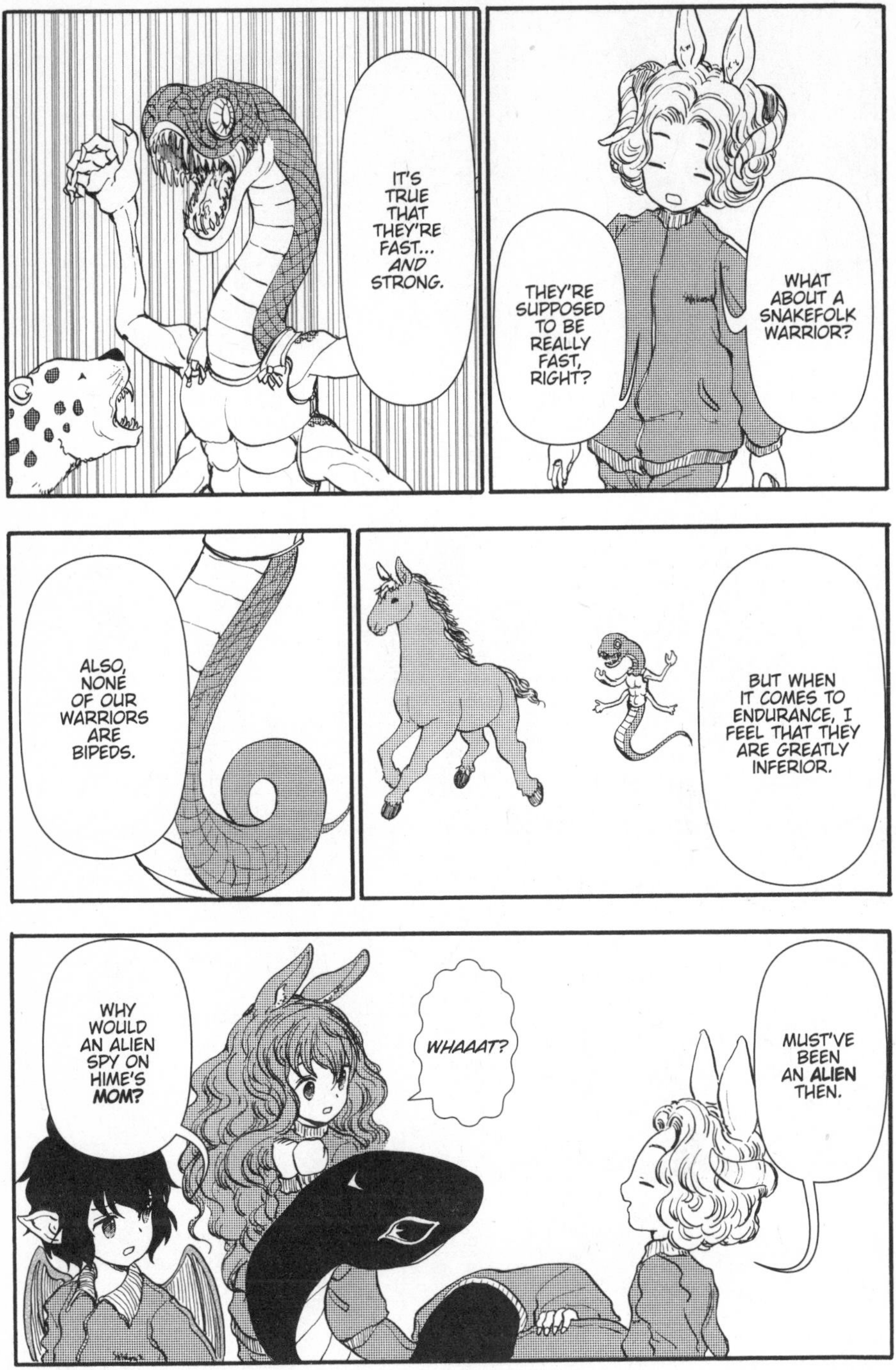
WHAT ABOUT A SNAKEFOLK WARRIOR?
THEY'RE SUPPOSED TO BE REALLY FAST, RIGHT?
IT'S TRUE THAT THEY'RE FAST... *AND* STRONG.
BUT WHEN IT COMES TO ENDURANCE, I FEEL THAT THEY ARE GREATLY INFERIOR.
ALSO, NONE OF OUR WARRIORS ARE BIPEDS.
MUST'VE BEEN AN **ALIEN** THEN.
WHAAAT?
WHY WOULD AN ALIEN SPY ON HIME'S **MOM**?

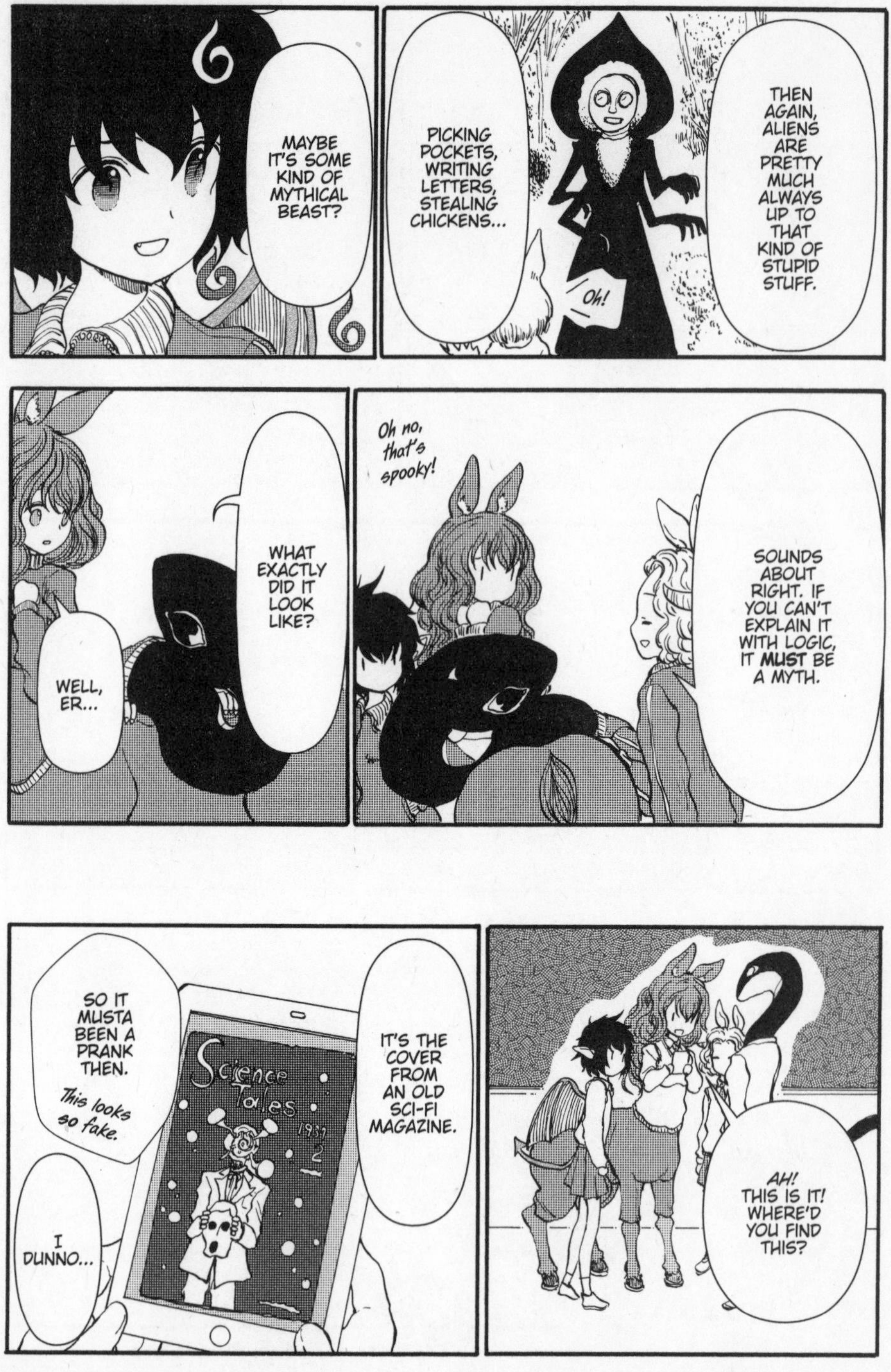
THEN AGAIN, ALIENS ARE PRETTY MUCH ALWAYS UP TO THAT KIND OF STUPID STUFF.
Oh!
PICKING POCKETS, WRITING LETTERS, STEALING CHICKENS...
MAYBE IT'S SOME KIND OF MYTHICAL BEAST?
SOUNDS ABOUT RIGHT. IF YOU CAN'T EXPLAIN IT WITH LOGIC, IT **MUST** BE A MYTH.
Oh no, that's spooky!
WHAT EXACTLY DID IT LOOK LIKE?
WELL, ER...
AH! THIS IS IT! WHERE'D YOU FIND THIS?
IT'S THE COVER FROM AN OLD SCI-FI MAGAZINE.
Science Tales
SO IT MUSTA BEEN A PRANK THEN.
This looks so fake.
I DUNNO...

A Centaur's Life

GENETICS MADE EASY: LESSON 1
WHAT IS HEREDITY?

HEREDITY IS THE PHENOMENON BY WHICH THE CHARACTERISTICS OF PARENTS ARE PASSED ON TO OFFSPRING. THE CHILD OF A FROG IS OF COURSE A FROG. LIKEWISE, THAT OF A TREE FROG IS A TREE FROG; THAT OF A SPOTTED FROG IS A SPOTTED FROG. AS A PERHAPS MORE RELATABLE EXAMPLE, CONSIDER HOW KIDS' FACES TEND TO RESEMBLE THOSE OF THEIR PARENTS OR BROTHERS AND SISTERS. IN MOST CASES, THEY ALSO TEND TO SHARE THE SAME BODY TYPE AS ONE OF THEIR PARENTS. HOW THESE CHARACTERISTICS ARE PASSED DOWN IS FAMOUSLY EXPLAINED BY MENDEL'S LAWS. WE WON'T WRITE THEM ALL HERE, BUT SUFFICE IT TO SAY THAT HEREDITY IS GOVERNED BY RULES. GENES ACT AS THE INTERMEDIARY WHICH MAKES HEREDITY POSSIBLE.

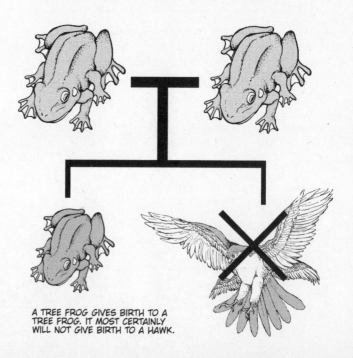

A TREE FROG GIVES BIRTH TO A TREE FROG. IT MOST CERTAINLY WILL NOT GIVE BIRTH TO A HAWK.

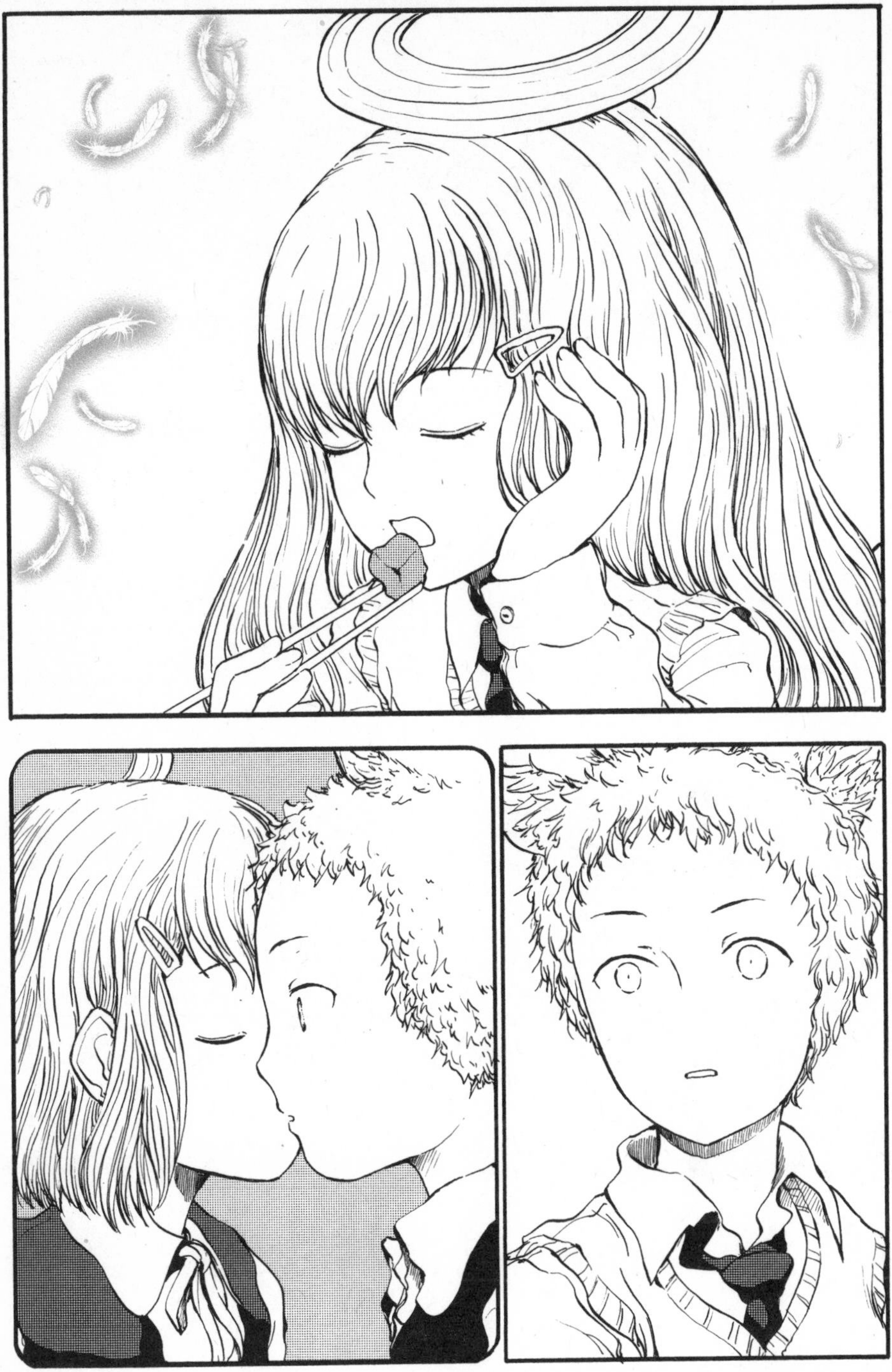

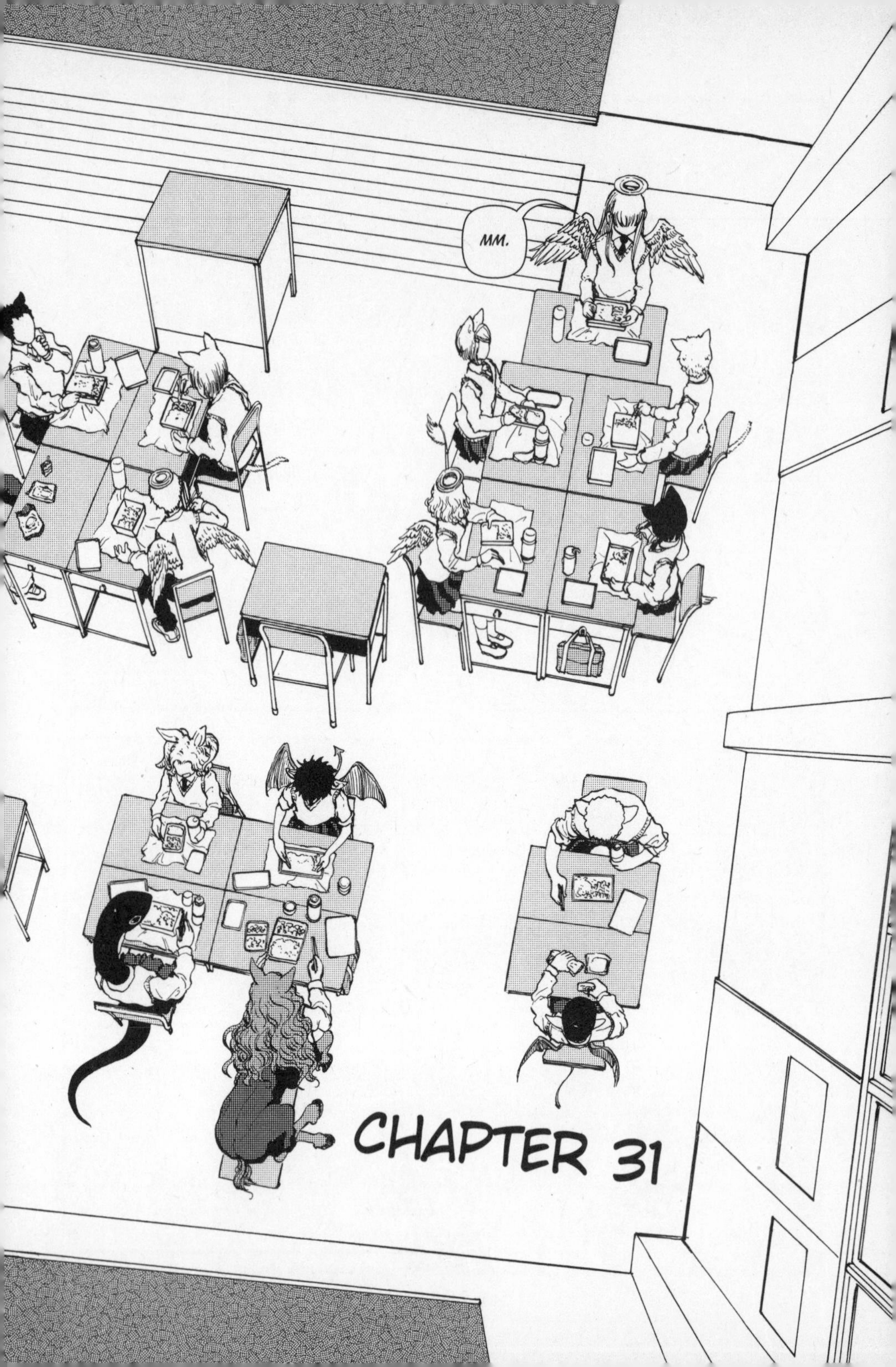
MM.
CHAPTER 31

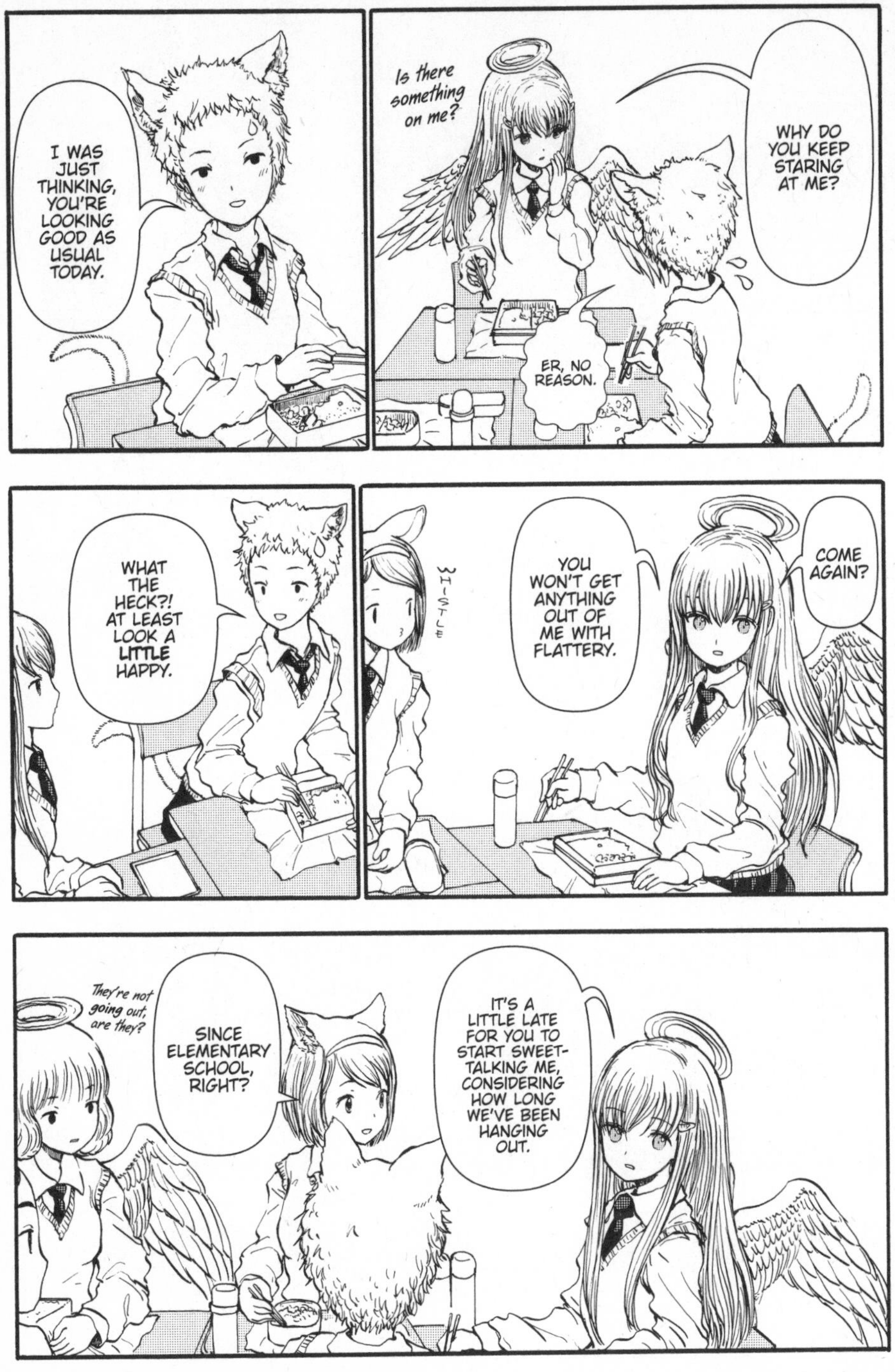
WHY DO YOU KEEP STARING AT ME?
Is there something on me?
ER, NO REASON.
I WAS JUST THINKING, YOU'RE LOOKING GOOD AS USUAL TODAY.
COME AGAIN?
YOU WON'T GET ANYTHING OUT OF ME WITH FLATTERY.
WHISTLE
WHAT THE HECK?! AT LEAST LOOK A LITTLE HAPPY.
IT'S A LITTLE LATE FOR YOU TO START SWEET-TALKING ME, CONSIDERING HOW LONG WE'VE BEEN HANGING OUT.
SINCE ELEMENTARY SCHOOL, RIGHT?
They're not going out, are they?

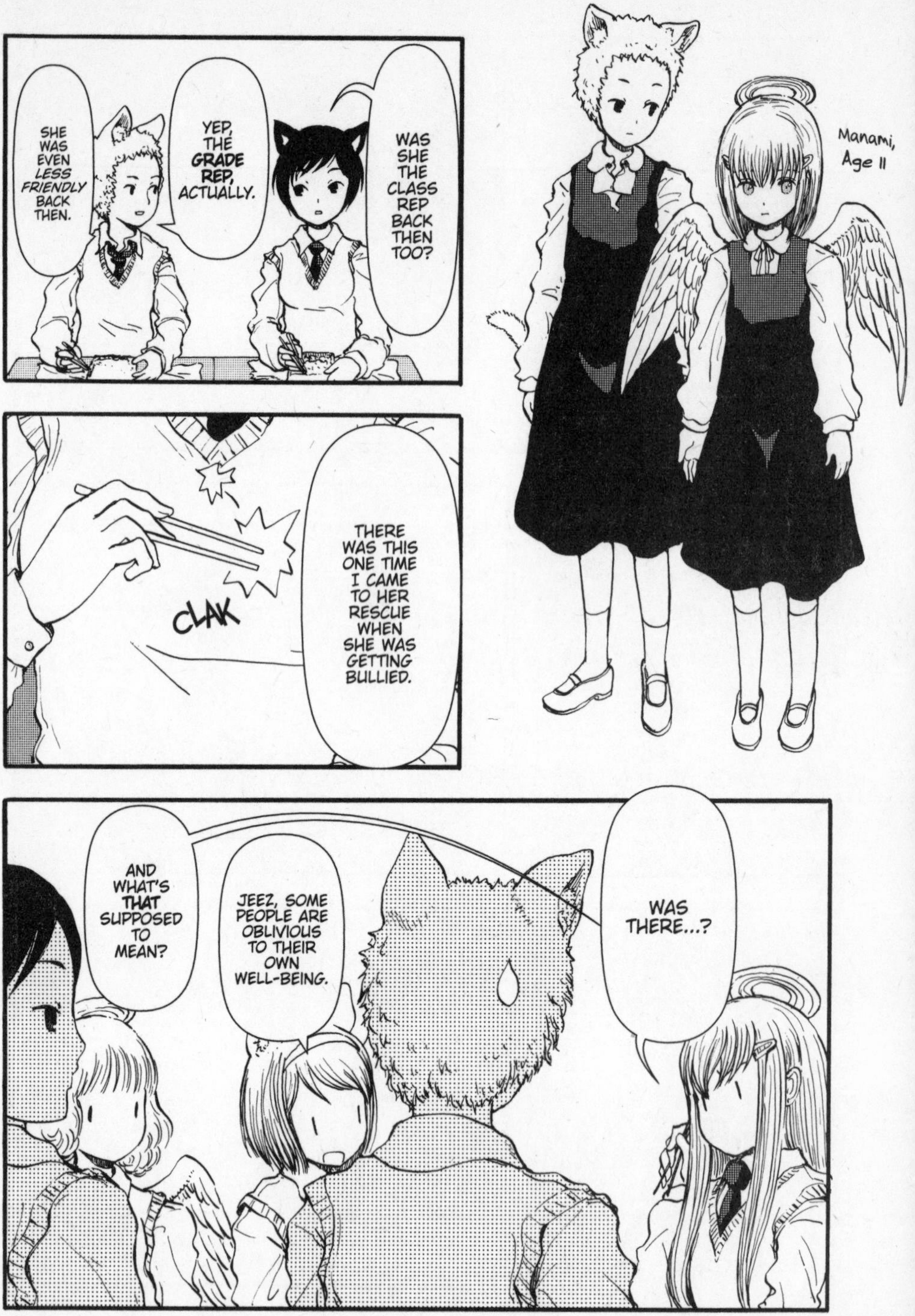
Manami, Age 11
WAS SHE THE CLASS REP BACK THEN TOO?
YEP, THE GRADE REP, ACTUALLY.
SHE WAS EVEN LESS FRIENDLY BACK THEN.
THERE WAS THIS ONE TIME I CAME TO HER RESCUE WHEN SHE WAS GETTING BULLIED.
CLAK
WAS THERE...?
JEEZ, SOME PEOPLE ARE OBLIVIOUS TO THEIR OWN WELL-BEING.
AND WHAT'S THAT SUPPOSED TO MEAN?

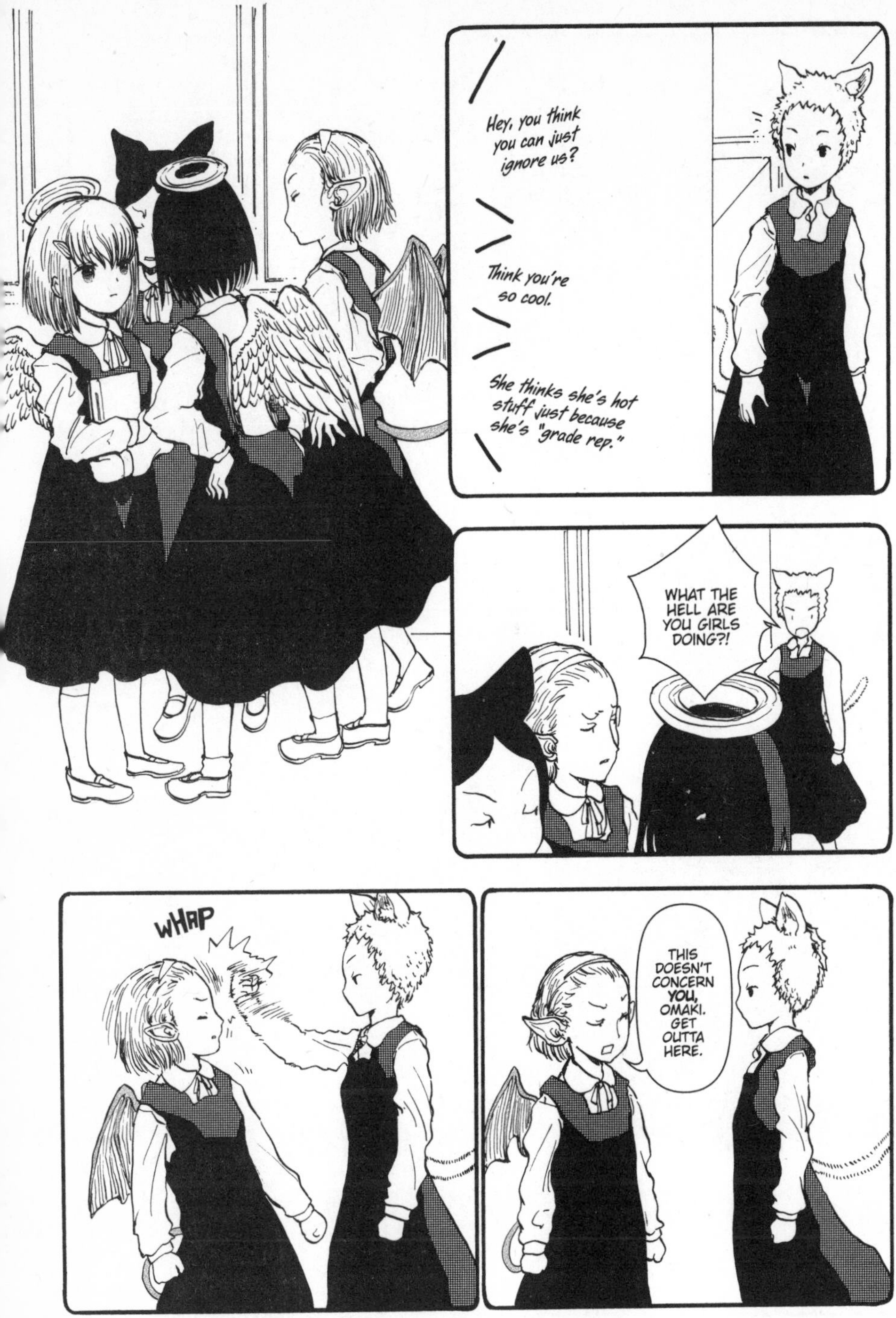
Hey, you think you can just ignore us?
Think you're so cool.
She thinks she's hot stuff just because she's "grade rep."
WHAT THE HELL ARE YOU GIRLS DOING?!
THIS DOESN'T CONCERN YOU, OMAKI. GET OUTTA HERE.
WHAP

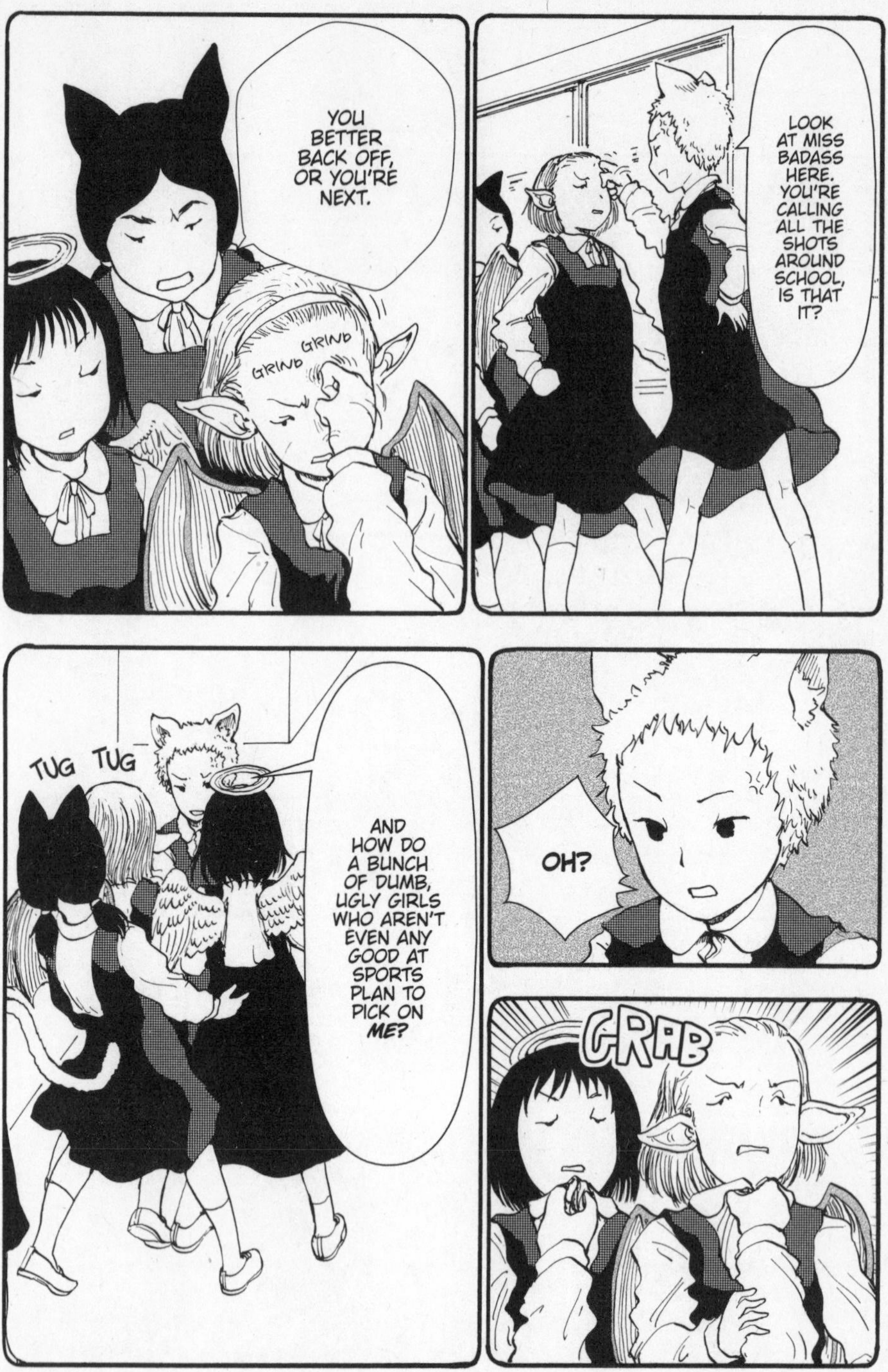
LOOK AT MISS BADASS HERE. YOU'RE CALLING ALL THE SHOTS AROUND SCHOOL, IS THAT IT?
YOU BETTER BACK OFF, OR YOU'RE NEXT.
GRIND GRIND
OH?
GRAB
AND HOW DO A BUNCH OF DUMB, UGLY GIRLS WHO AREN'T EVEN ANY GOOD AT SPORTS PLAN TO PICK ON *ME*?
TUG TUG

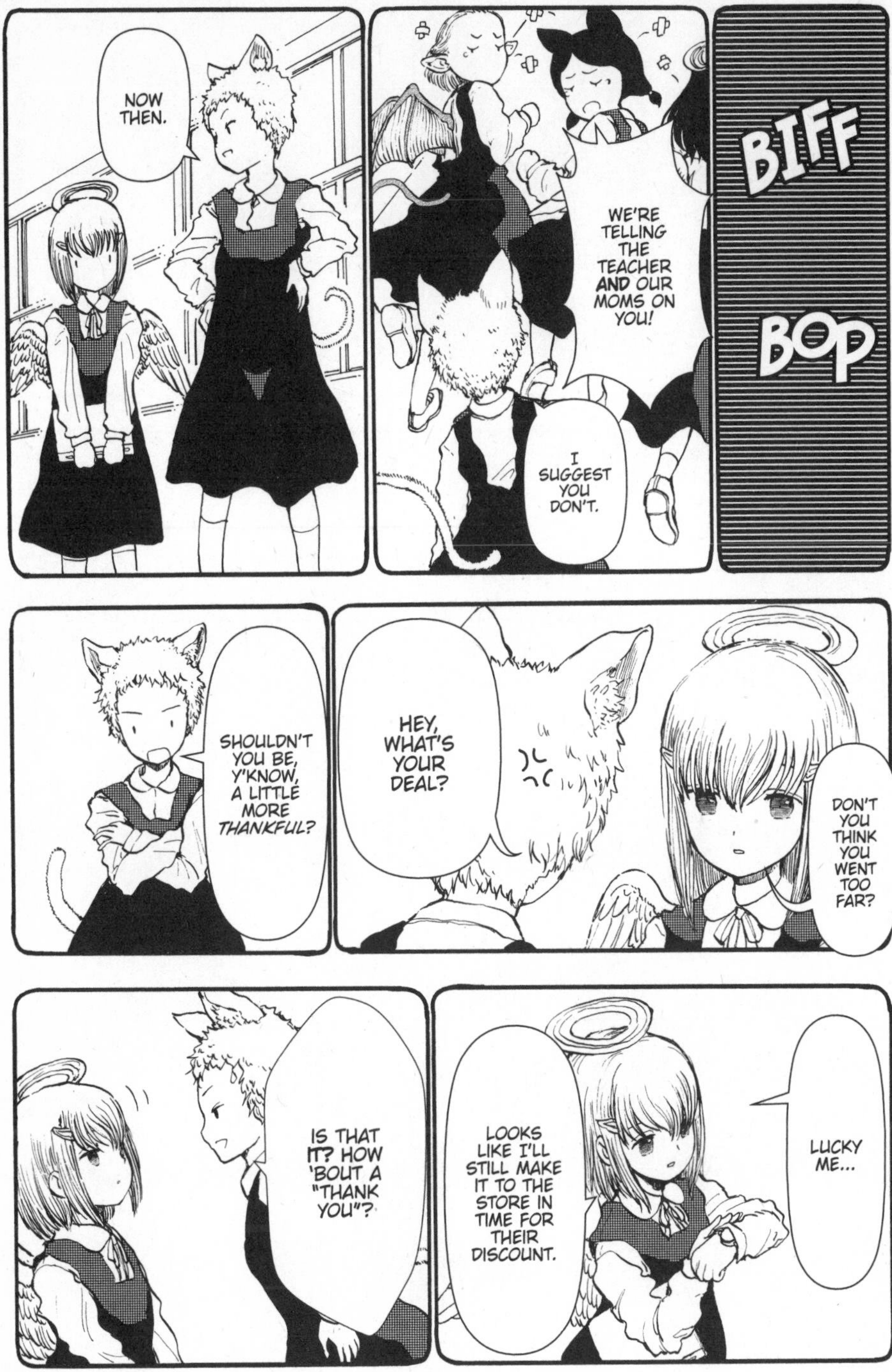
BIFF
BOP
WE'RE TELLING THE TEACHER AND OUR MOMS ON YOU!
I SUGGEST YOU DON'T.
NOW THEN.
DON'T YOU THINK YOU WENT TOO FAR?
HEY, WHAT'S YOUR DEAL?
SHOULDN'T YOU BE, Y'KNOW, A LITTLE MORE *THANKFUL*?
LUCKY ME...
LOOKS LIKE I'LL STILL MAKE IT TO THE STORE IN TIME FOR THEIR DISCOUNT.
IS THAT IT? HOW 'BOUT A "THANK YOU"?

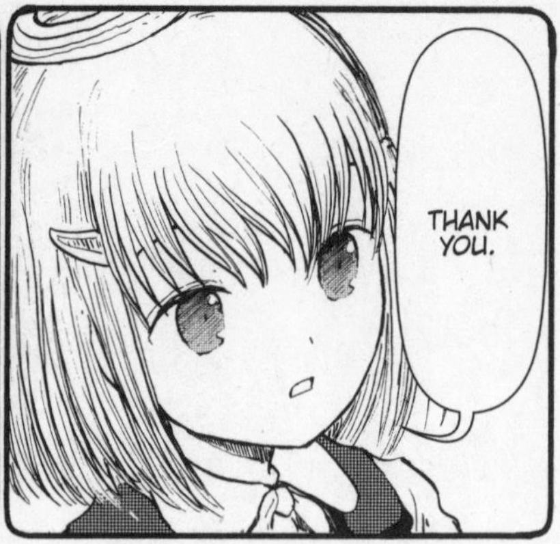
THANK YOU.

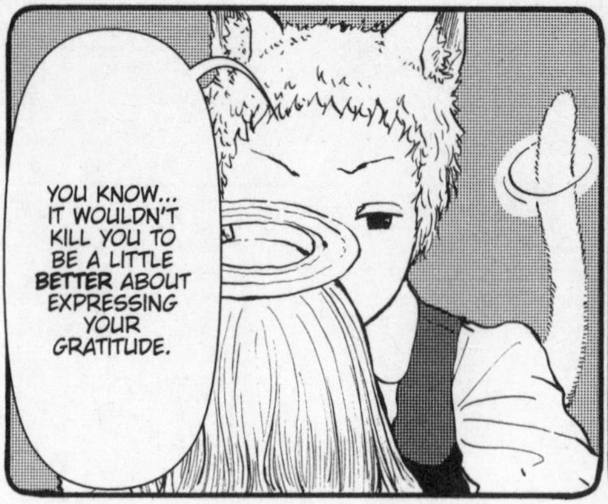
YOU KNOW... IT WOULDN'T KILL YOU TO BE A LITTLE **BETTER** ABOUT EXPRESSING YOUR GRATITUDE.

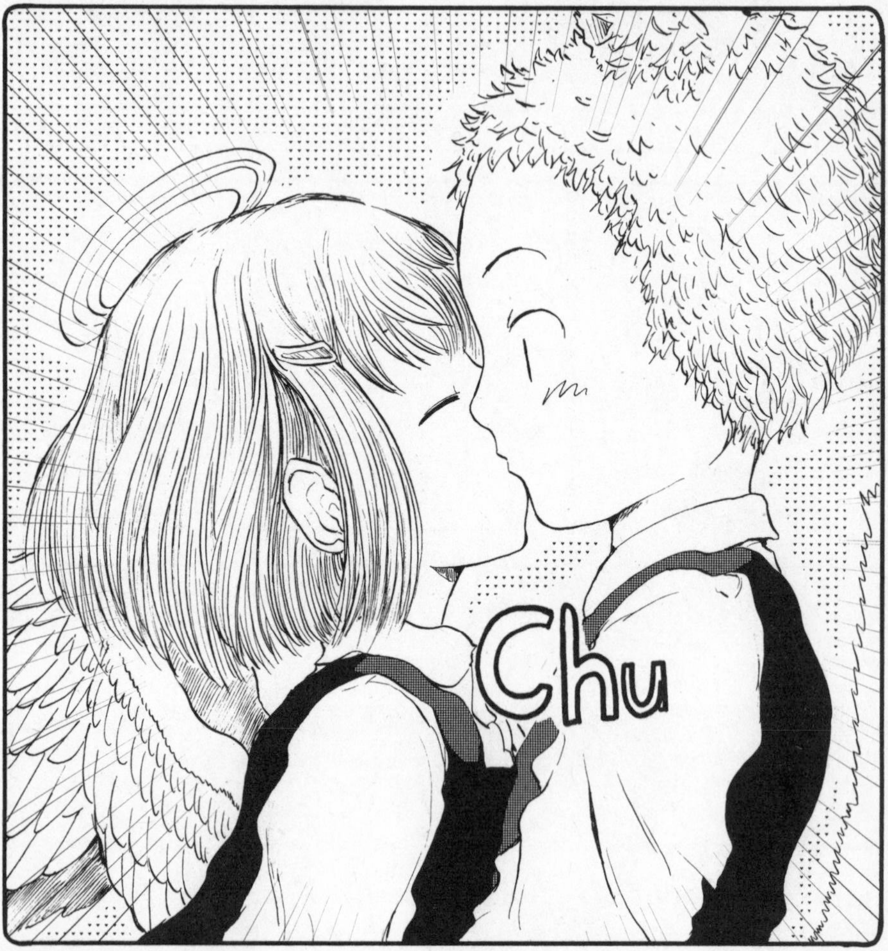
Chu

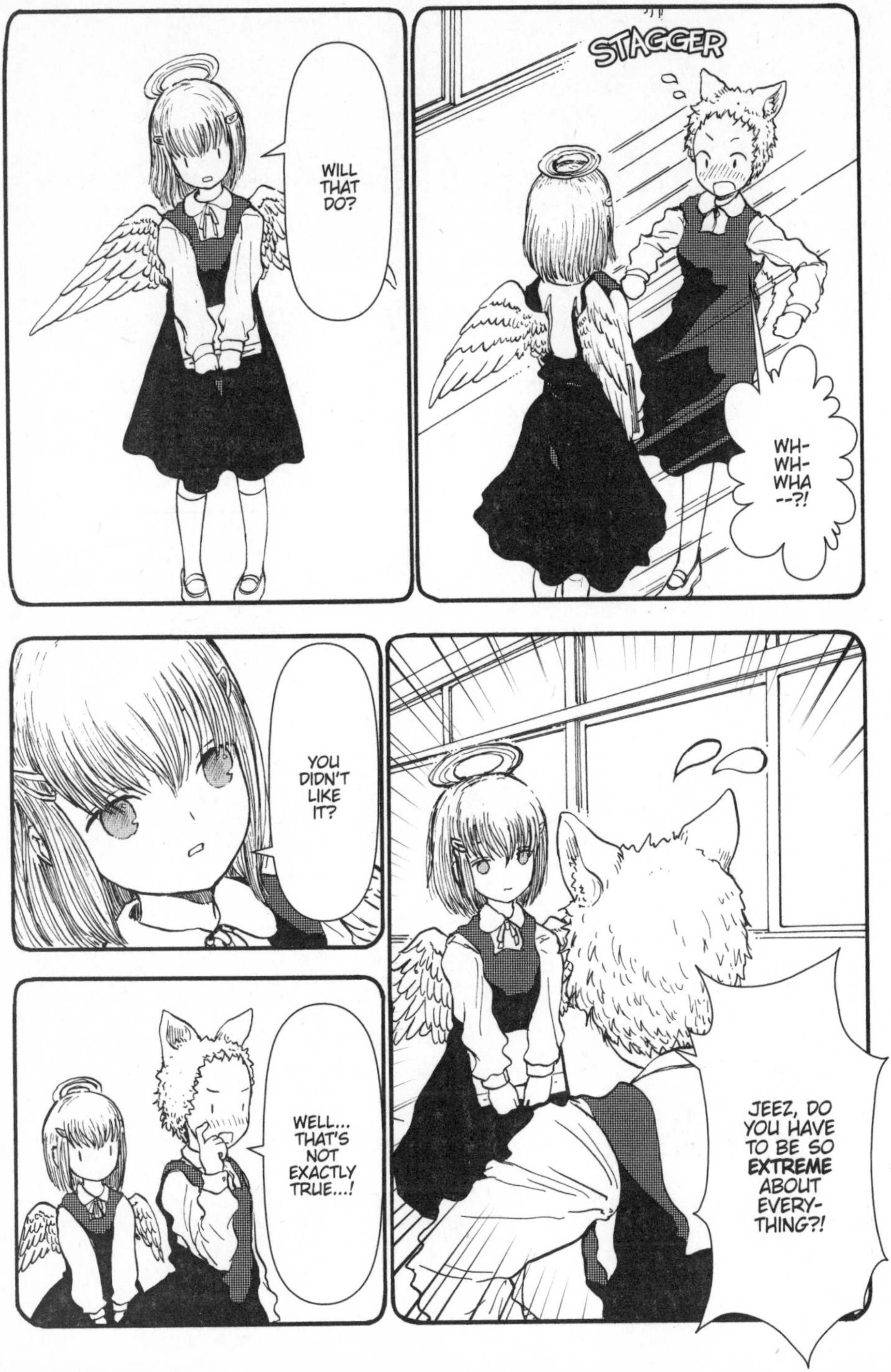
STAGGER
WH-WH-WHA--?!
WILL THAT DO?
JEEZ, DO YOU HAVE TO BE SO **EXTREME** ABOUT EVERY-THING?!
YOU DIDN'T LIKE IT?
WELL... THAT'S NOT EXACTLY TRUE...!

MITAMA, YOUR HOUSE IS A SHRINE?

MM-HM.

Little sisters?

I'm home.

BIG SIS- TER!

SCAMPER SCAMPER

SMOOCH

Were you good today?

GLOMP

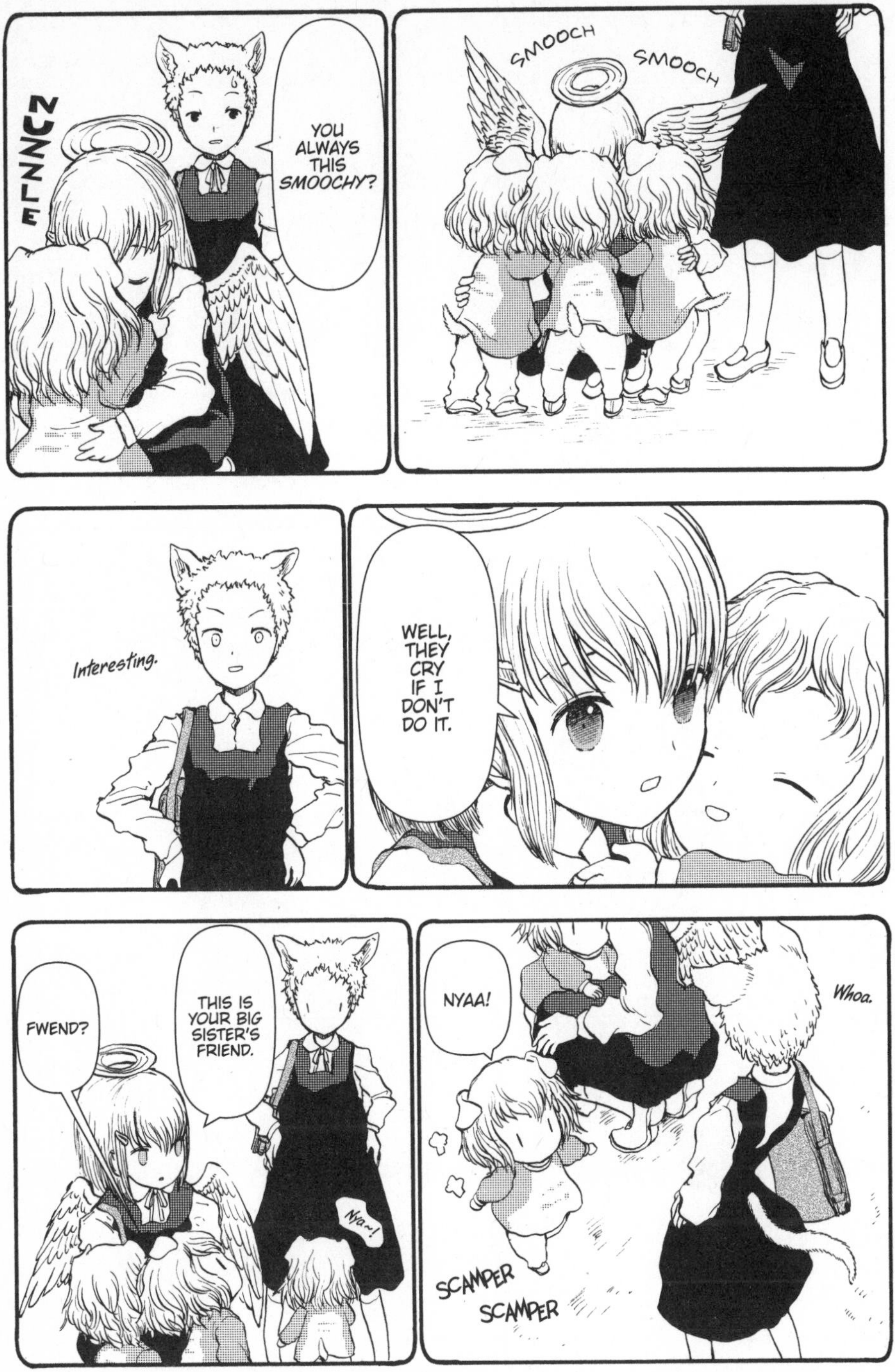
SMOOCH
SMOOCH
NUZZLE
YOU ALWAYS THIS SMOOCHY?
WELL, THEY CRY IF I DON'T DO IT.
Interesting.
Whoa.
NYAA!
SCAMPER
SCAMPER
THIS IS YOUR BIG SISTER'S FRIEND.
FWEND?
Nya~!

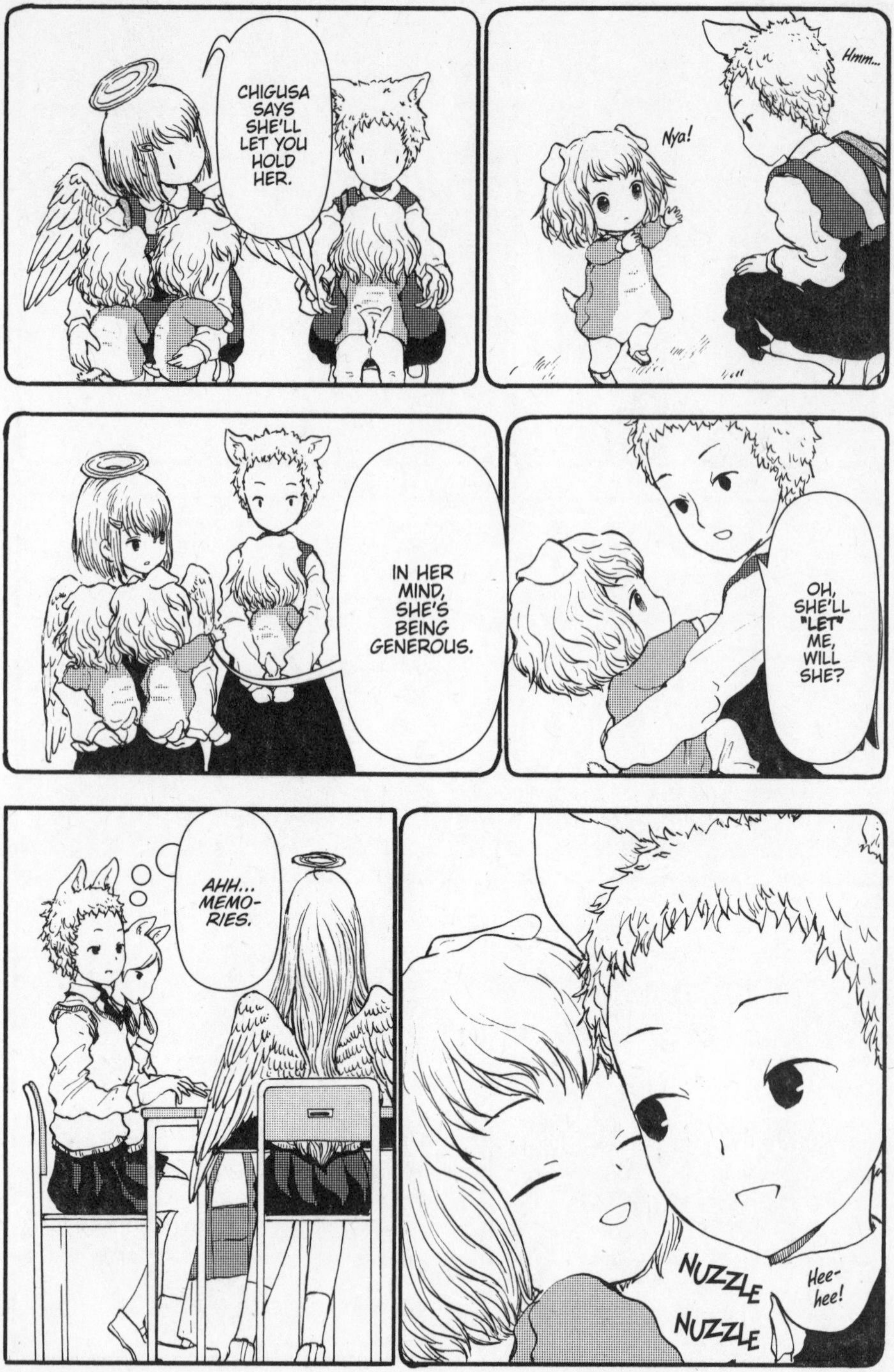
Hmm...
Nya!
CHIGUSA SAYS SHE'LL LET YOU HOLD HER.
OH, SHE'LL "LET" ME, WILL SHE?
IN HER MIND, SHE'S BEING GENEROUS.
Hee-hee!
NUZZLE NUZZLE
AHH... MEMORIES.

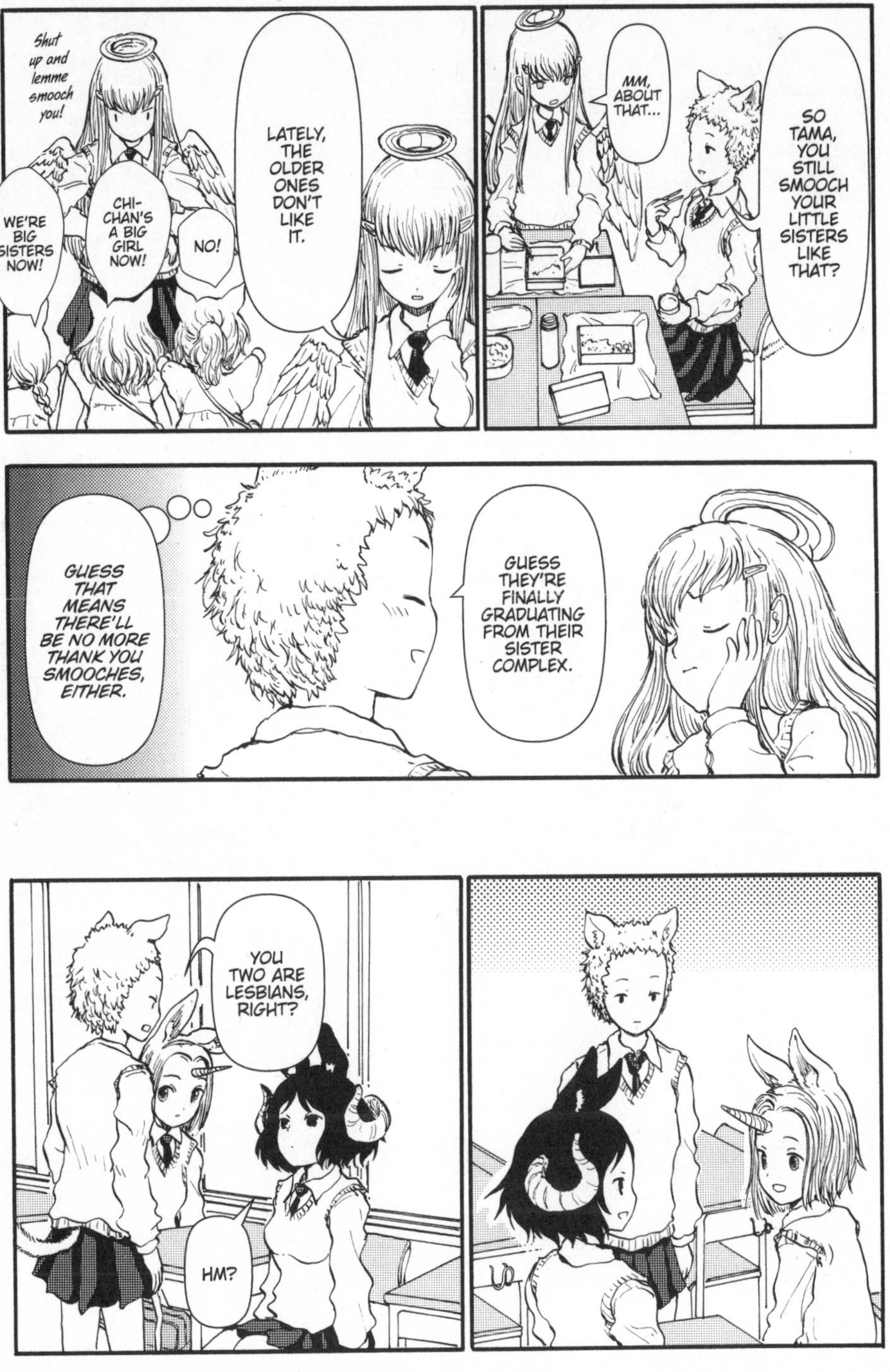
SO TAMA, YOU STILL SMOOCH YOUR LITTLE SISTERS LIKE THAT?
MM, ABOUT THAT...
LATELY, THE OLDER ONES DON'T LIKE IT.
Shut up and lemme smooch you!
NO!
CHI-CHAN'S A BIG GIRL NOW!
WE'RE BIG SISTERS NOW!
GUESS THEY'RE FINALLY GRADUATING FROM THEIR SISTER COMPLEX.
GUESS THAT MEANS THERE'LL BE NO MORE THANK YOU SMOOCHES, EITHER.
YOU TWO ARE LESBIANS, RIGHT?
HM?

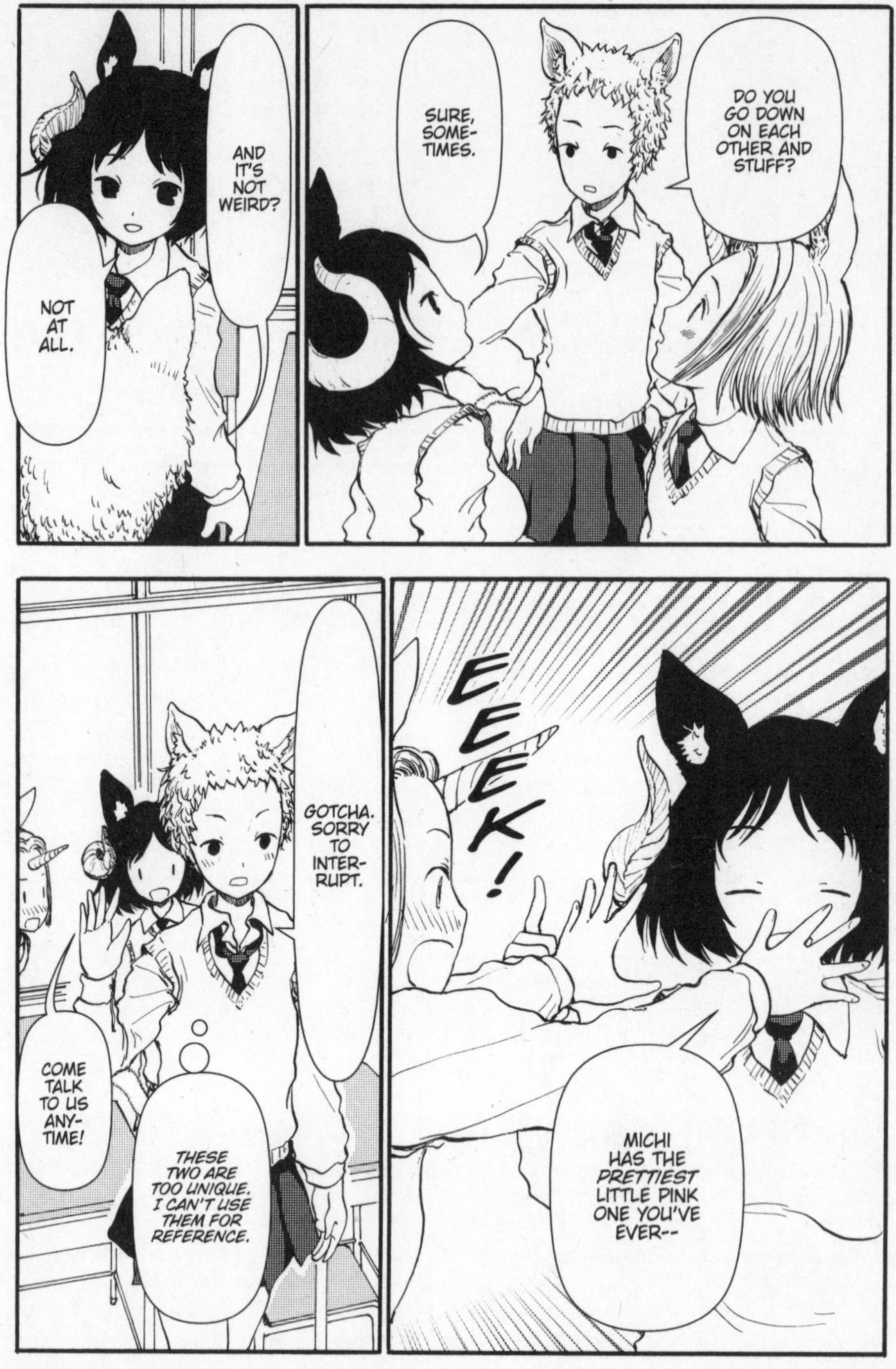

DO YOU GO DOWN ON EACH OTHER AND STUFF?
SURE, SOME-TIMES.
AND IT'S NOT WEIRD?
NOT AT ALL.
EEEEK!
MICHI HAS THE *PRETTIEST* LITTLE PINK ONE YOU'VE EVER--
GOTCHA. SORRY TO INTER-RUPT.
COME TALK TO US ANY-TIME!
THESE TWO ARE TOO UNIQUE. I CAN'T USE THEM FOR REFERENCE.

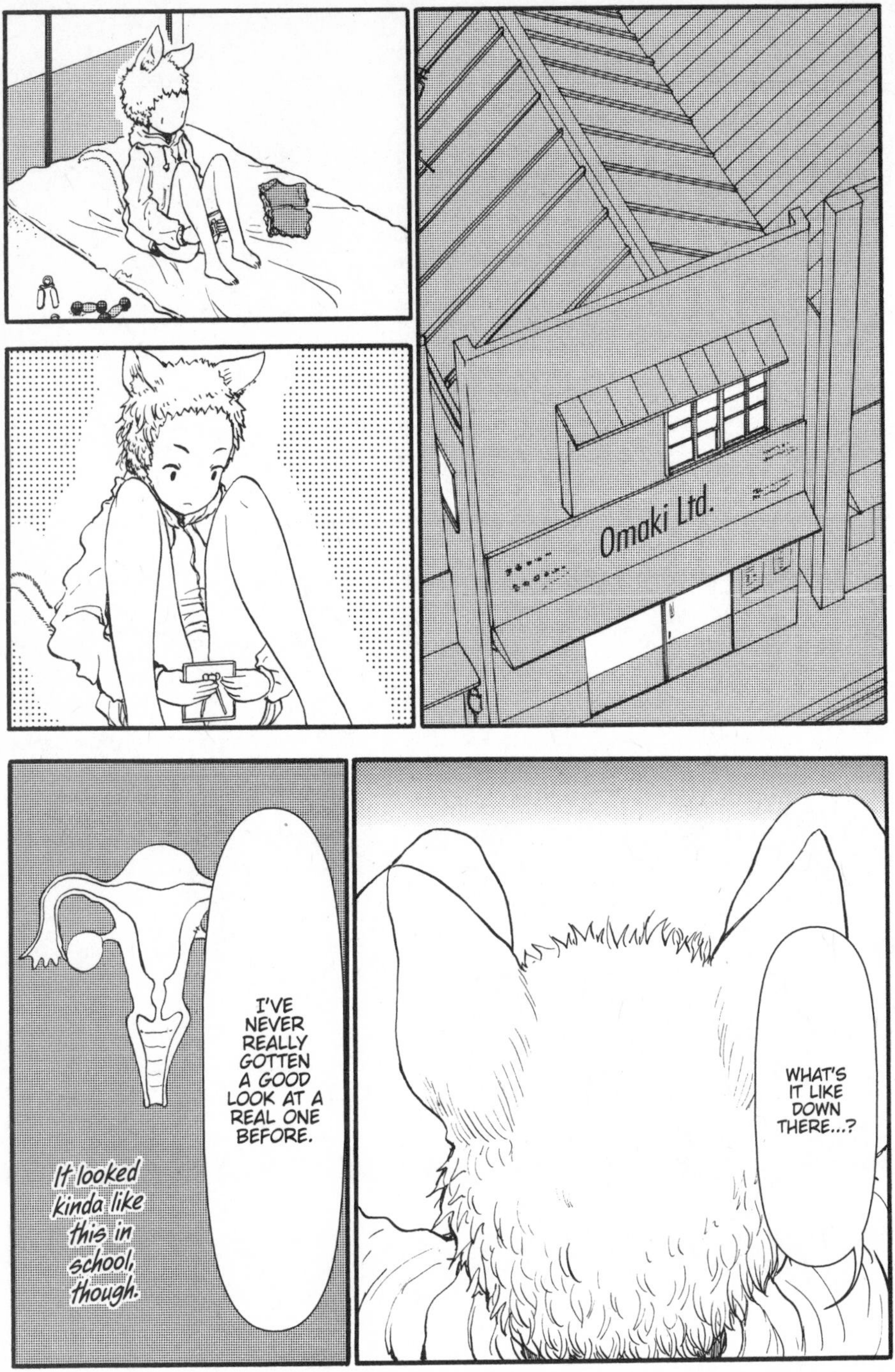
Omaki Ltd.
WHAT'S IT LIKE DOWN THERE...?
I'VE NEVER REALLY GOTTEN A GOOD LOOK AT A REAL ONE BEFORE.
It looked kinda like this in school, though.

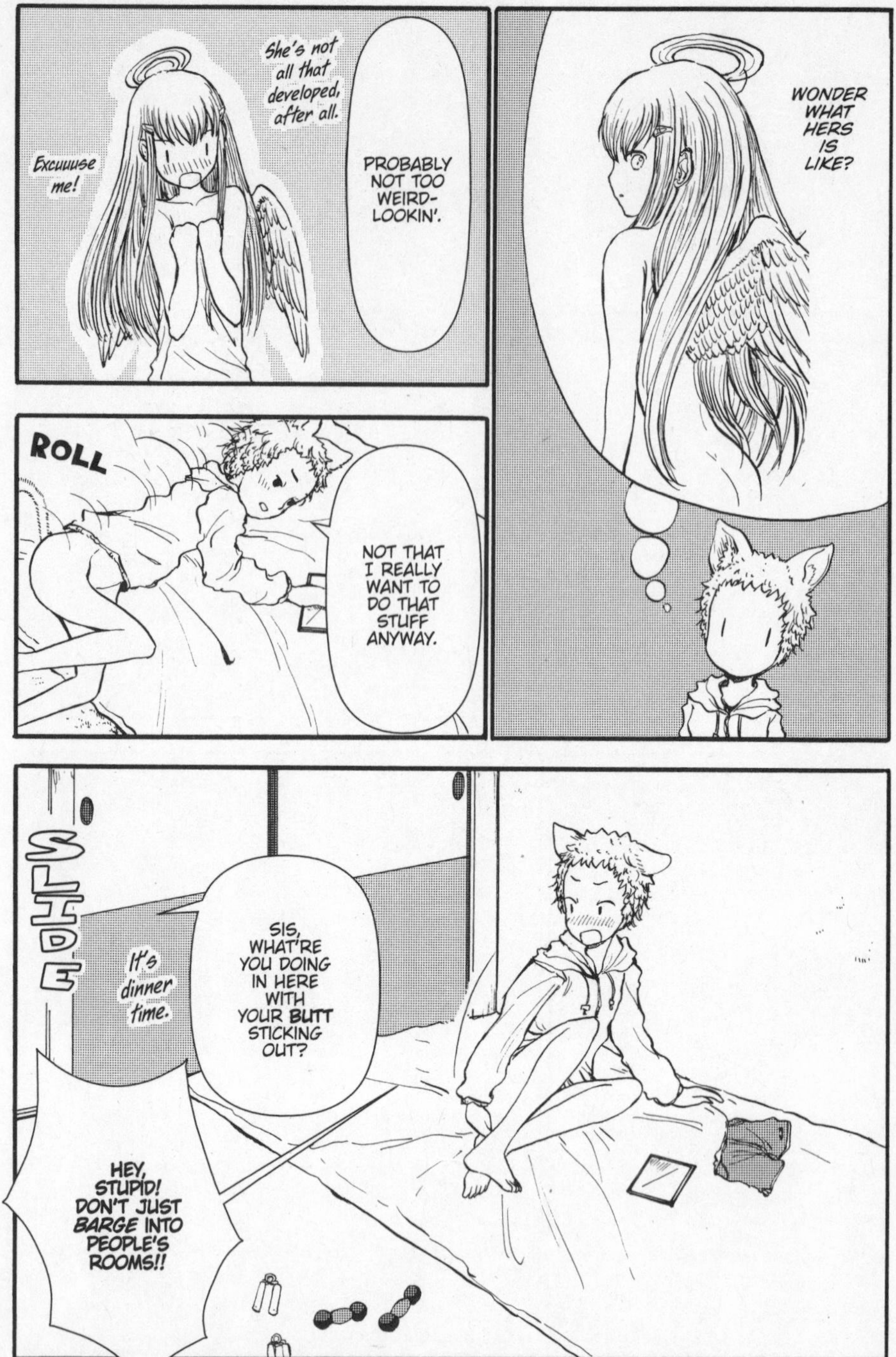
WONDER WHAT HERS IS LIKE?
PROBABLY NOT TOO WEIRD-LOOKIN'.
She's not all that developed, after all.
Excuuuse me!
ROLL
NOT THAT I REALLY WANT TO DO THAT STUFF ANYWAY.
SIS, WHAT'RE YOU DOING IN HERE WITH YOUR BUTT STICKING OUT?
It's dinner time.
SLIDE
HEY, STUPID! DON'T JUST BARGE INTO PEOPLE'S ROOMS!!

A Centaur's Life

GENETICS MADE EASY: LESSON 2
HOW ARE HUMAN CHARACTERISTICS PASSED DOWN?

WITH FACIAL STRUCTURE, FOR EXAMPLE, YOU MIGHT HAVE A PERSON WHOSE BROW AND NOSE RESEMBLE THAT OF THEIR FATHER, WHILE THEIR EYES AND JAWLINE MATCH THAT OF THEIR MOTHER. THIS PERSON HAS INHERITED THESE FACIAL FEATURES FROM THEIR RESPECTIVE PARENTS. NOW LET'S IMAGINE YOU HAVE AN ANGELFOLK FATHER AND A GOATFOLK MOTHER. WOULD THAT MEAN THEIR CHILD WOULD HAVE BOTH WINGS AND HORNS? THE ANSWER IS NO-- THE CHILD WOULD HAVE *EITHER* WINGS OR HORNS. IN OTHER WORDS, THE CHILD WE BE BORN EITHER AS AN ANGELFOLK OR A GOATFOLK (THERE ARE EXCEPTIONS, BUT WE'LL SAVE THOSE FOR LATER). WHY MIGHT THAT BE?

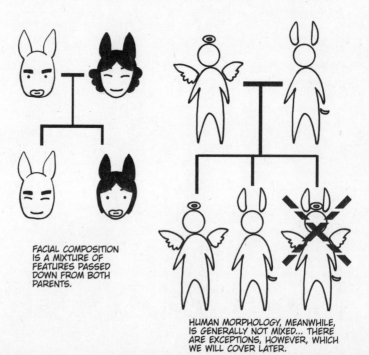

FACIAL COMPOSITION IS A MIXTURE OF FEATURES PASSED DOWN FROM BOTH PARENTS.

HUMAN MORPHOLOGY, MEANWHILE, IS GENERALLY NOT MIXED... THERE ARE EXCEPTIONS, HOWEVER, WHICH WE WILL COVER LATER.

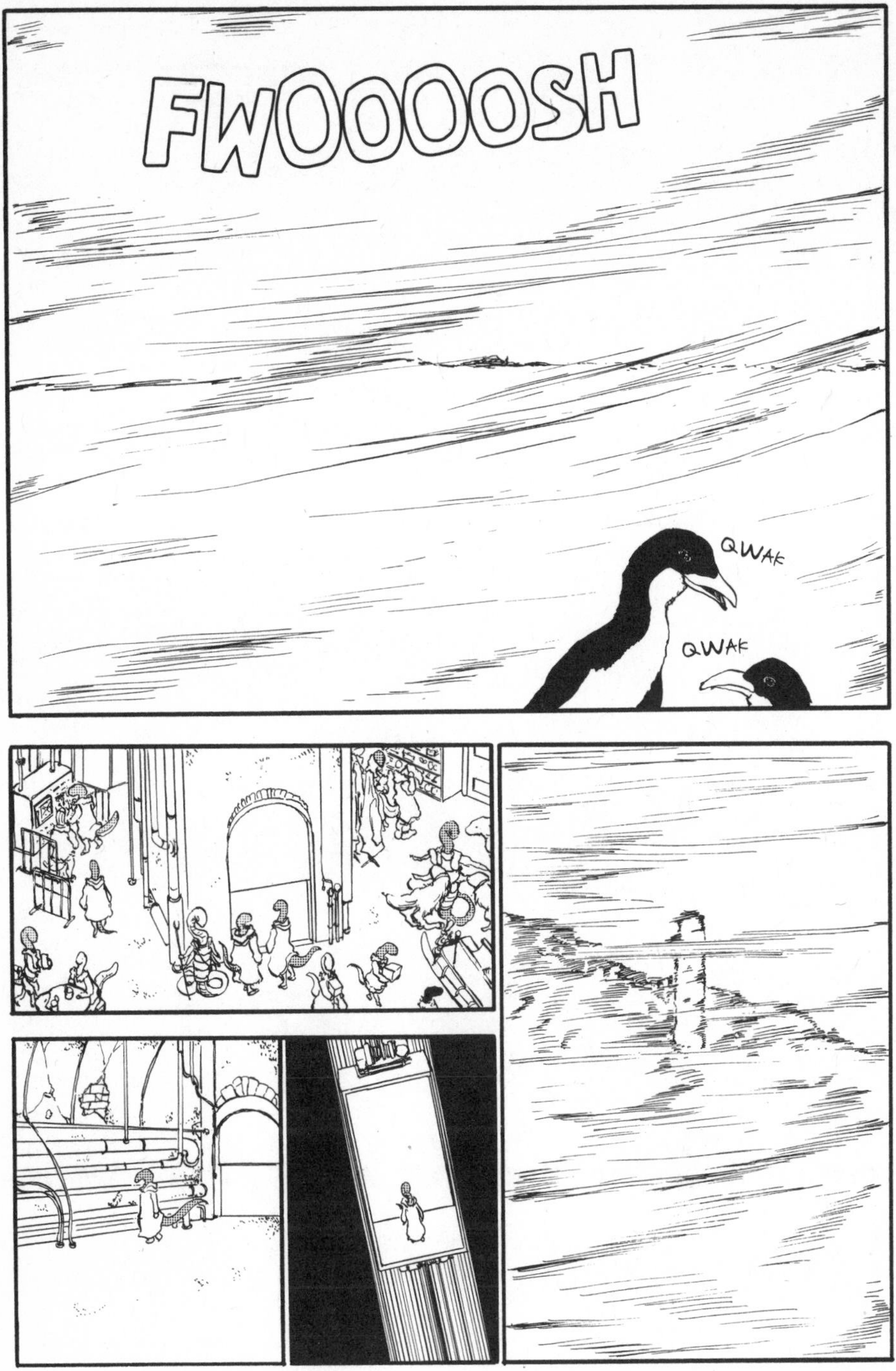
FWOOOOSH
QWAK
QWAK

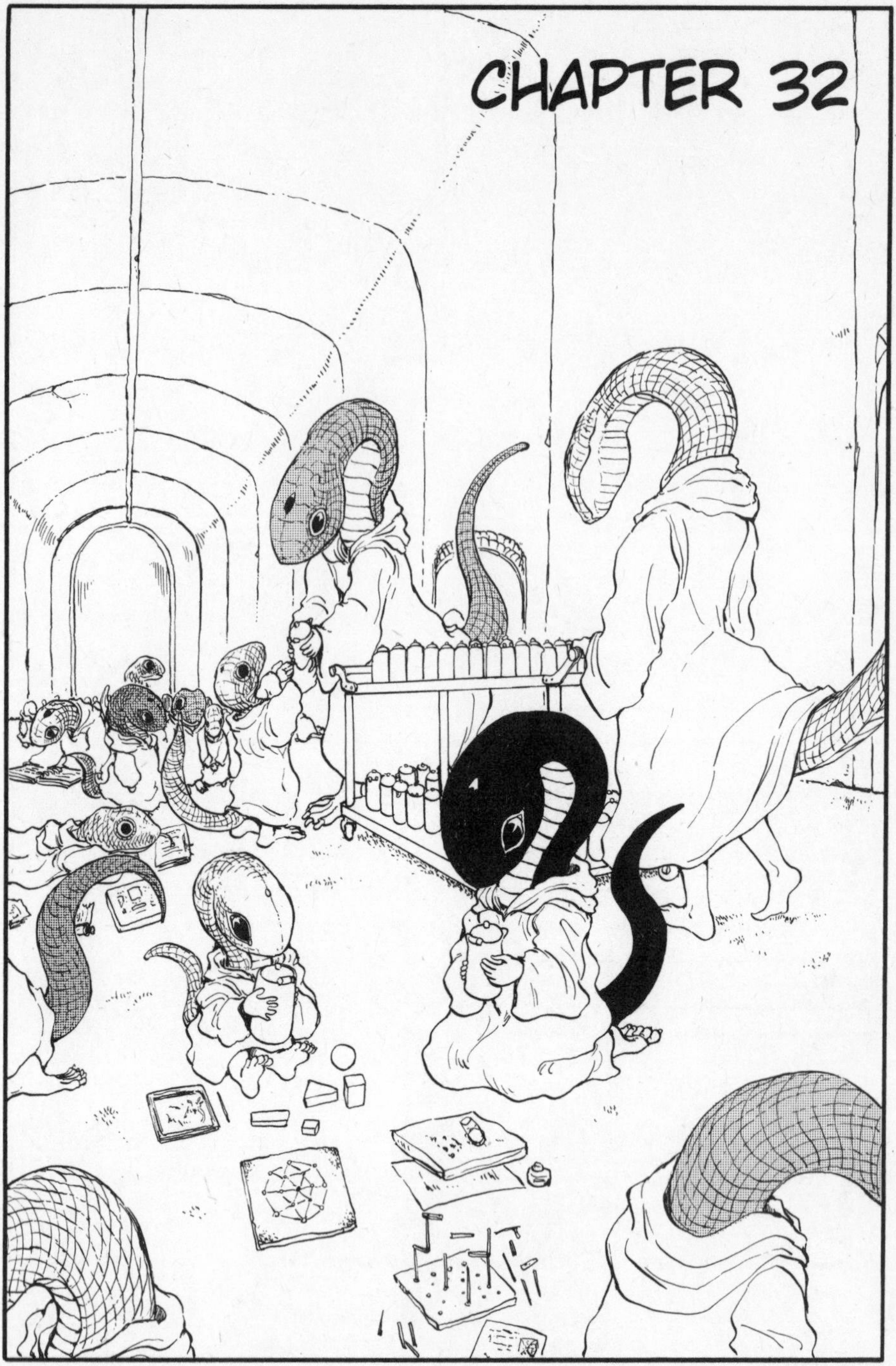
CHAPTER 32

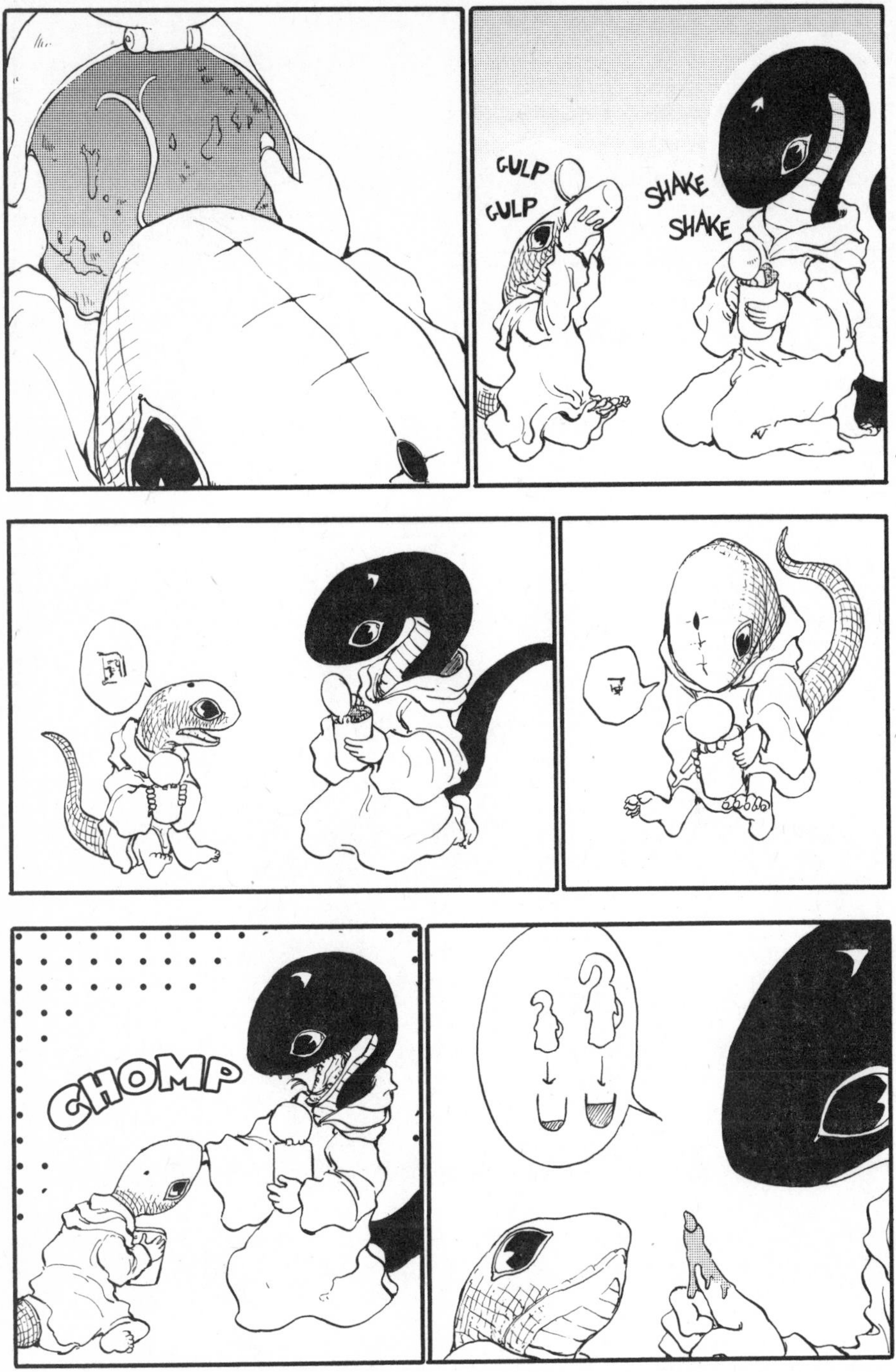
SHAKE SHAKE
GULP GULP
CHOMP

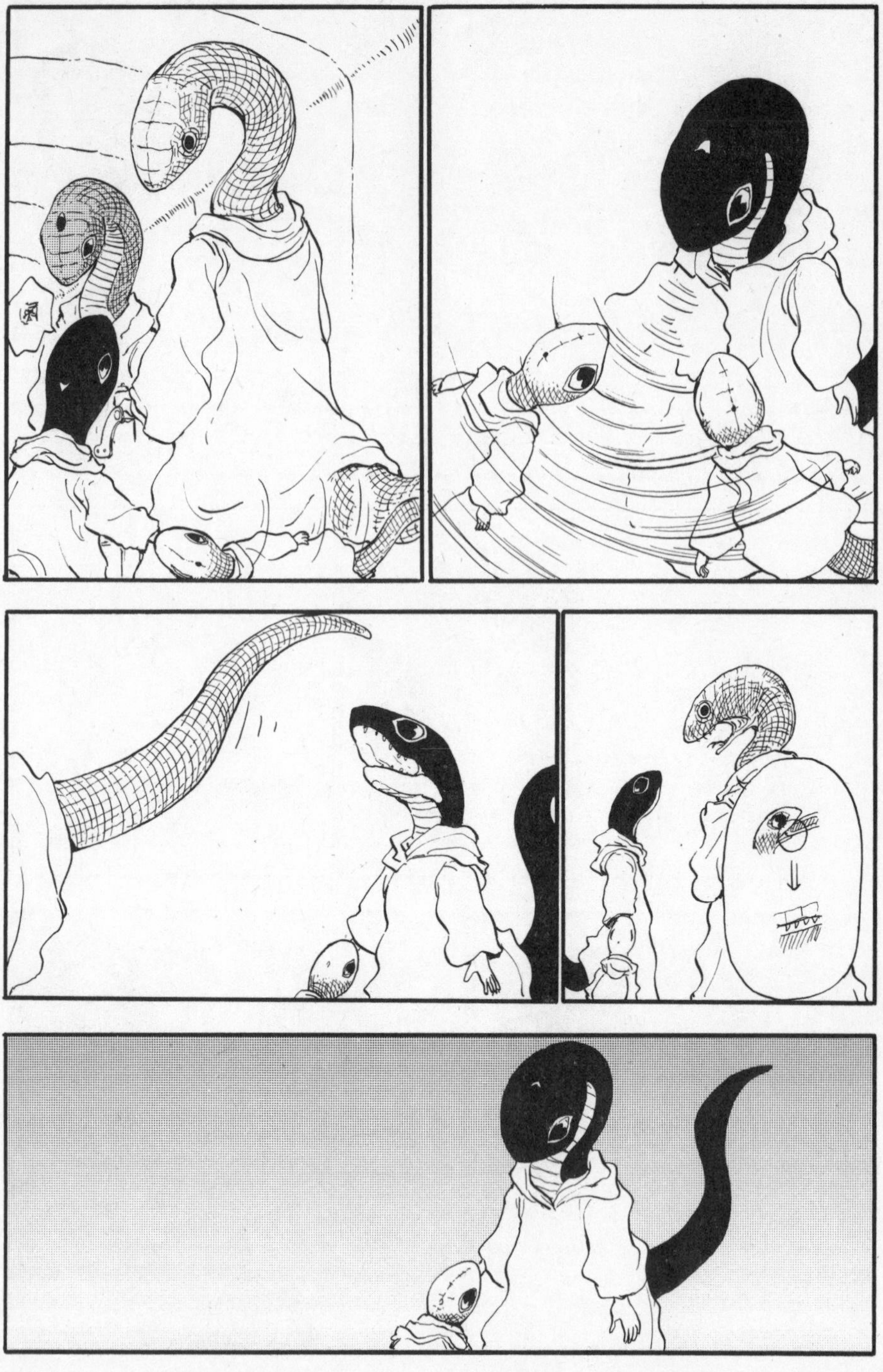

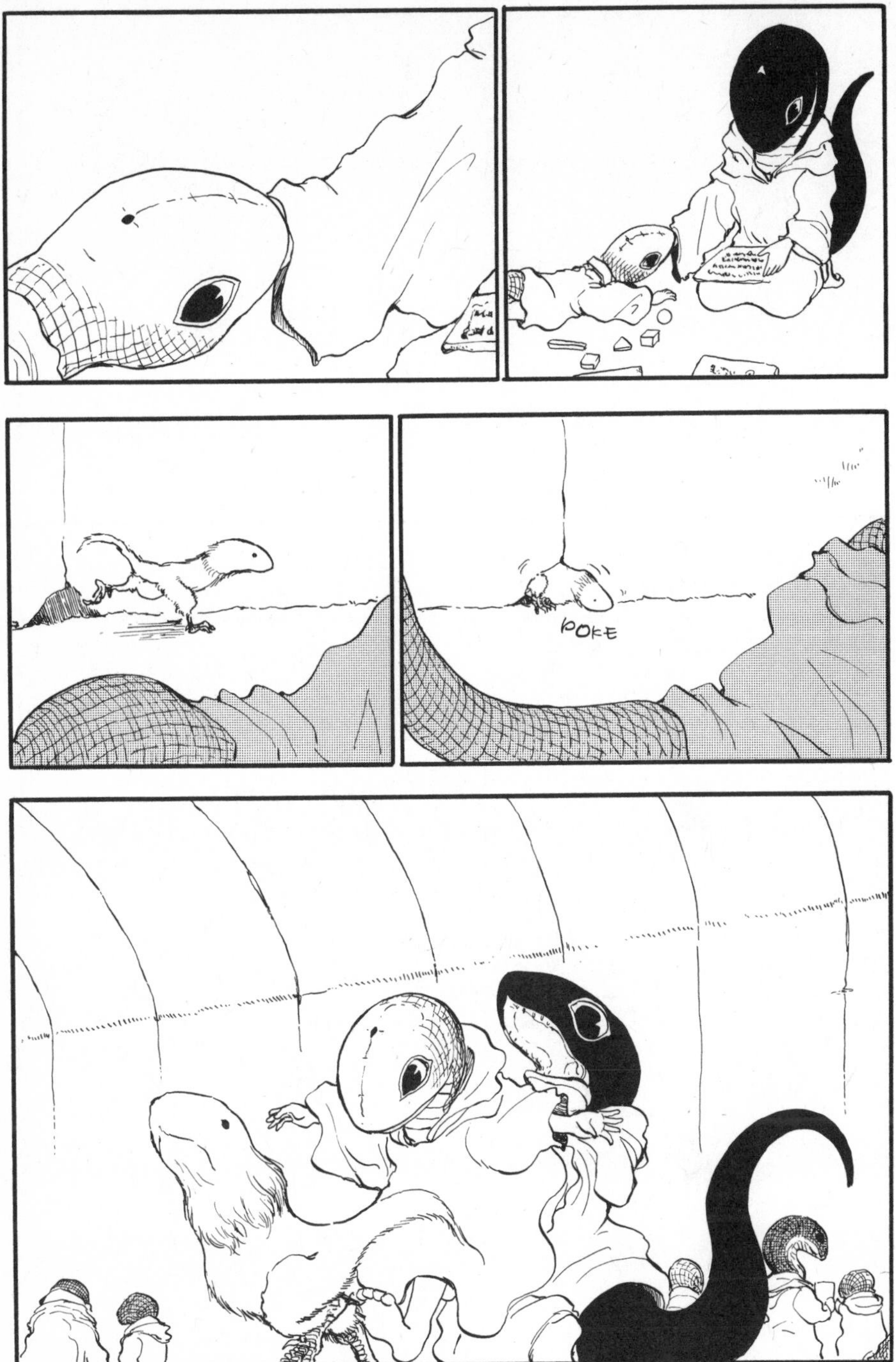
POKE

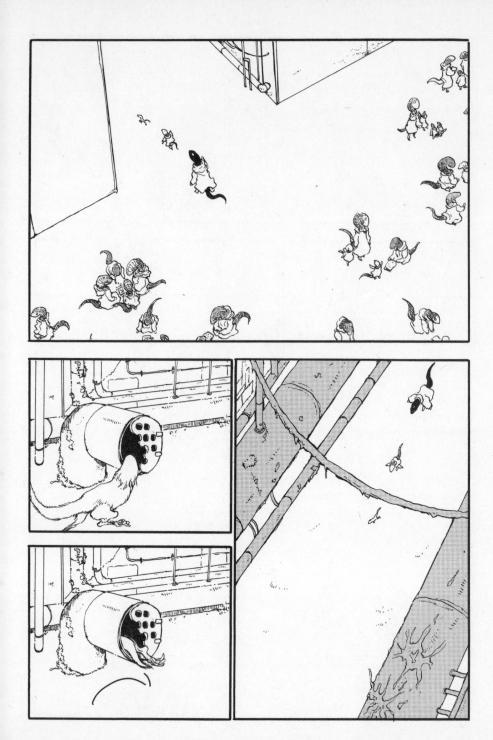

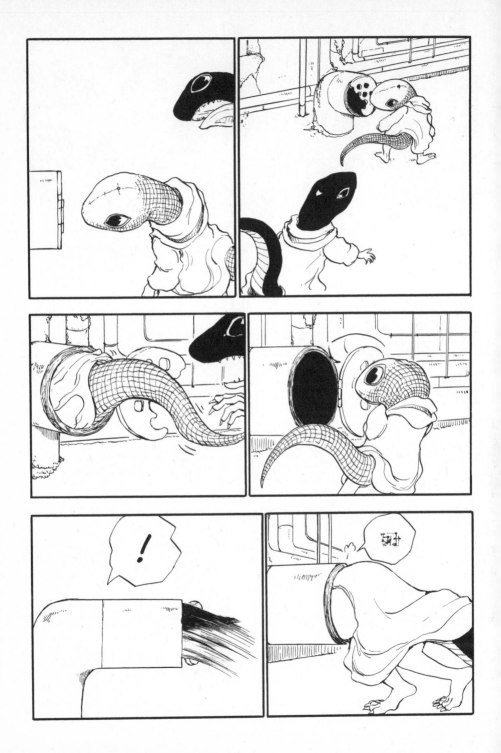

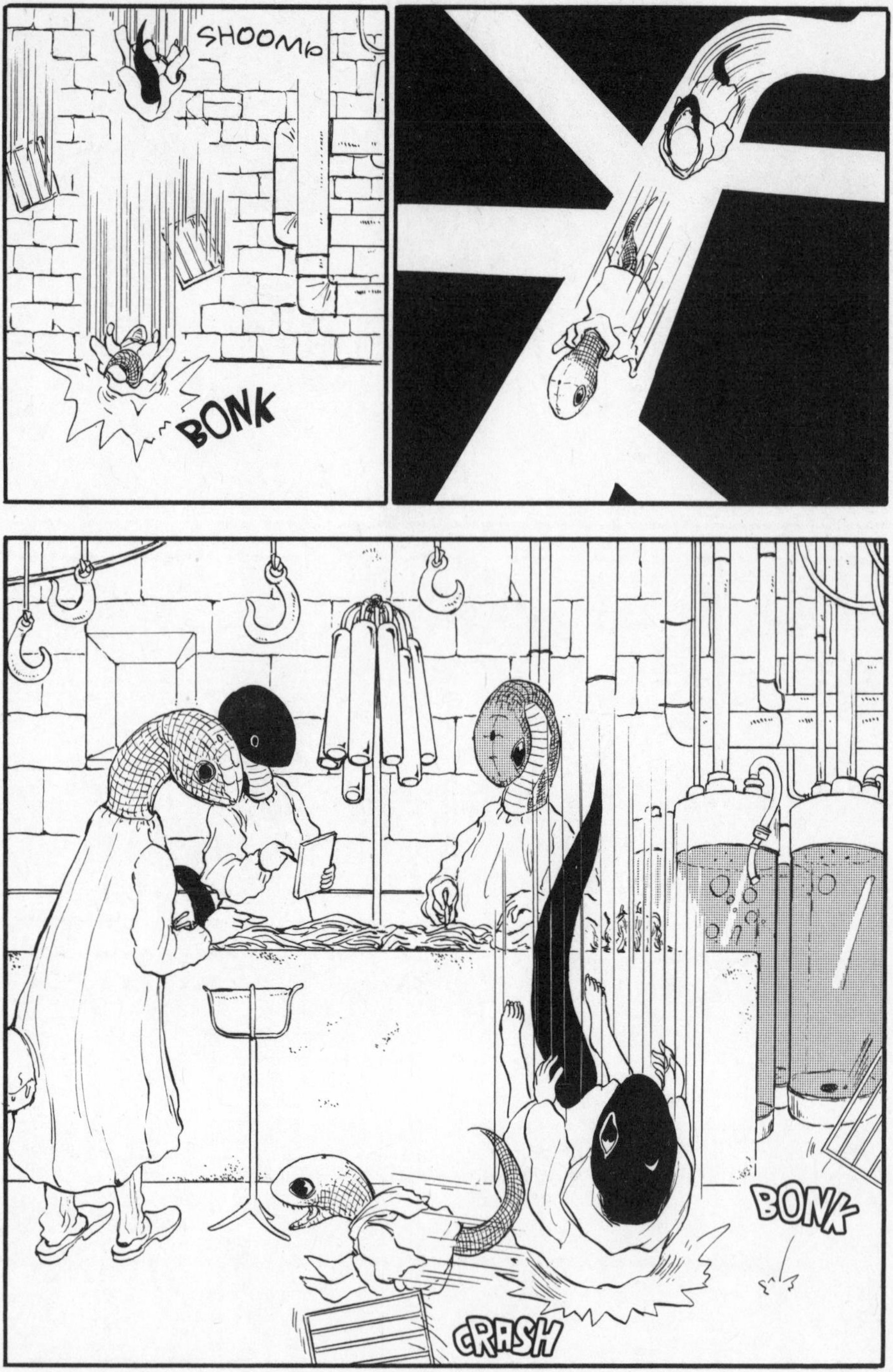
SHOOMP
BONK
BONK
CRASH

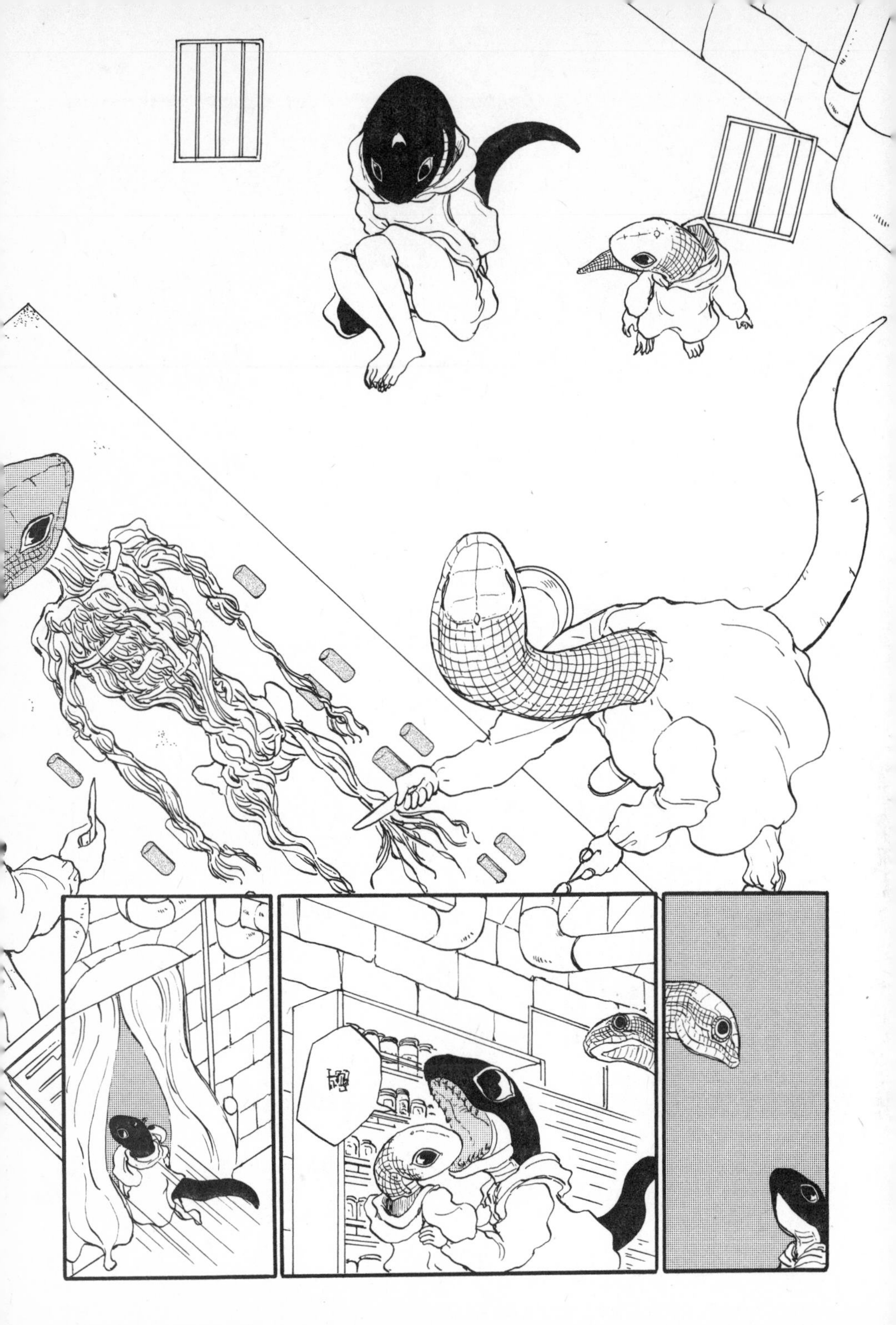

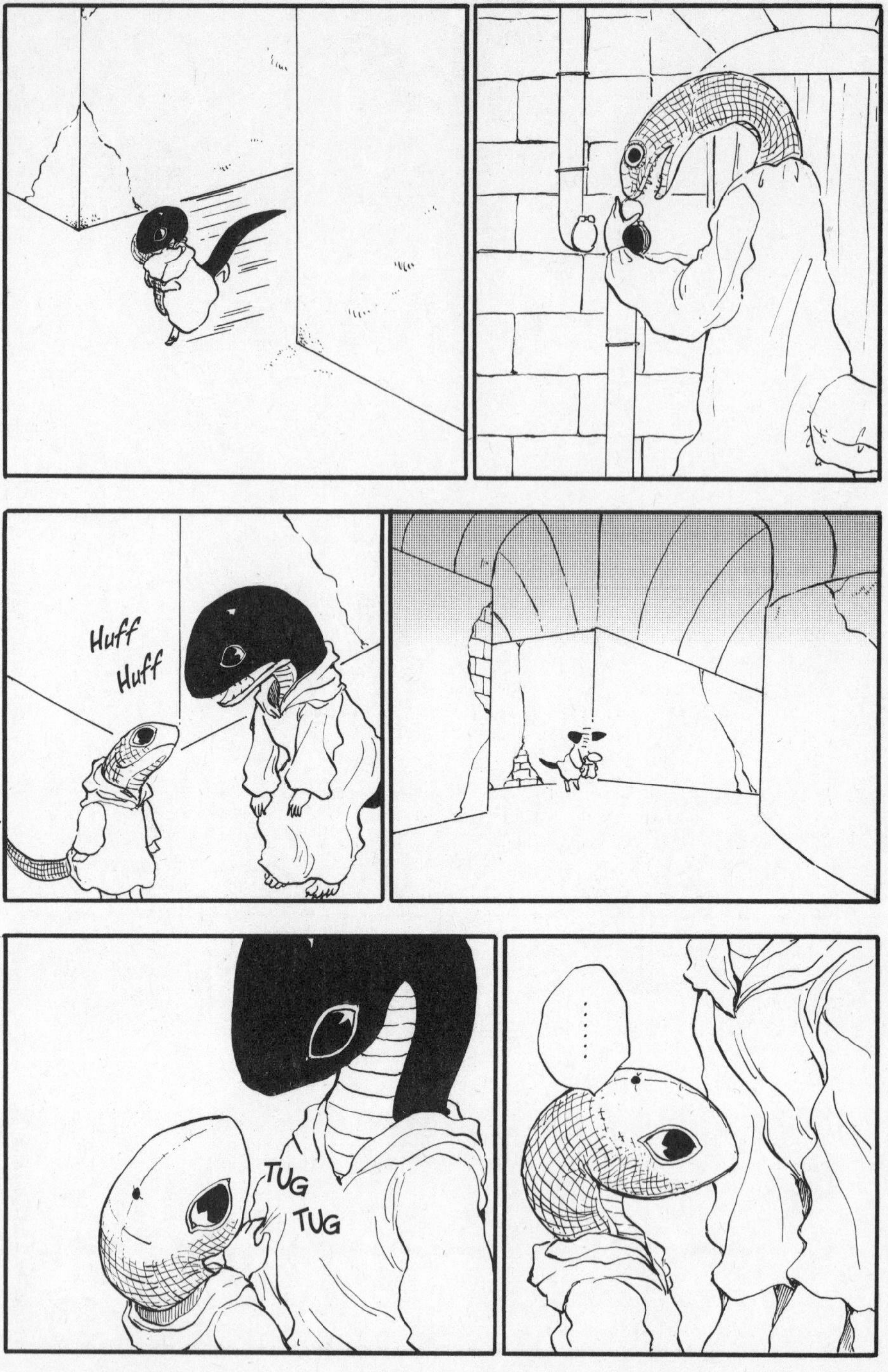
Huff
Huff
……
TUG
TUG

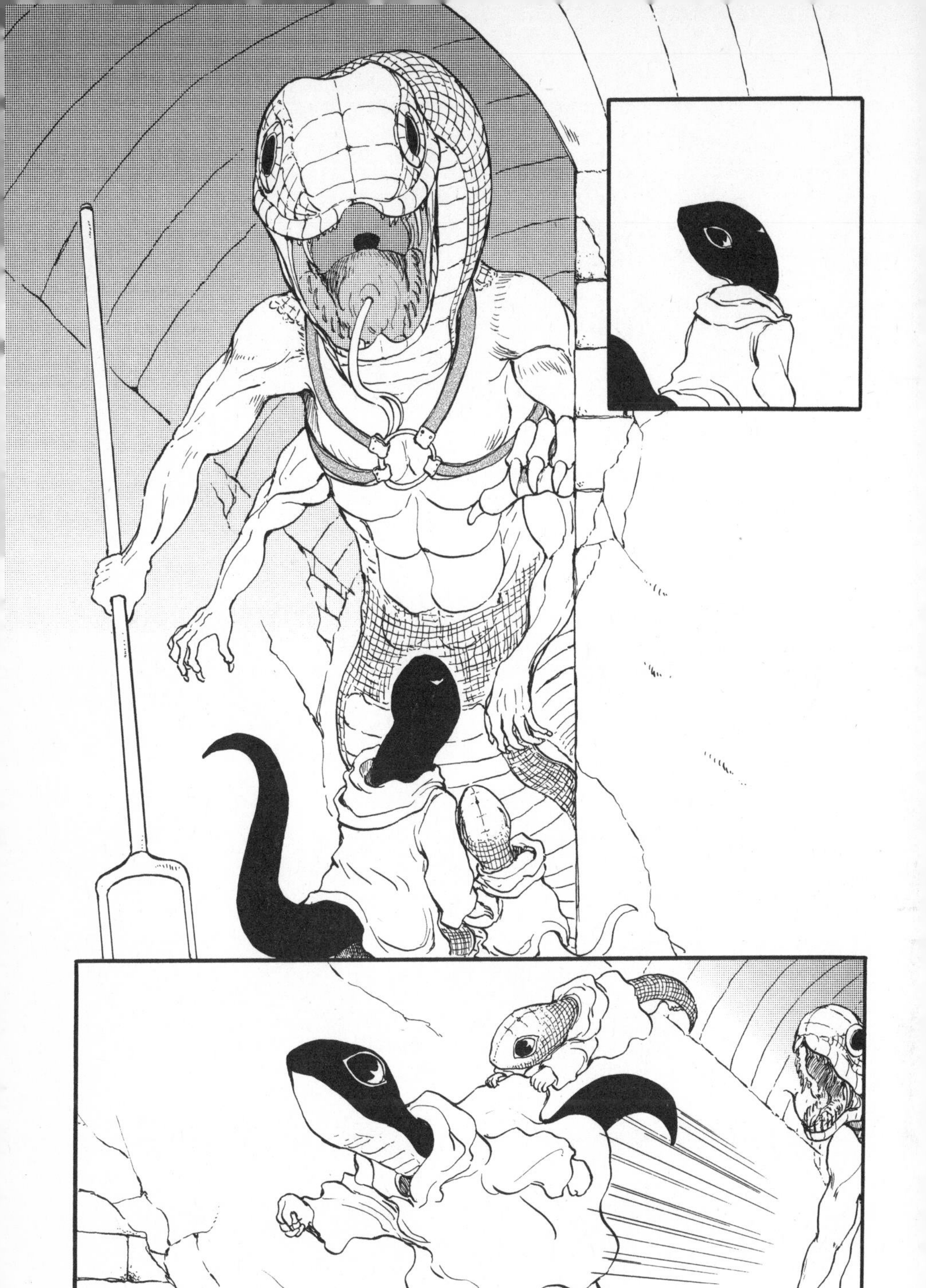

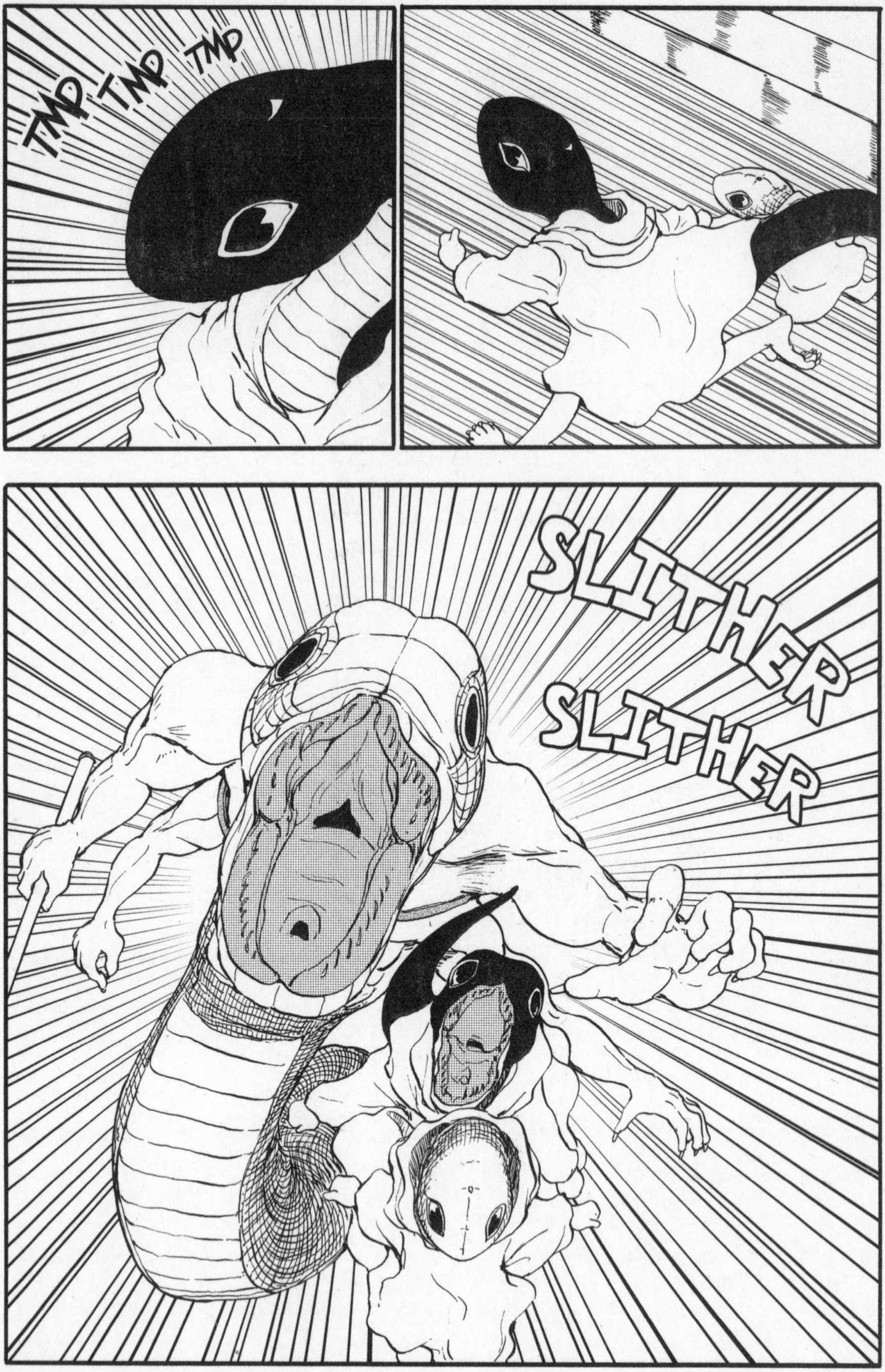
TMP TMP TMP
SLITHER SLITHER

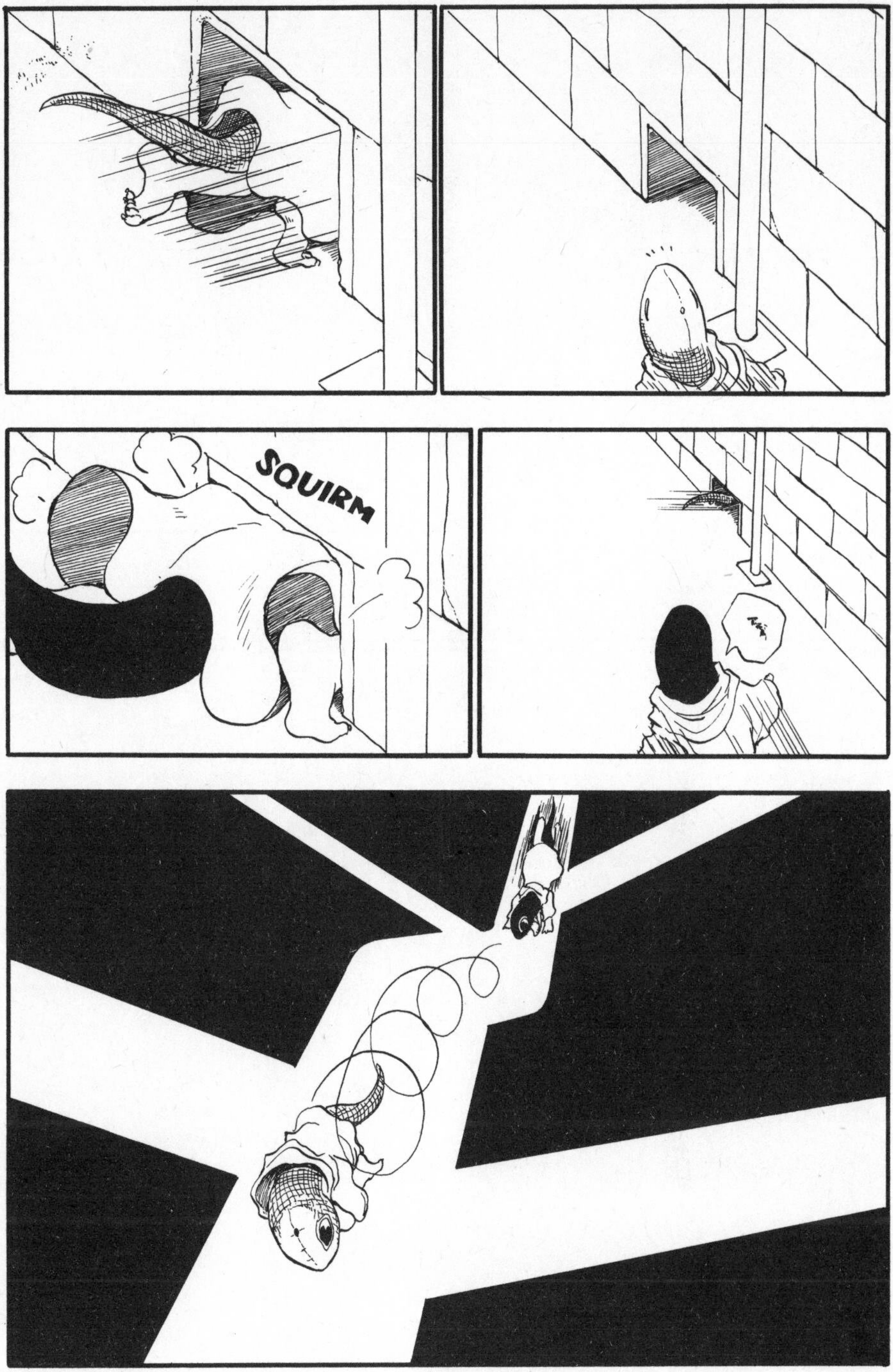
SQUIRM

SPLOOSH
SPLISH
SPLASH
SLOP
SPLOOOSH

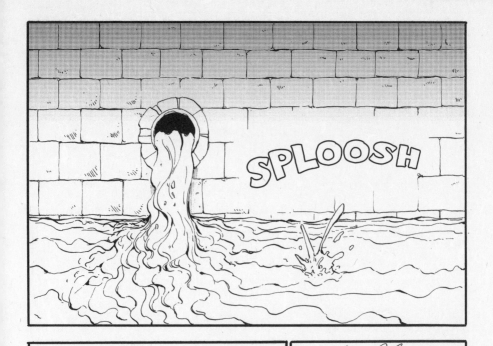

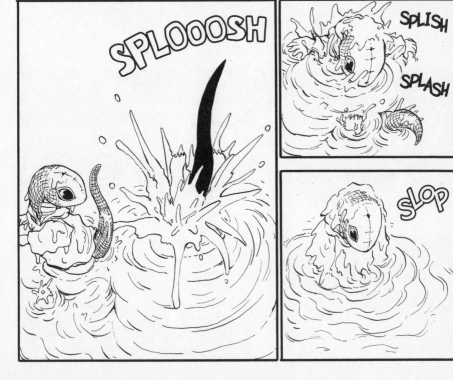

SLITHER
?
RAAWR
SLITHERRR
K-CHAK
GRAWR

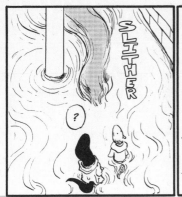

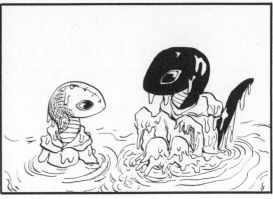

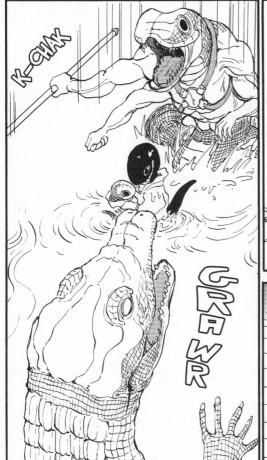

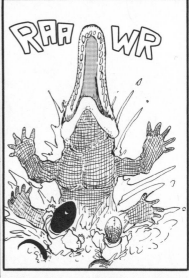

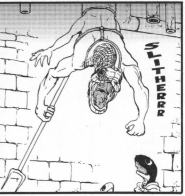

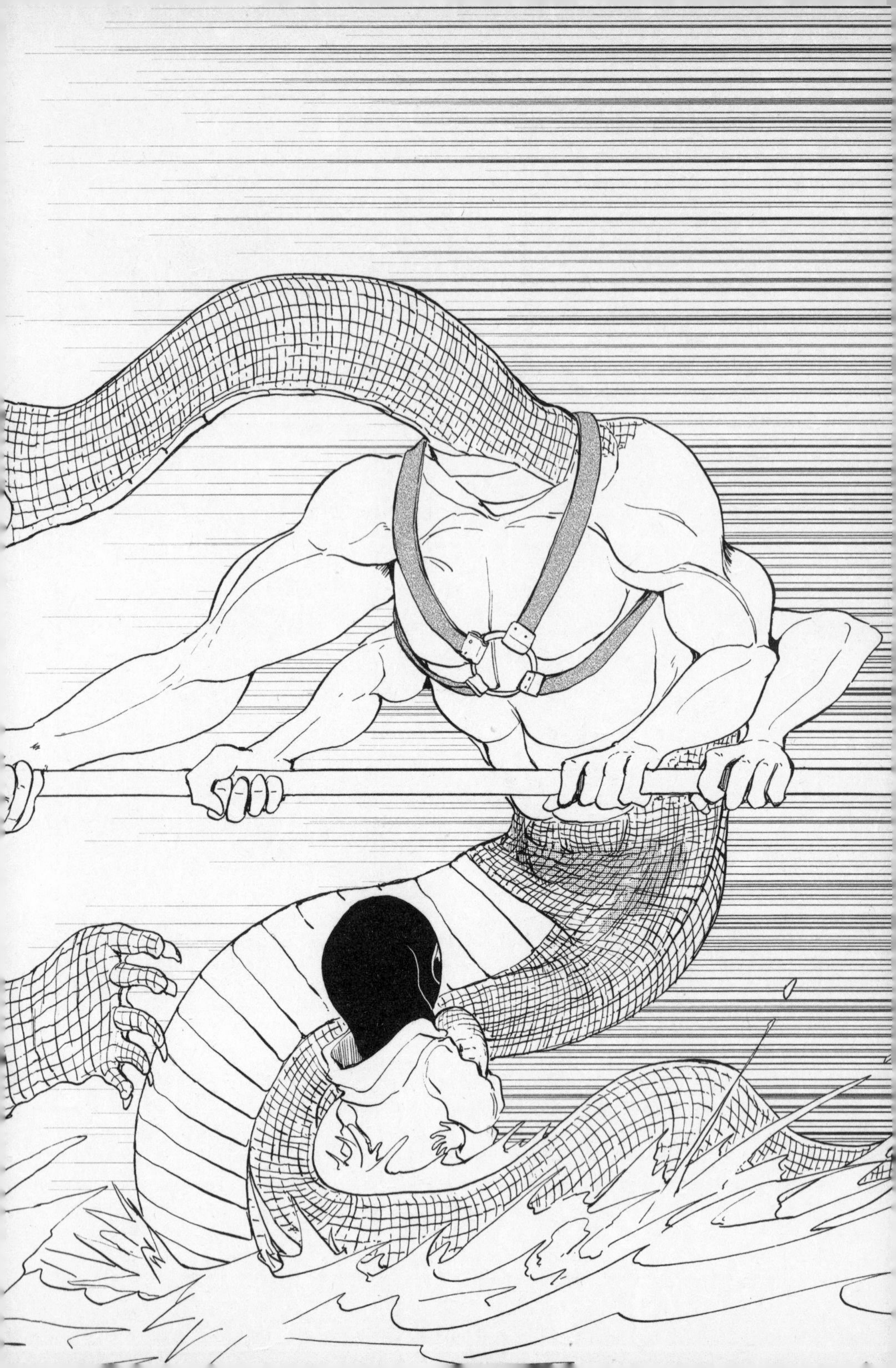

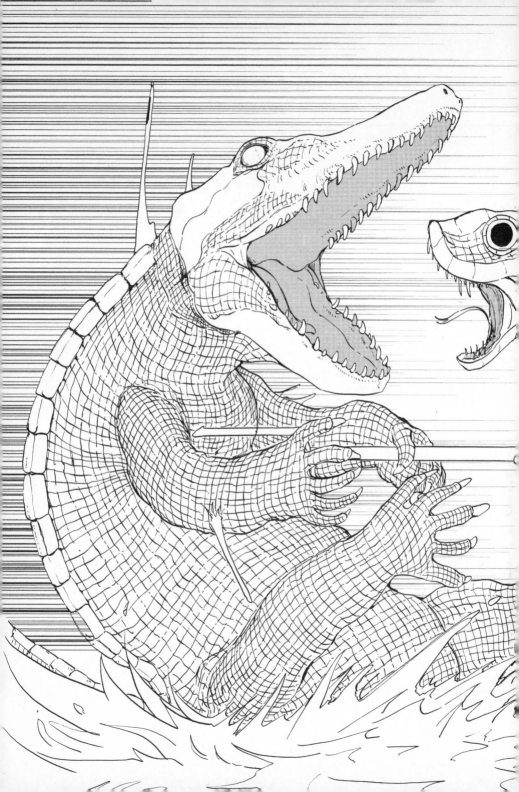

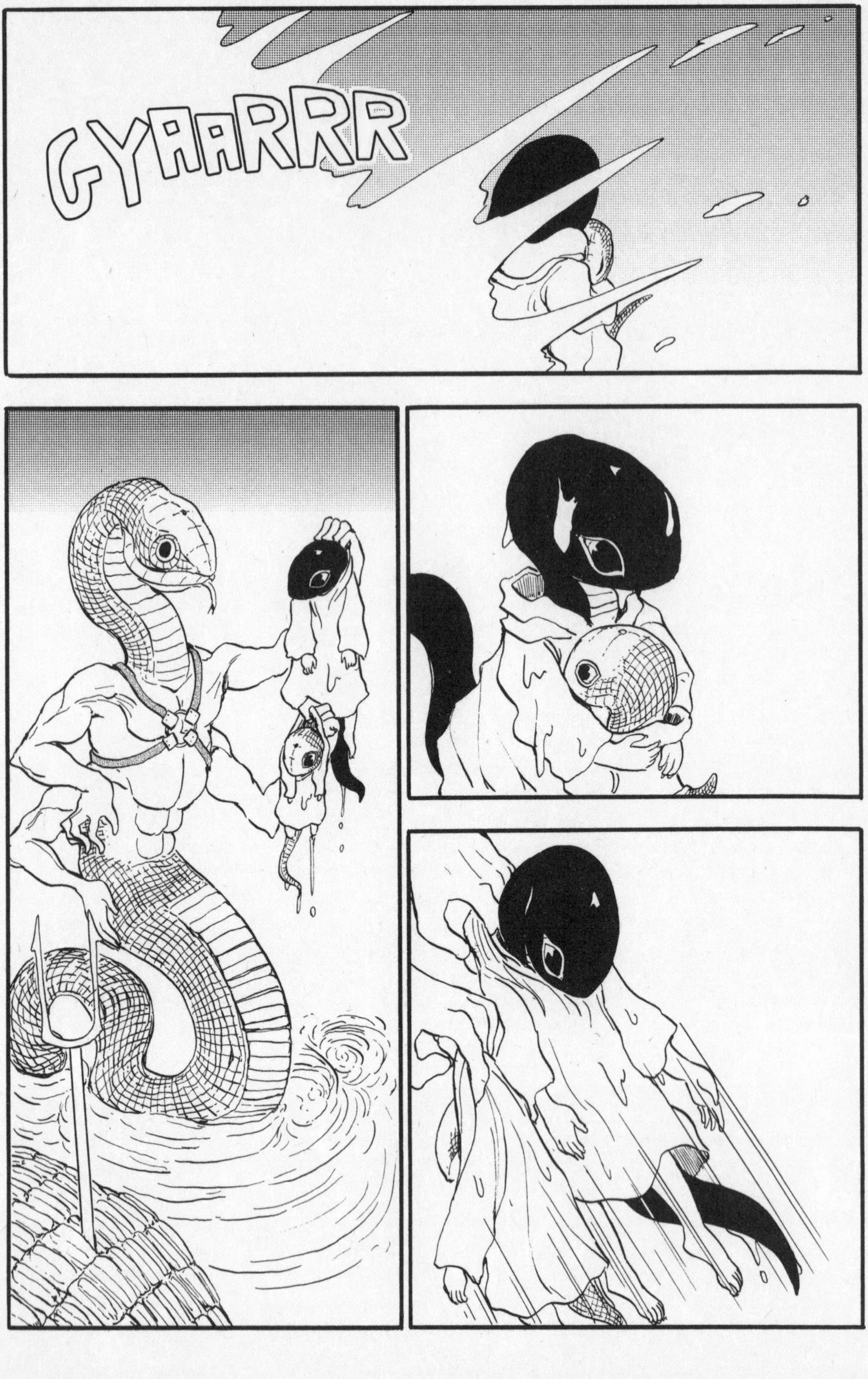
GYAARRR

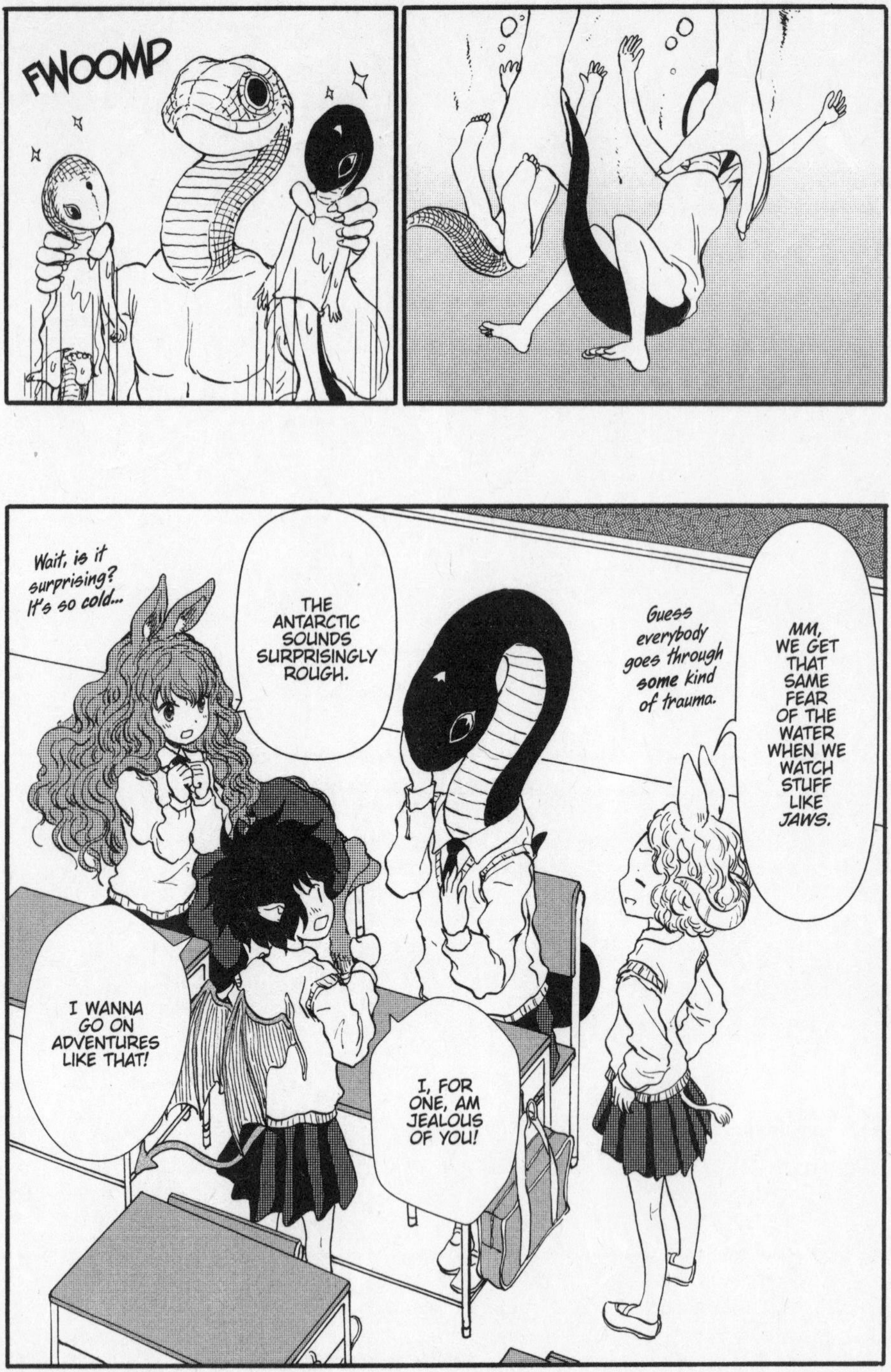
FWOOMP
MM, WE GET THAT SAME FEAR OF THE WATER WHEN WE WATCH STUFF LIKE JAWS.
Guess everybody goes through some kind of trauma.
THE ANTARCTIC SOUNDS SURPRISINGLY ROUGH.
Wait, is it surprising? It's so cold...
I, FOR ONE, AM JEALOUS OF YOU!
I WANNA GO ON ADVENTURES LIKE THAT!

A Centaur's Life

GENETICS MADE EASY: LESSON 3
A SYSTEM FOR
PASSING DOWN
CHARACTERISTICS

PREVIOUSLY, WE NOTED THAT IT IS GENES THAT MAKE HEREDITY POSSIBLE. GENES ARE INFORMATION STORED IN YOUR DNA--THE NUCLEIC ACID FOUND IN THE CELLS THAT MAKE UP YOUR BODY. DNA IS COMPOSED OF FOUR BASE SUBSTANCES (ADENINE, GUANINE, CYTOSINE, AND THYMINE), THE ARRANGEMENT OF WHICH FORMS A SORT OF CODE, WORKING LIKE A COMPUTER PROGRAM TO RECORD THE TRAITS OF A LIVING THING.

WITHIN THESE GENES LIE THE CODES THAT CREATE HORNS OR WINGS. SO WHY IS IT, THEN, THAT A CHILD WHO HAS RECEIVED THE GENES TO MAKE WINGS FROM A PARENT WOULD THEN GO ON TO BE BORN A WINGLESS GOATFOLK?

THE ANSWER IS THAT WITHIN YOUR GENES, THERE IS A PARTICULAR CODE WHICH ULTIMATELY DETERMINES YOUR RACE (RACE-DETERMINING GENES). IF THIS CODE DETERMINES THAT YOU ARE ANGELFOLK, THEN YOU WILL NOT BE BORN WITH HORNS, EVEN IF YOU HAVE THE GENE FOR HORNS. ONLY YOUR WING GENES WILL FUNCTION. CONVERSELY, IF YOUR RACE-DETERMINING GENES DICTATE THAT YOU ARE GOATFOLK, YOUR WING-GENERATING GENES WILL BE IGNORED.

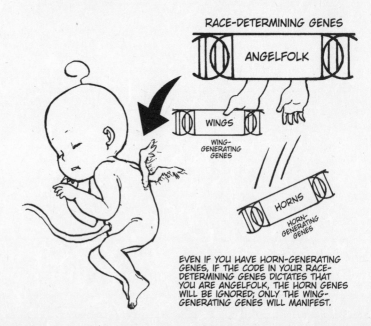

RACE-DETERMINING GENES

ANGELFOLK

WINGS

WING-
GENERATING
GENES

HORNS

HORN-
GENERATING
GENES

EVEN IF YOU HAVE HORN-GENERATING GENES, IF THE CODE IN YOUR RACE-DETERMINING GENES DICTATES THAT YOU ARE ANGELFOLK, THE HORN GENES WILL BE IGNORED; ONLY THE WING-GENERATING GENES WILL MANIFEST.

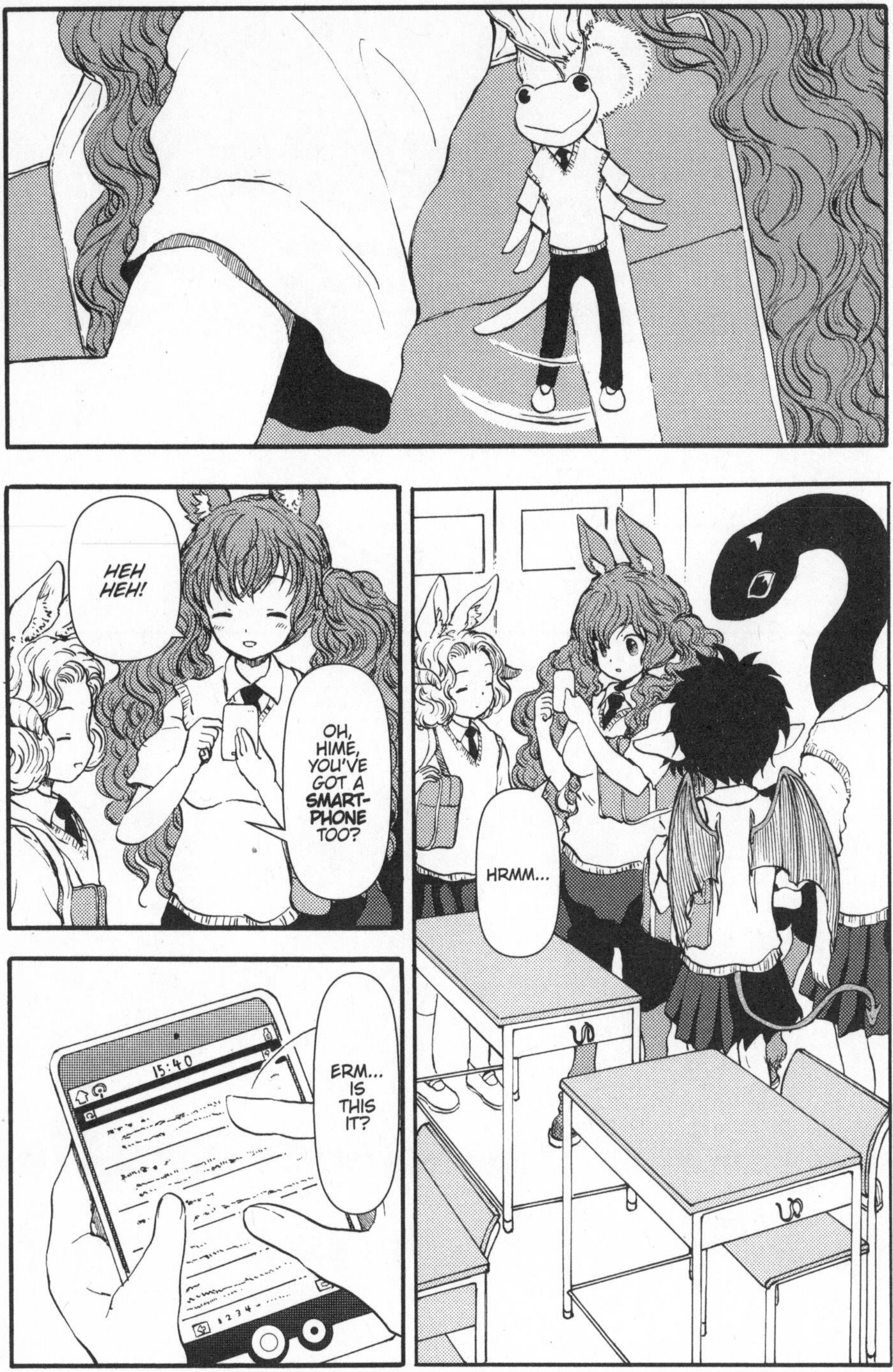
HRMM...
OH, HIME, YOU'VE GOT A SMARTPHONE TOO?
HEH HEH!
ERM... IS THIS IT?
15:40

CHAPTER 33

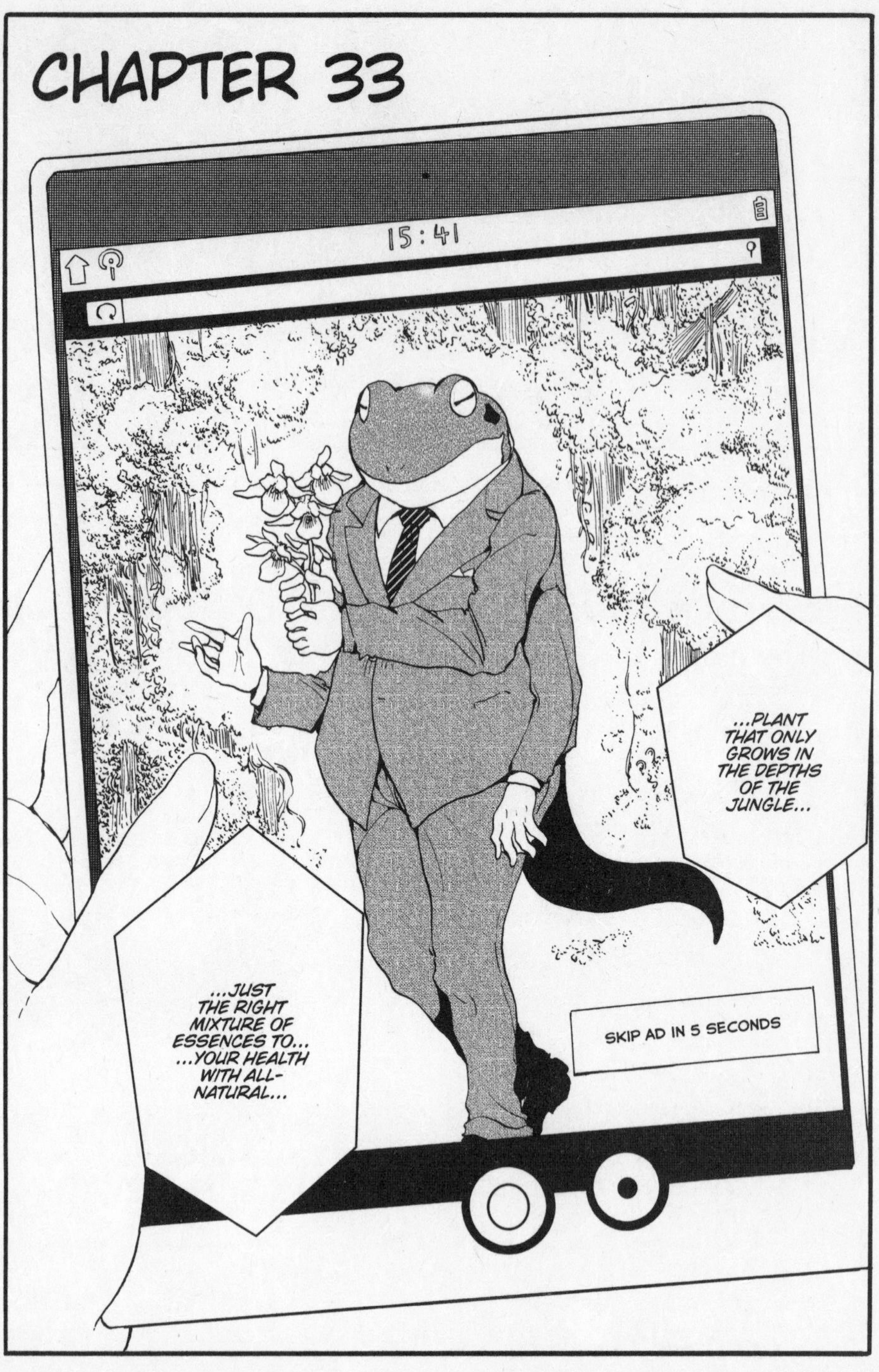
15:41
...PLANT THAT ONLY GROWS IN THE DEPTHS OF THE JUNGLE...
SKIP AD IN 5 SECONDS
...JUST THE RIGHT MIXTURE OF ESSENCES TO... ...YOUR HEALTH WITH ALL-NATURAL...

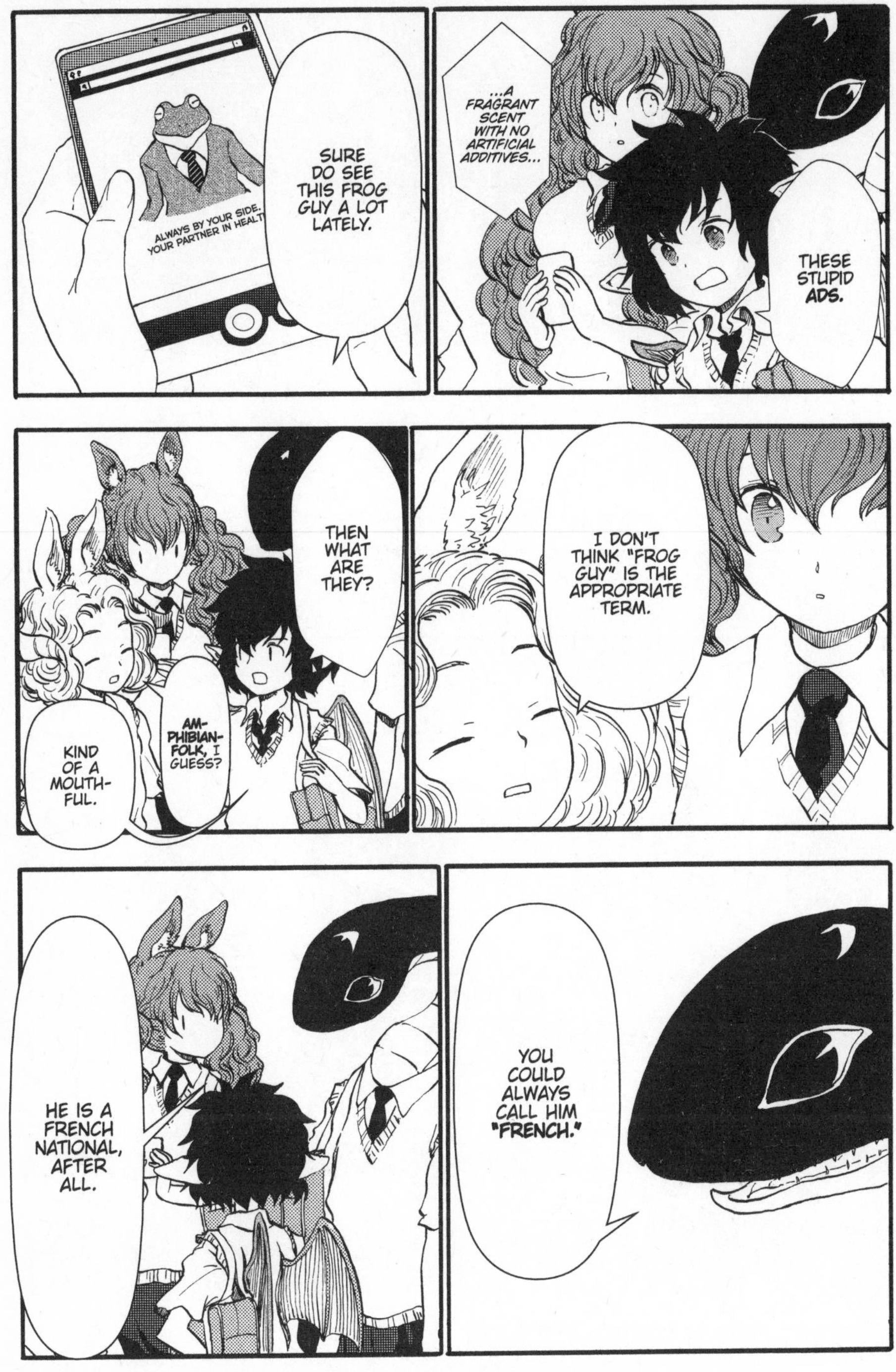
...A FRAGRANT SCENT WITH NO ARTIFICIAL ADDITIVES...
THESE STUPID ADS.
ALWAYS BY YOUR SIDE. YOUR PARTNER IN HEALT
SURE DO SEE THIS FROG GUY A LOT LATELY.
I DON'T THINK "FROG GUY" IS THE APPROPRIATE TERM.
THEN WHAT ARE THEY?
AM-PHIBIAN-FOLK, I GUESS?
KIND OF A MOUTH-FUL.
YOU COULD ALWAYS CALL HIM "FRENCH."
HE IS A FRENCH NATIONAL, AFTER ALL.

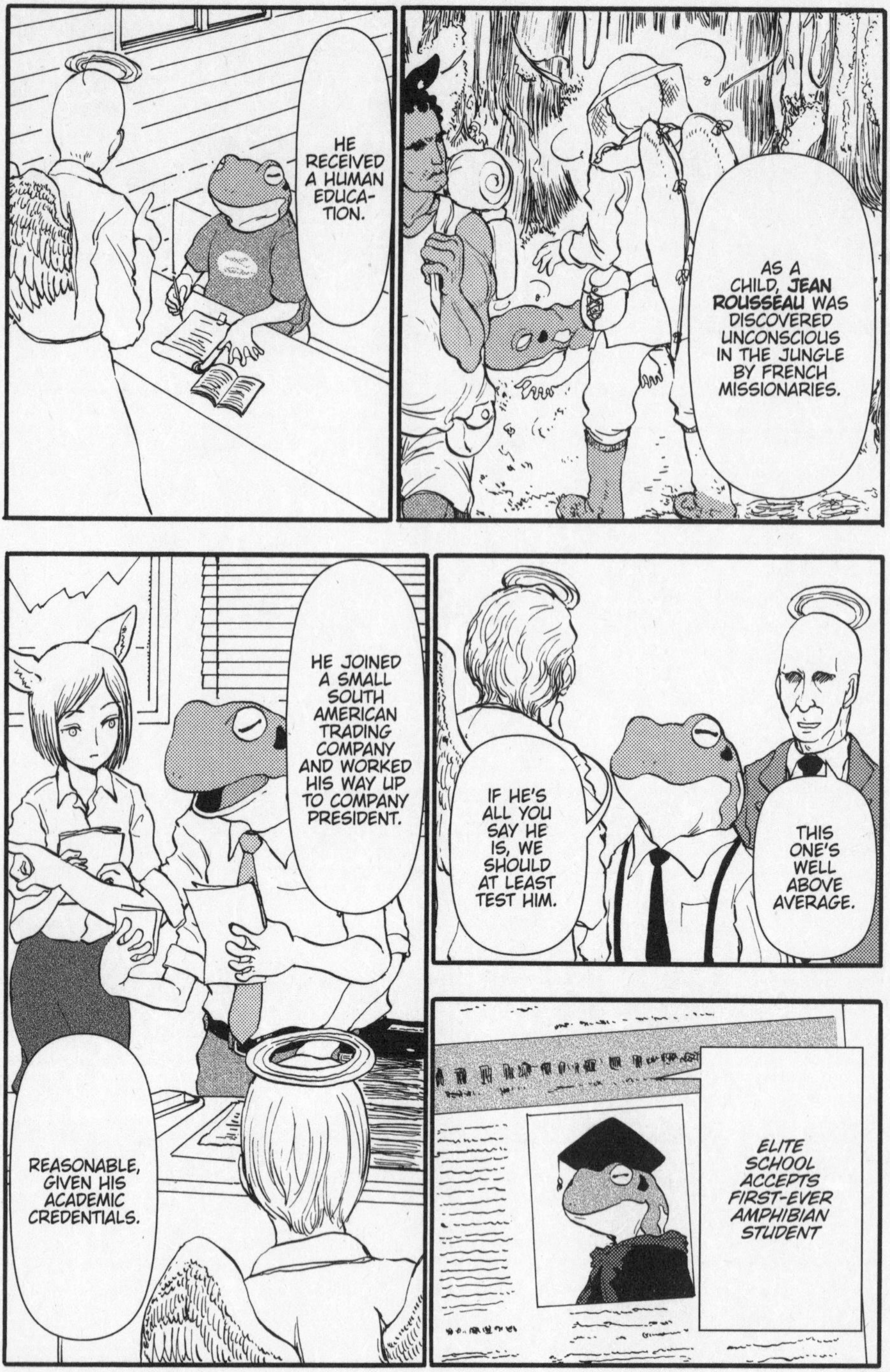
AS A CHILD, JEAN ROUSSEAU WAS DISCOVERED UNCONSCIOUS IN THE JUNGLE BY FRENCH MISSIONARIES.
HE RECEIVED A HUMAN EDUCATION.
THIS ONE'S WELL ABOVE AVERAGE.
IF HE'S ALL YOU SAY HE IS, WE SHOULD AT LEAST TEST HIM.
ELITE SCHOOL ACCEPTS FIRST-EVER AMPHIBIAN STUDENT
HE JOINED A SMALL SOUTH AMERICAN TRADING COMPANY AND WORKED HIS WAY UP TO COMPANY PRESIDENT.
REASONABLE, GIVEN HIS ACADEMIC CREDENTIALS.

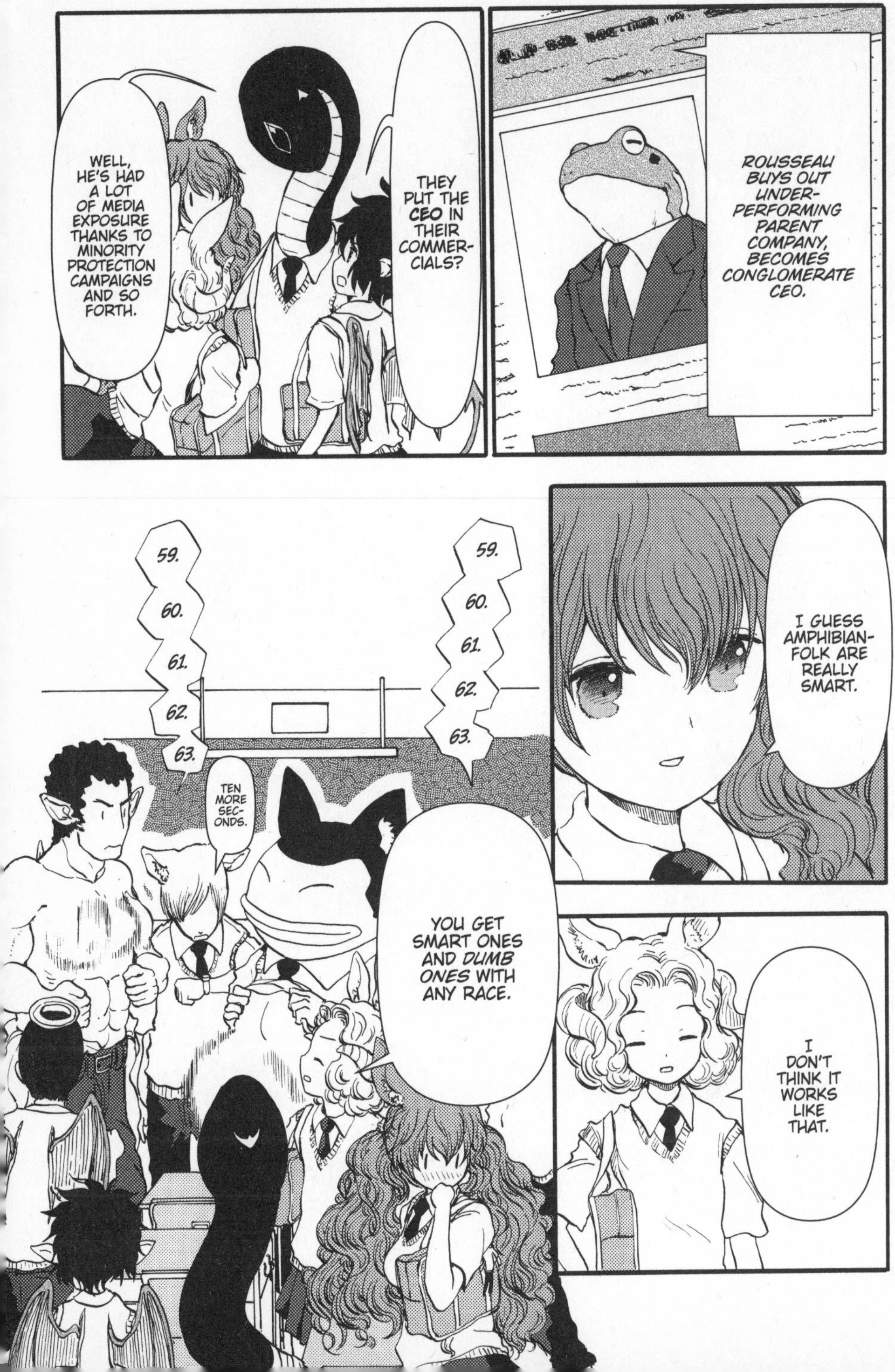
ROUSSEAU BUYS OUT UNDER-PERFORMING PARENT COMPANY, BECOMES CONGLOMERATE CEO.
THEY PUT THE CEO IN THEIR COMMERCIALS?
WELL, HE'S HAD A LOT OF MEDIA EXPOSURE THANKS TO MINORITY PROTECTION CAMPAIGNS AND SO FORTH.
I GUESS AMPHIBIAN-FOLK ARE REALLY SMART.
YOU GET SMART ONES AND *DUMB ONES* WITH ANY RACE.
I DON'T THINK IT WORKS LIKE THAT.
59.
60.
61.
62.
63.
59.
60.
61.
62.
63.
TEN MORE SECONDS.

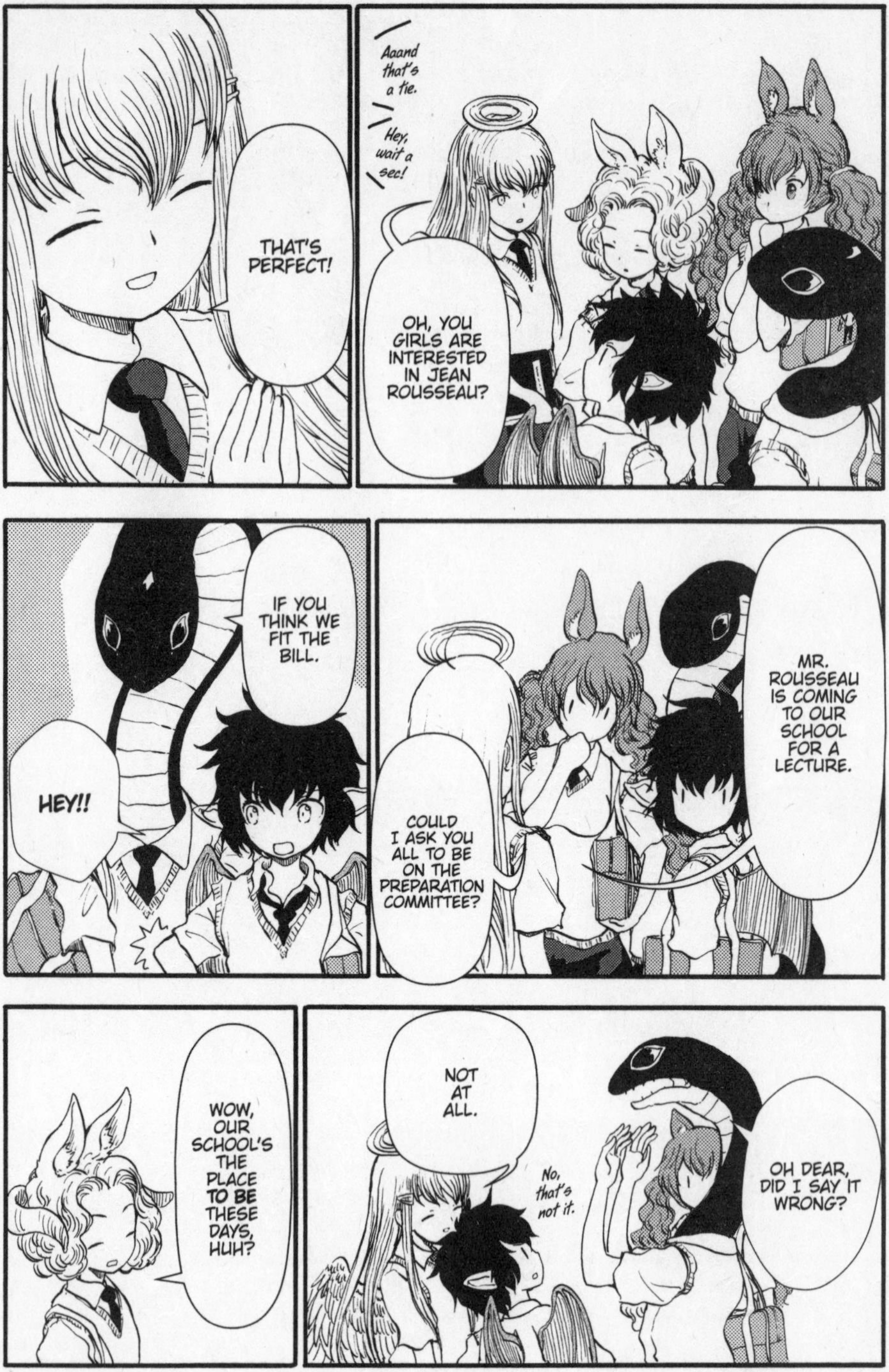
Aaand that's a tie.
Hey, wait a sec!
OH, YOU GIRLS ARE INTERESTED IN JEAN ROUSSEAU?
THAT'S PERFECT!
MR. ROUSSEAU IS COMING TO OUR SCHOOL FOR A LECTURE.
COULD I ASK YOU ALL TO BE ON THE PREPARATION COMMITTEE?
IF YOU THINK WE FIT THE BILL.
HEY!!
OH DEAR, DID I SAY IT WRONG?
NOT AT ALL.
No, that's not it.
WOW, OUR SCHOOL'S THE PLACE TO BE THESE DAYS, HUH?

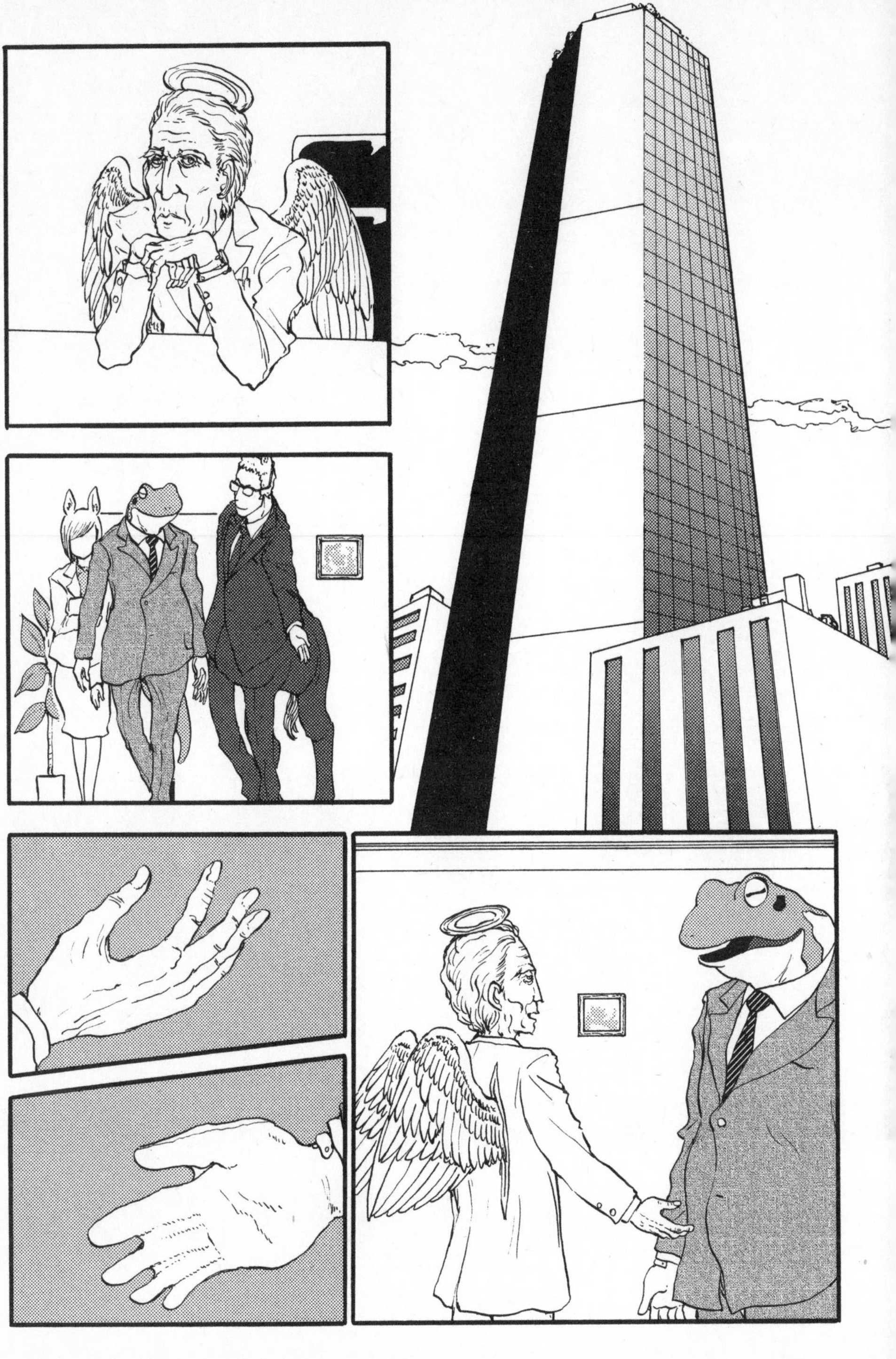

DON'T YOU SUPPOSE IT'S RUDE TO SHAKE HANDS WITH YOUR *GLOVES* STILL ON?

BUT MY HANDS ARE...

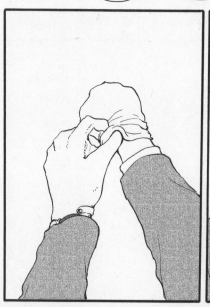

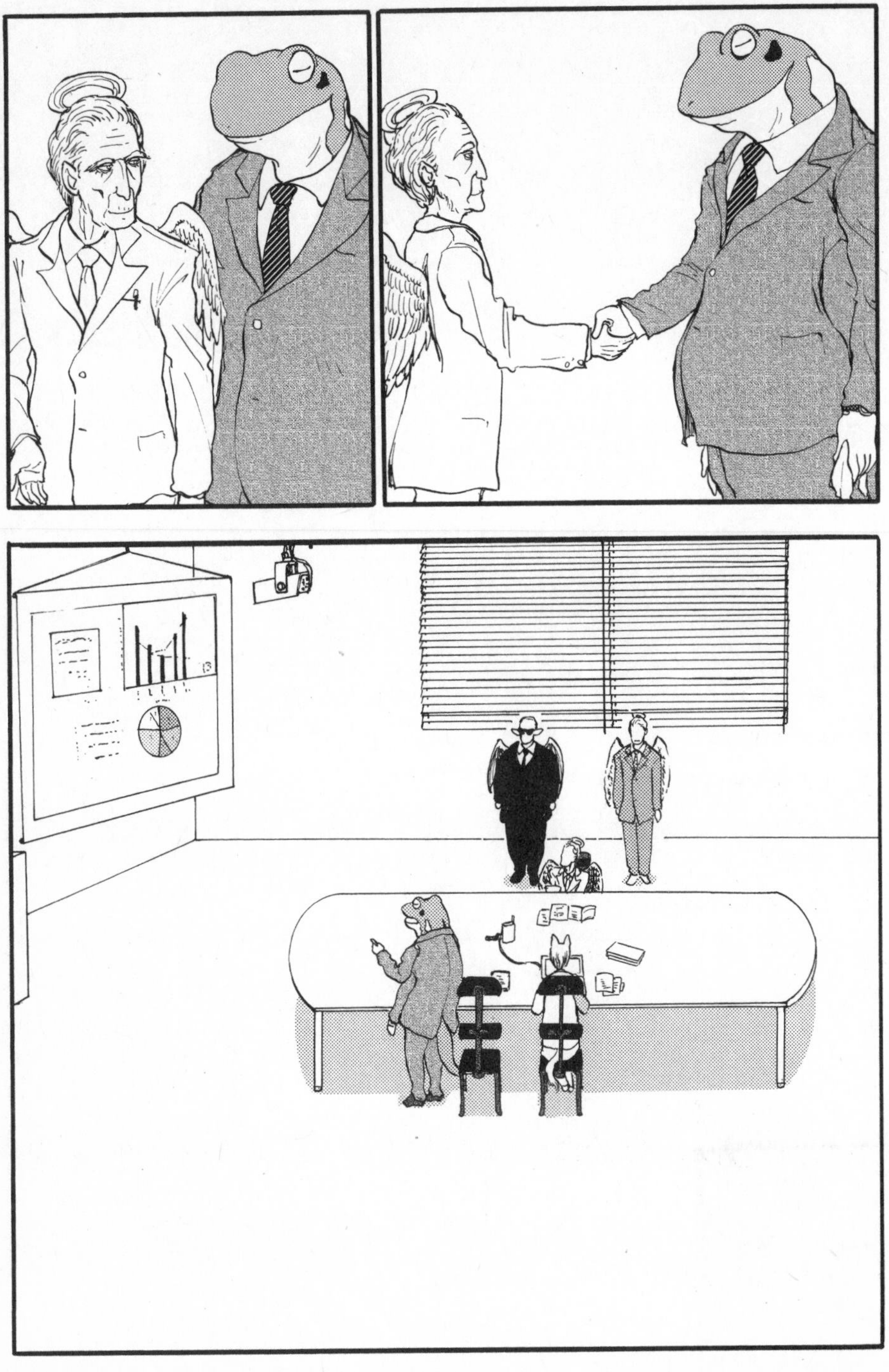

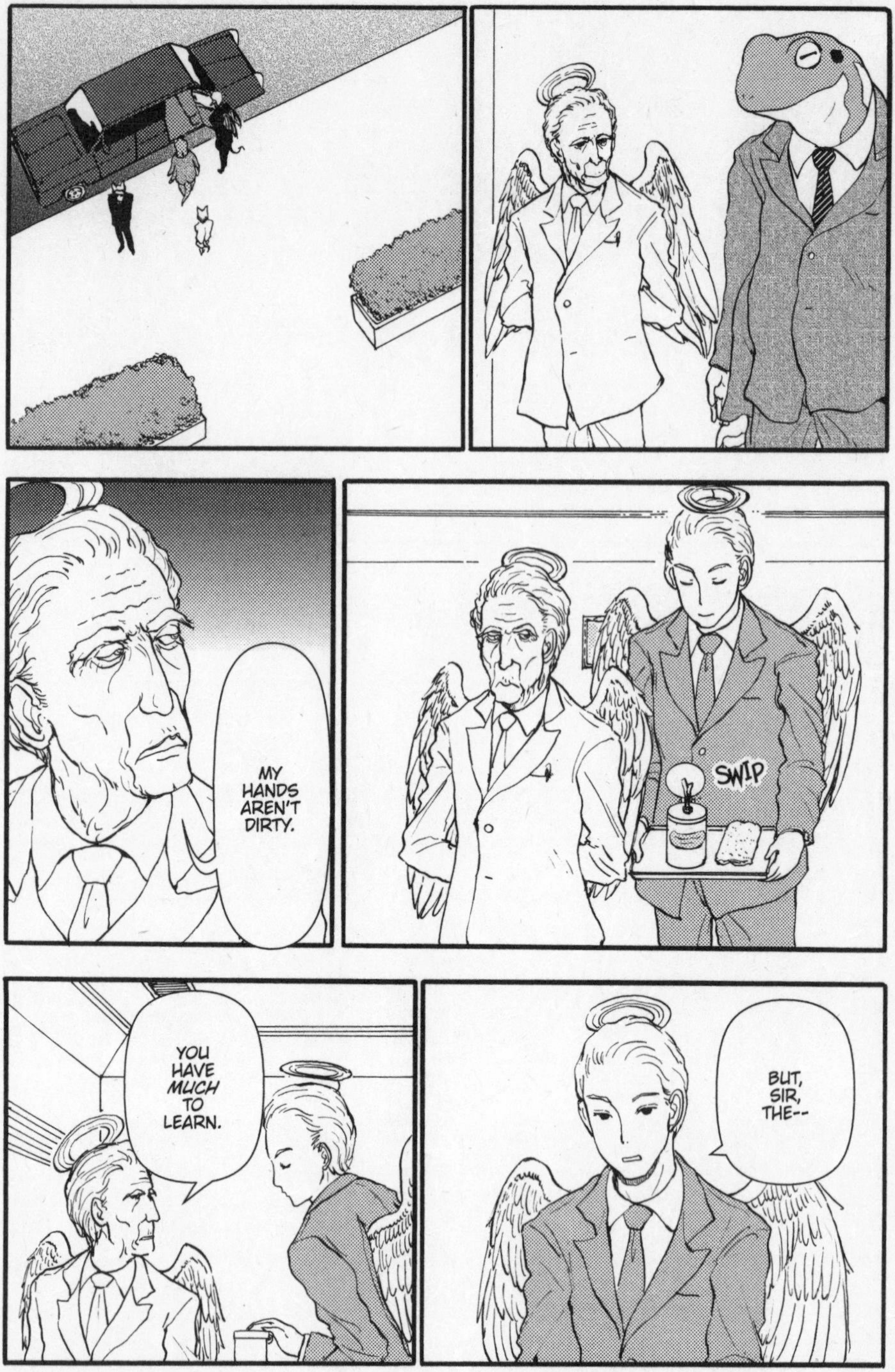
SWIP
MY HANDS AREN'T DIRTY.
BUT, SIR, THE--
YOU HAVE *MUCH* TO LEARN.

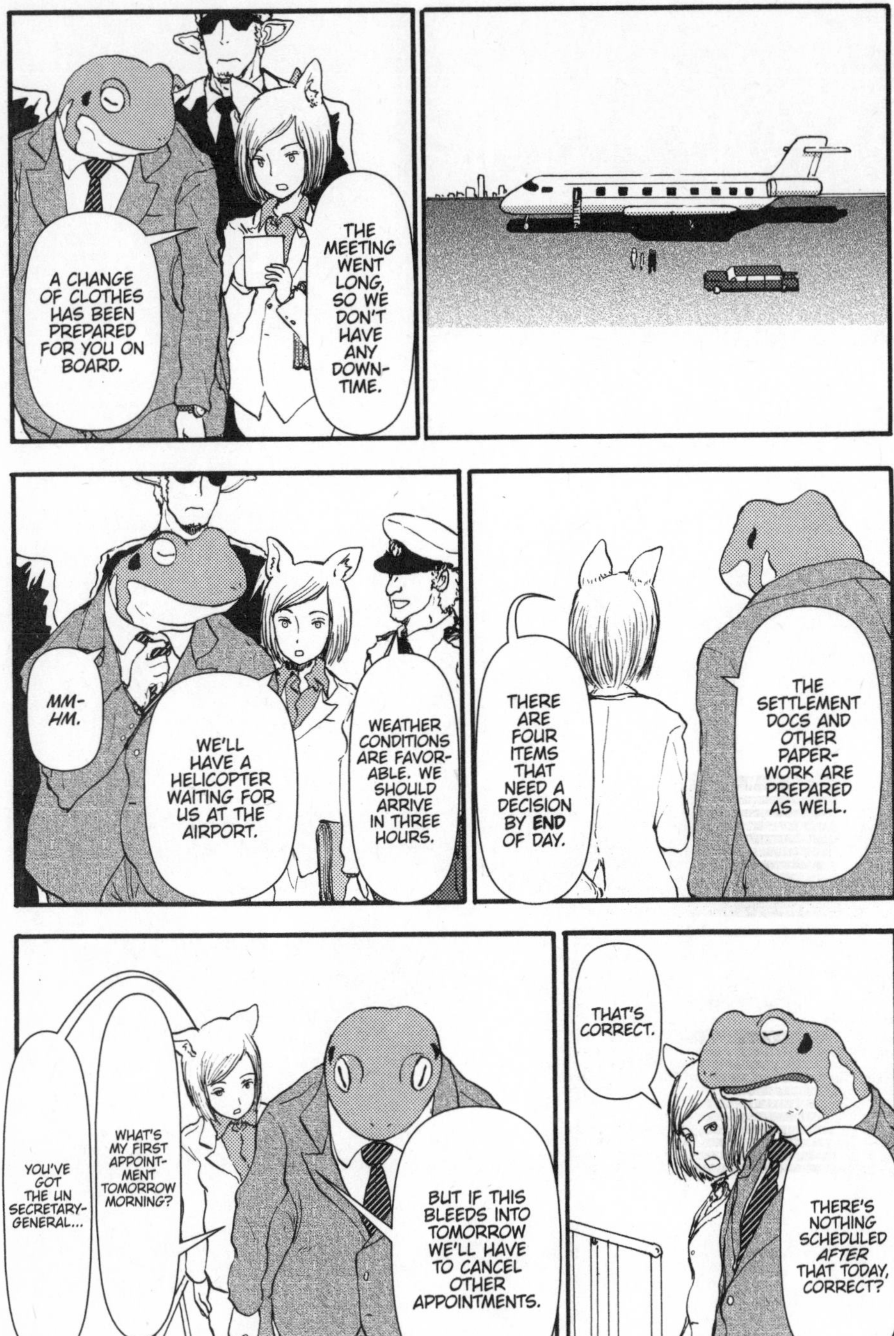
THE MEETING WENT LONG, SO WE DON'T HAVE ANY DOWN-TIME.
A CHANGE OF CLOTHES HAS BEEN PREPARED FOR YOU ON BOARD.
THE SETTLEMENT DOCS AND OTHER PAPER-WORK ARE PREPARED AS WELL.
THERE ARE FOUR ITEMS THAT NEED A DECISION BY **END** OF DAY.
WEATHER CONDITIONS ARE FAVOR-ABLE. WE SHOULD ARRIVE IN THREE HOURS.
WE'LL HAVE A HELICOPTER WAITING FOR US AT THE AIRPORT.
MM-HM.
THERE'S NOTHING SCHEDULED *AFTER* THAT TODAY, CORRECT?
THAT'S CORRECT.
BUT IF THIS BLEEDS INTO TOMORROW WE'LL HAVE TO CANCEL OTHER APPOINTMENTS.
WHAT'S MY FIRST APPOINTMENT TOMORROW MORNING?
YOU'VE GOT THE UN SECRETARY-GENERAL...

RUB
RUB

WOP
WOP
WOP

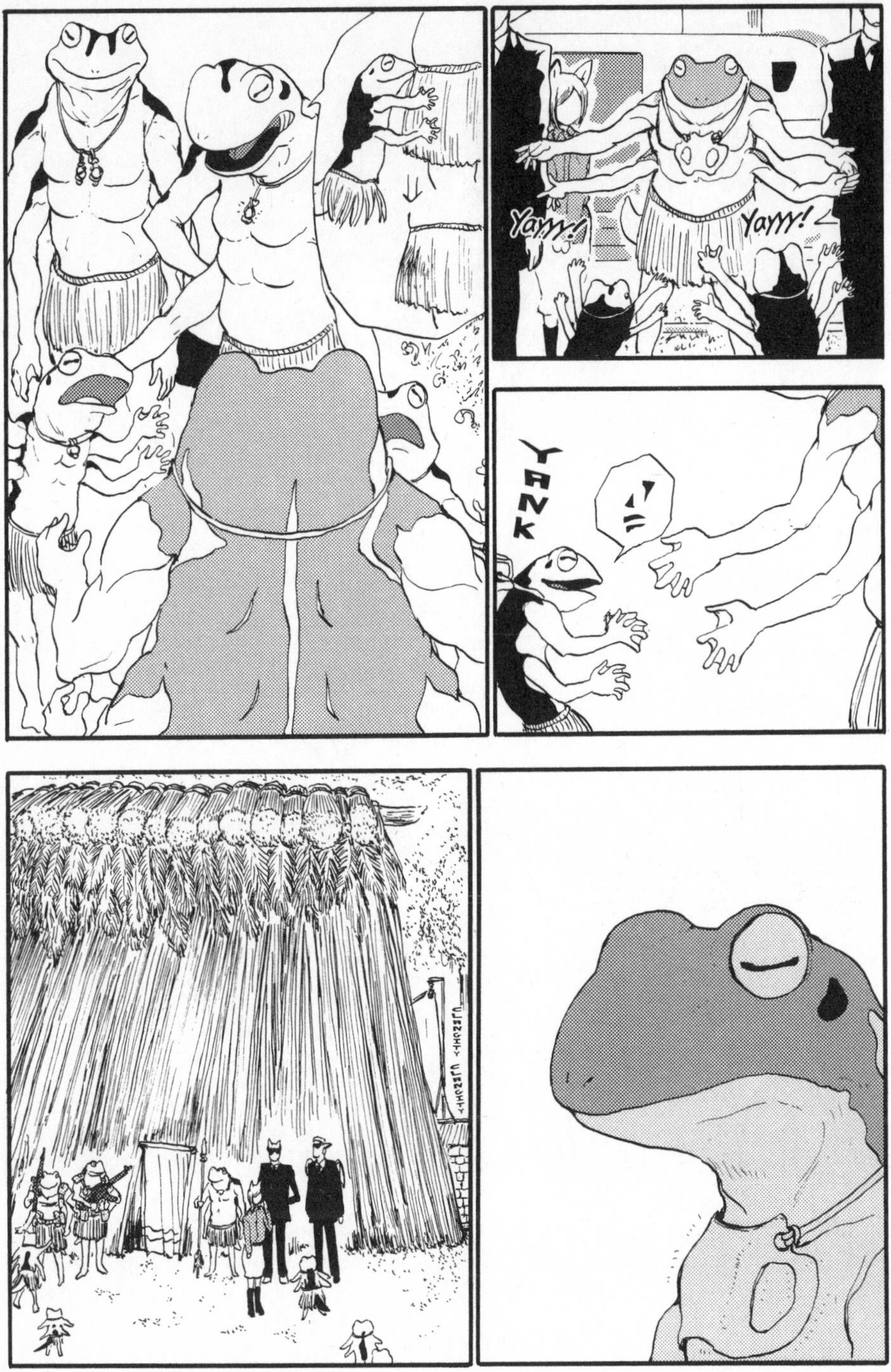
Yayyy!
Yayyy!
YANK
!?
CLANGITY CLANGITY

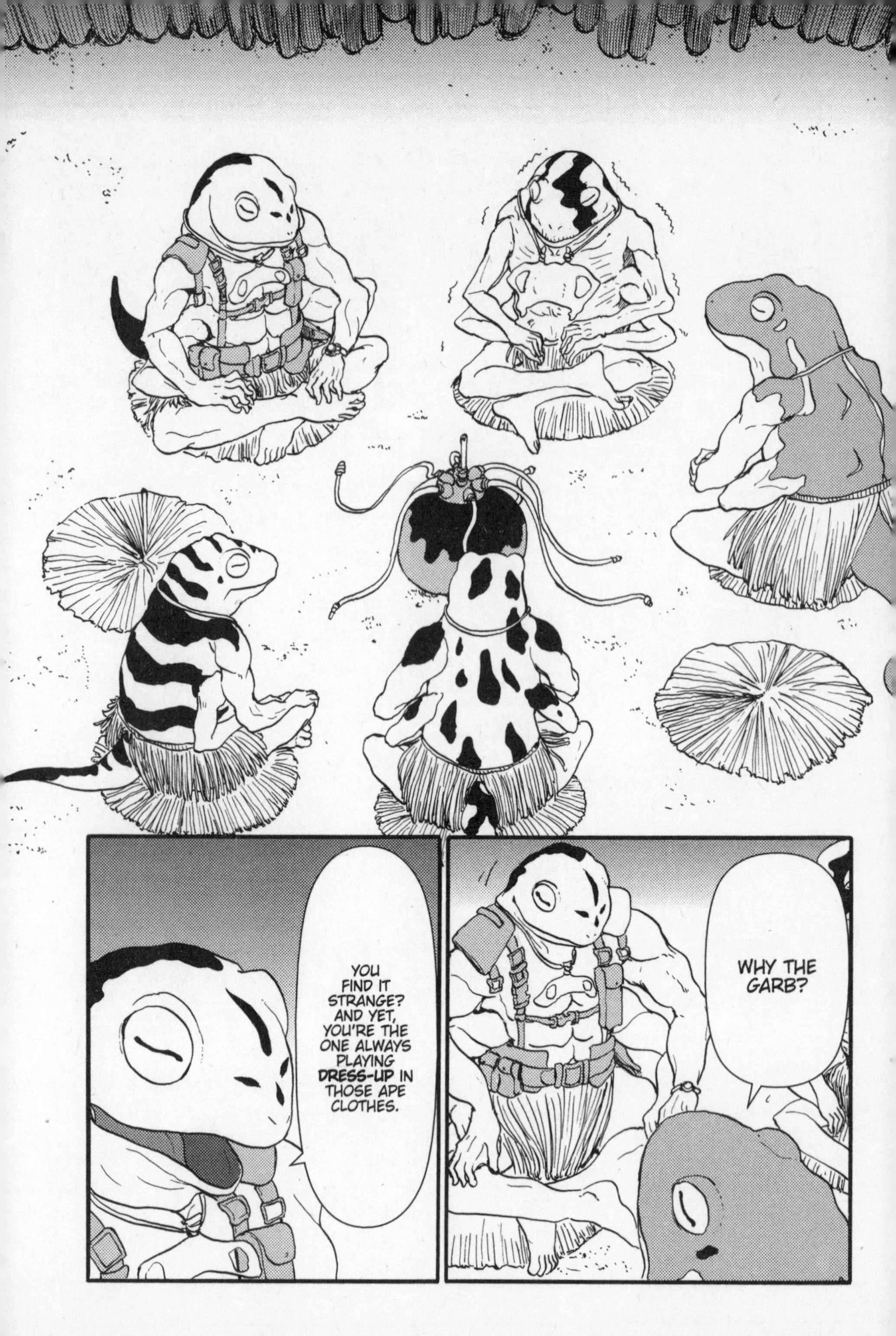
WHY THE GARB?
YOU FIND IT STRANGE? AND YET, YOU'RE THE ONE ALWAYS PLAYING **DRESS-UP** IN THOSE APE CLOTHES.

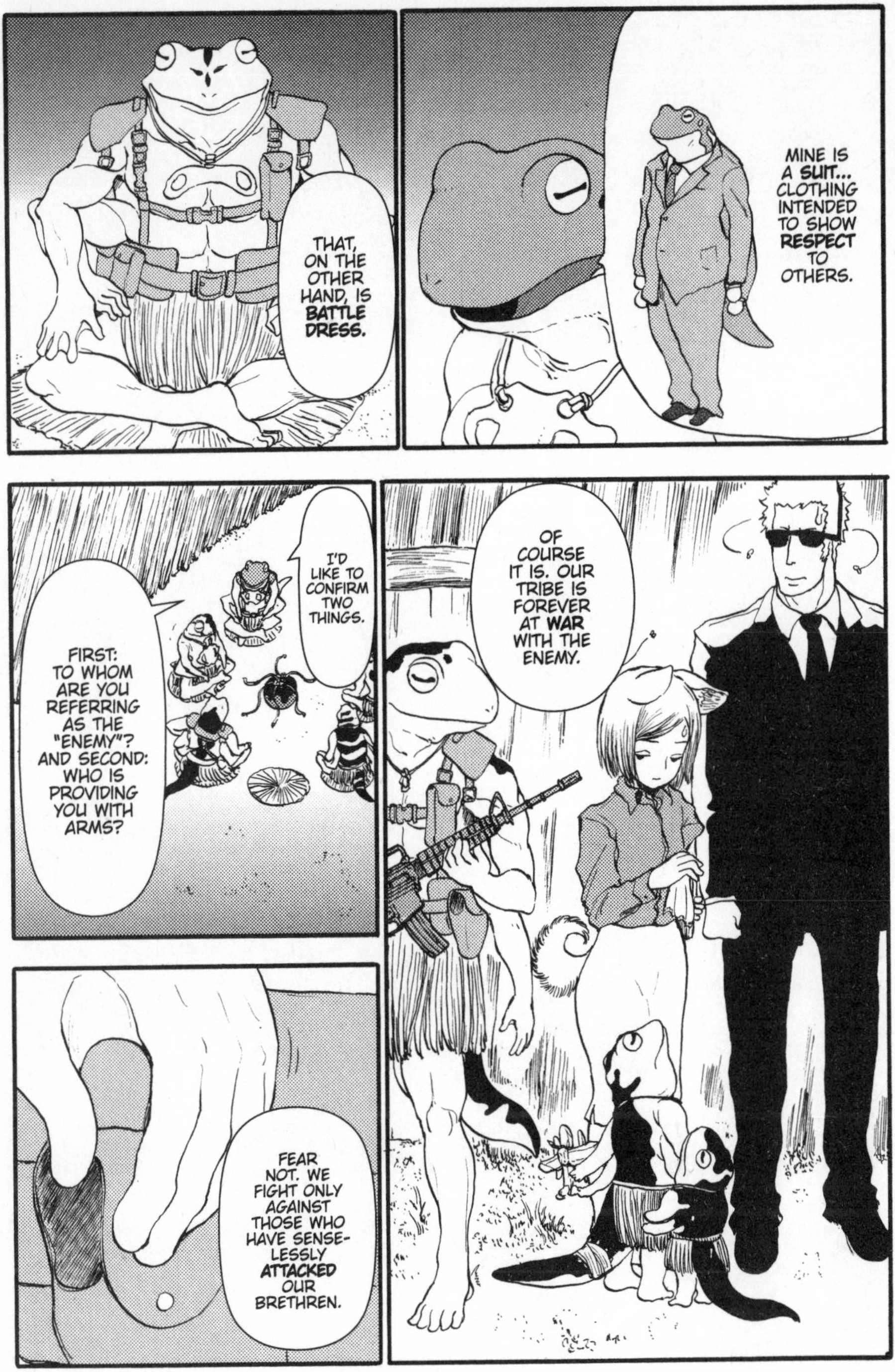
MINE IS A **SUIT...** CLOTHING INTENDED TO SHOW **RESPECT** TO OTHERS.
THAT, ON THE OTHER HAND, IS **BATTLE DRESS.**
OF COURSE IT IS. OUR TRIBE IS FOREVER AT **WAR** WITH THE ENEMY.
I'D LIKE TO CONFIRM TWO THINGS.
FIRST: TO WHOM ARE YOU REFERRING AS THE "ENEMY"? AND SECOND: WHO IS PROVIDING YOU WITH ARMS?
FEAR NOT. WE FIGHT ONLY AGAINST THOSE WHO HAVE SENSE-LESSLY **ATTACKED** OUR BRETHREN.

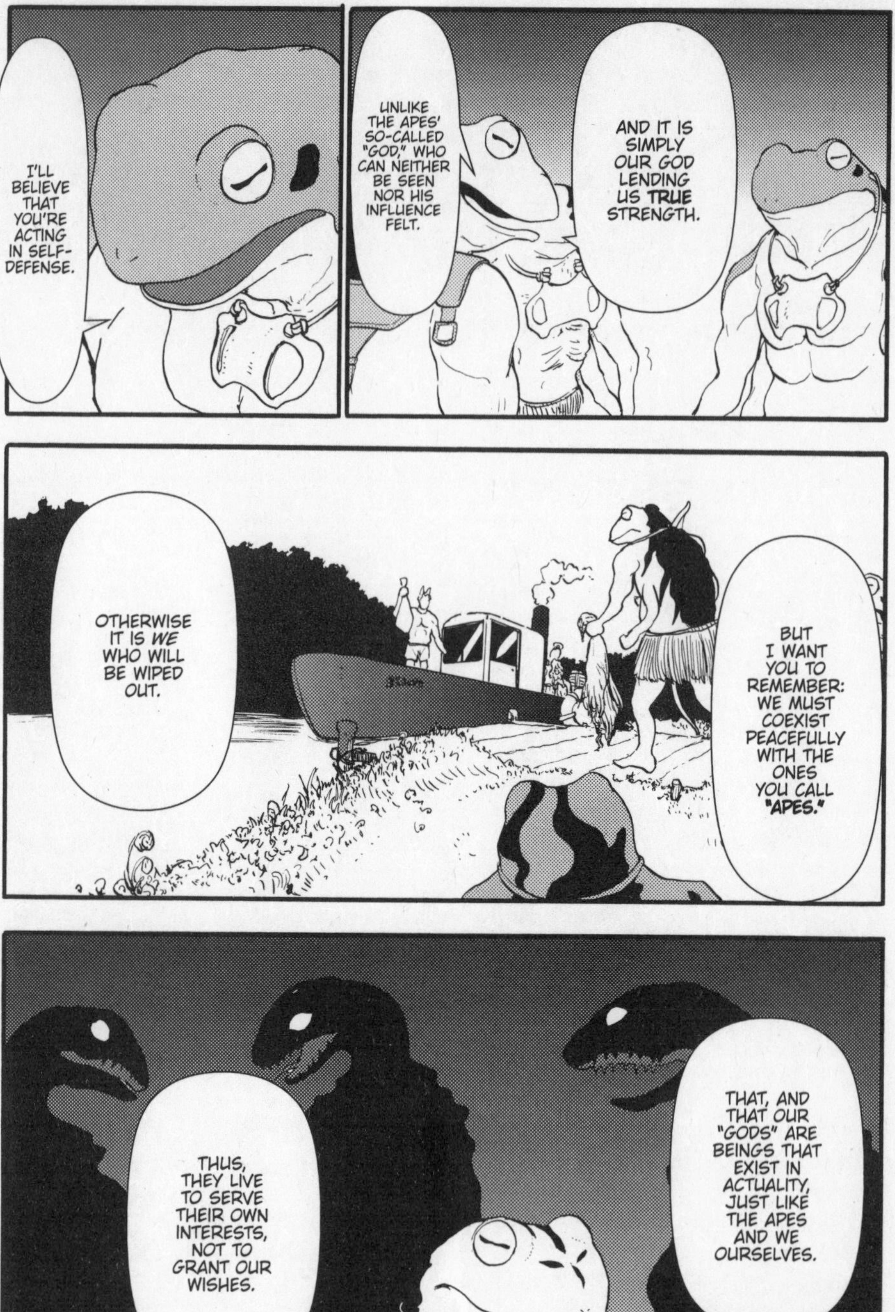
UNLIKE THE APES' SO-CALLED "GOD," WHO CAN NEITHER BE SEEN NOR HIS INFLUENCE FELT.
AND IT IS SIMPLY OUR GOD LENDING US **TRUE** STRENGTH.
I'LL BELIEVE THAT YOU'RE ACTING IN SELF-DEFENSE.
BUT I WANT YOU TO REMEMBER: WE MUST COEXIST PEACEFULLY WITH THE ONES YOU CALL **"APES."**
OTHERWISE IT IS *WE* WHO WILL BE WIPED OUT.
THAT, AND THAT OUR "GODS" ARE BEINGS THAT EXIST IN ACTUALITY, JUST LIKE THE APES AND WE OURSELVES.
THUS, THEY LIVE TO SERVE THEIR OWN INTERESTS, NOT TO GRANT OUR WISHES.

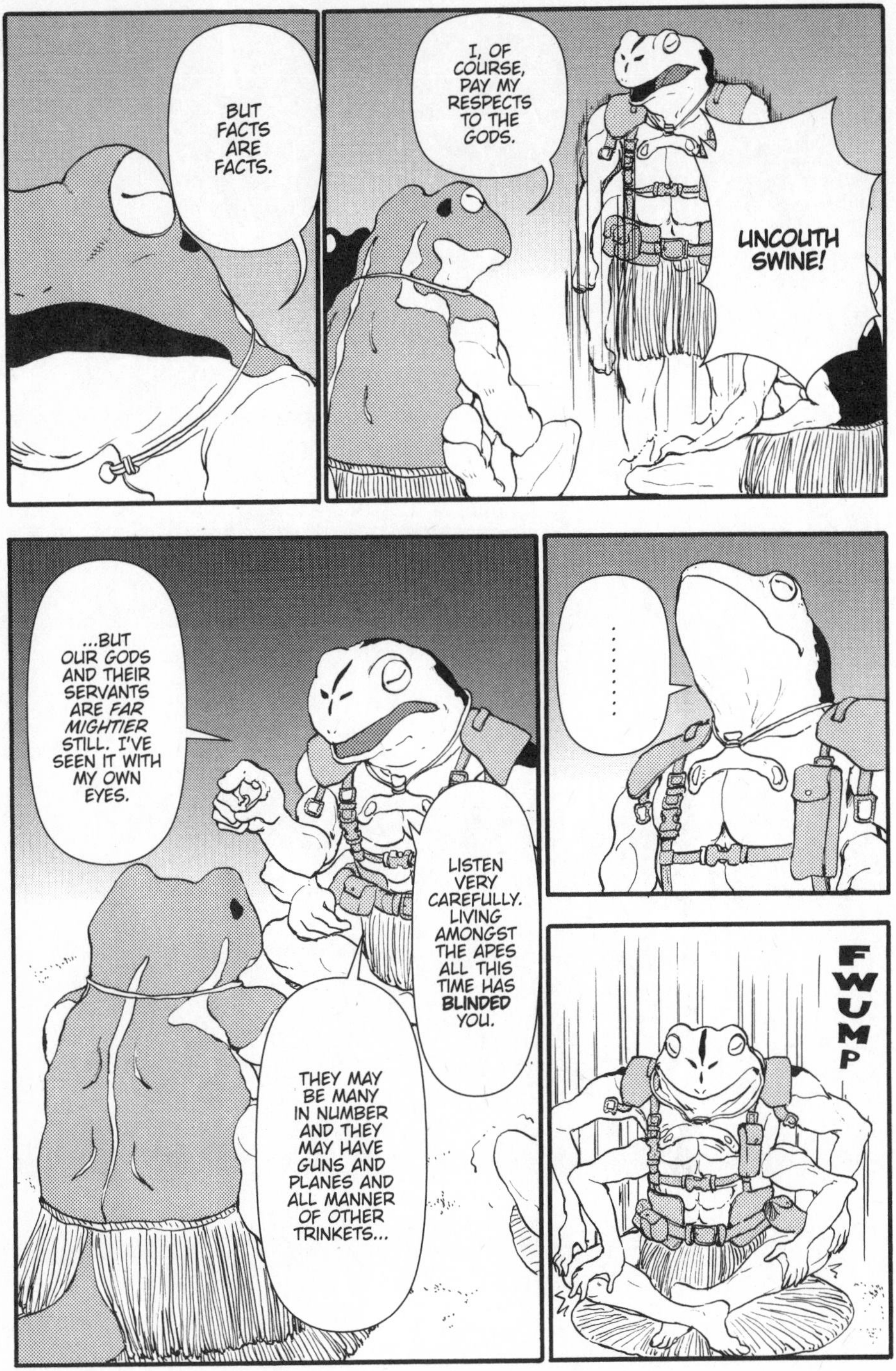
UNCOUTH SWINE!
I, OF COURSE, PAY MY RESPECTS TO THE GODS.
BUT FACTS ARE FACTS.
......
FWUMP
LISTEN VERY CAREFULLY. LIVING AMONGST THE APES ALL THIS TIME HAS **BLINDED** YOU.
THEY MAY BE MANY IN NUMBER AND THEY MAY HAVE GUNS AND PLANES AND ALL MANNER OF OTHER TRINKETS...
...BUT OUR GODS AND THEIR SERVANTS ARE *FAR MIGHTIER* STILL. I'VE SEEN IT WITH MY OWN EYES.

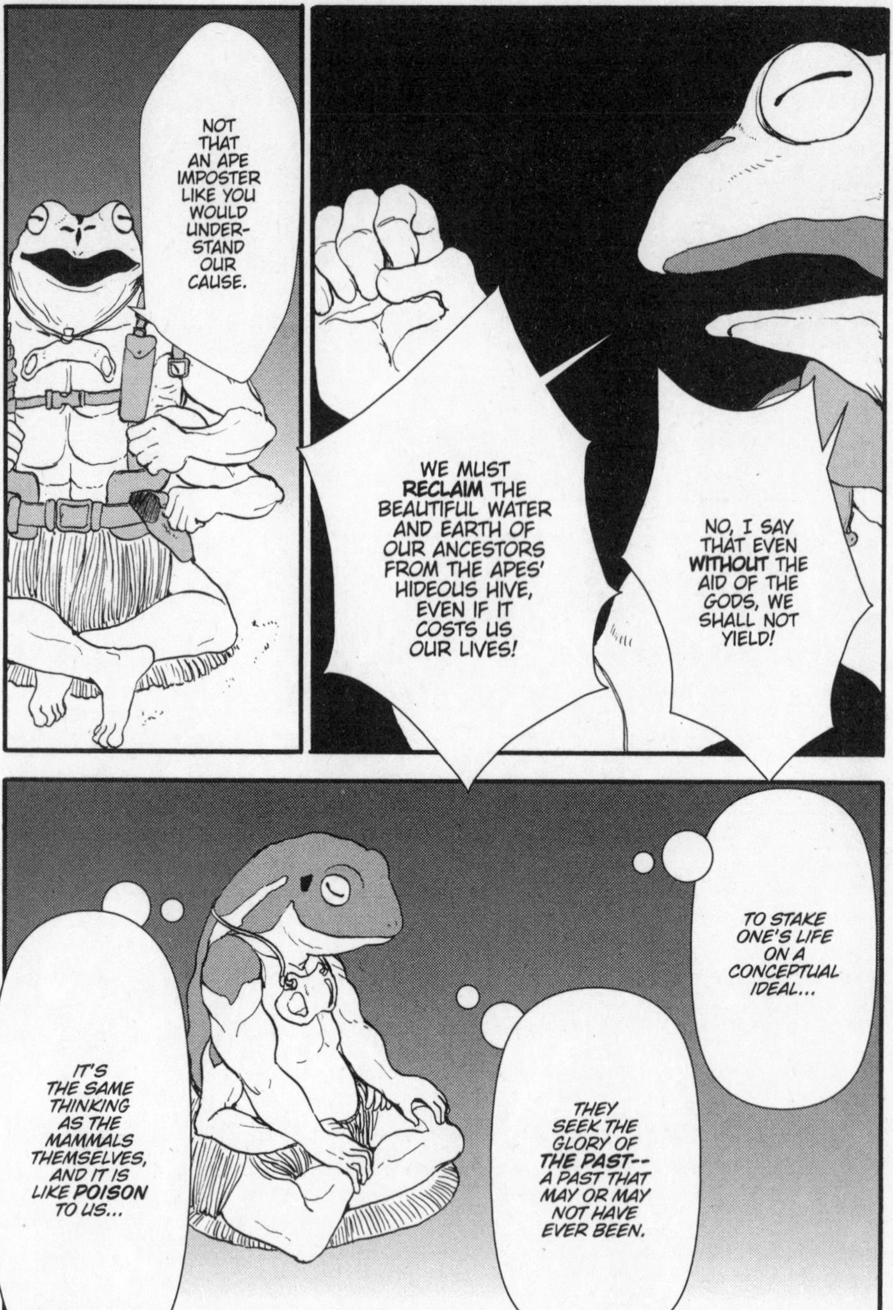
NO, I SAY THAT EVEN WITHOUT THE AID OF THE GODS, WE SHALL NOT YIELD!
WE MUST RECLAIM THE BEAUTIFUL WATER AND EARTH OF OUR ANCESTORS FROM THE APES' HIDEOUS HIVE, EVEN IF IT COSTS US OUR LIVES!
NOT THAT AN APE IMPOSTER LIKE YOU WOULD UNDER-STAND OUR CAUSE.
TO STAKE ONE'S LIFE ON A CONCEPTUAL IDEAL...
THEY SEEK THE GLORY OF THE PAST-- A PAST THAT MAY OR MAY NOT HAVE EVER BEEN.
IT'S THE SAME THINKING AS THE MAMMALS THEMSELVES, AND IT IS LIKE POISON TO US...

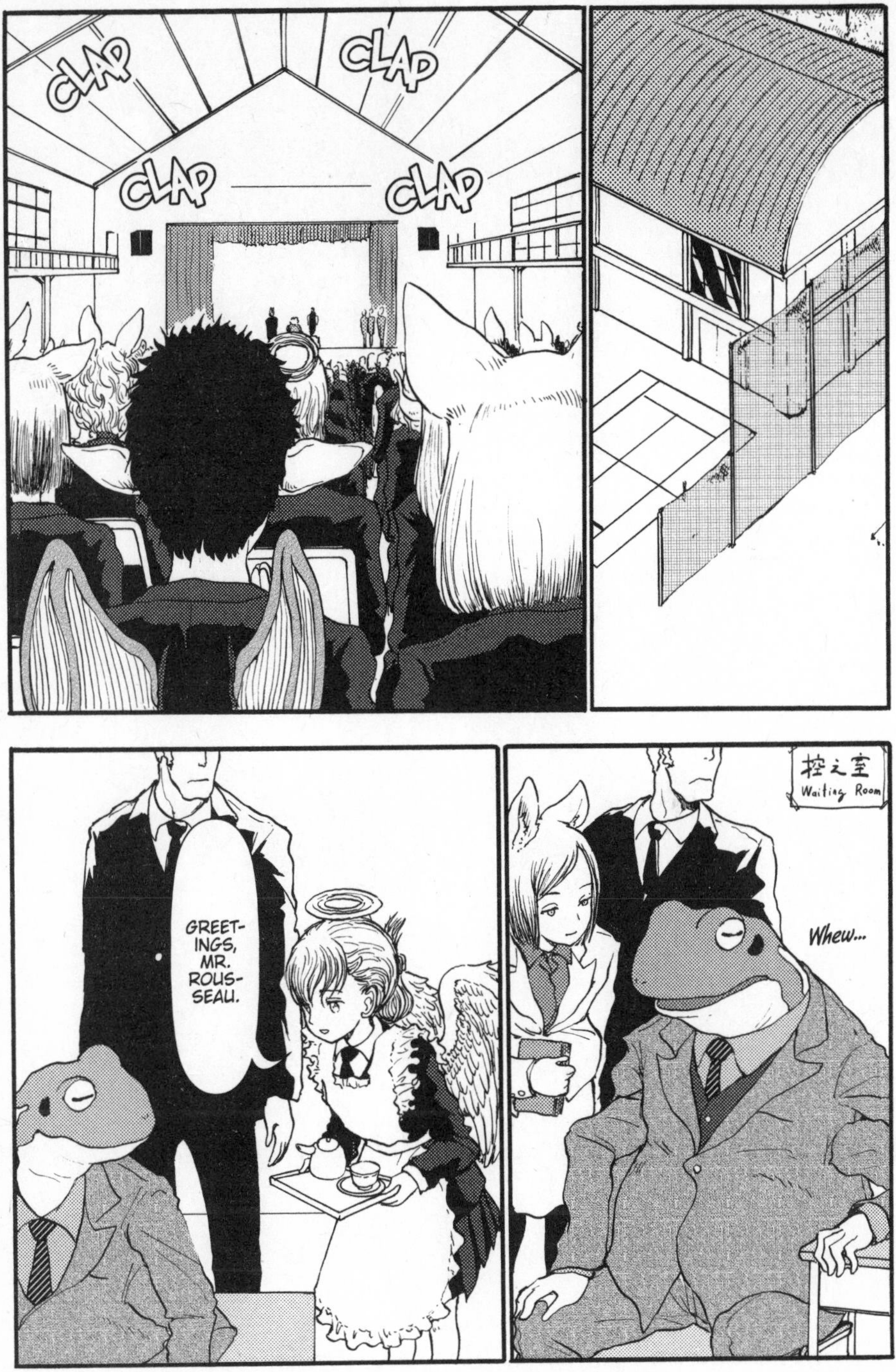
CLAP
CLAP
CLAP
CLAP
控え室
Waiting Room
Whew...
GREETINGS, MR. ROUSSEAU.

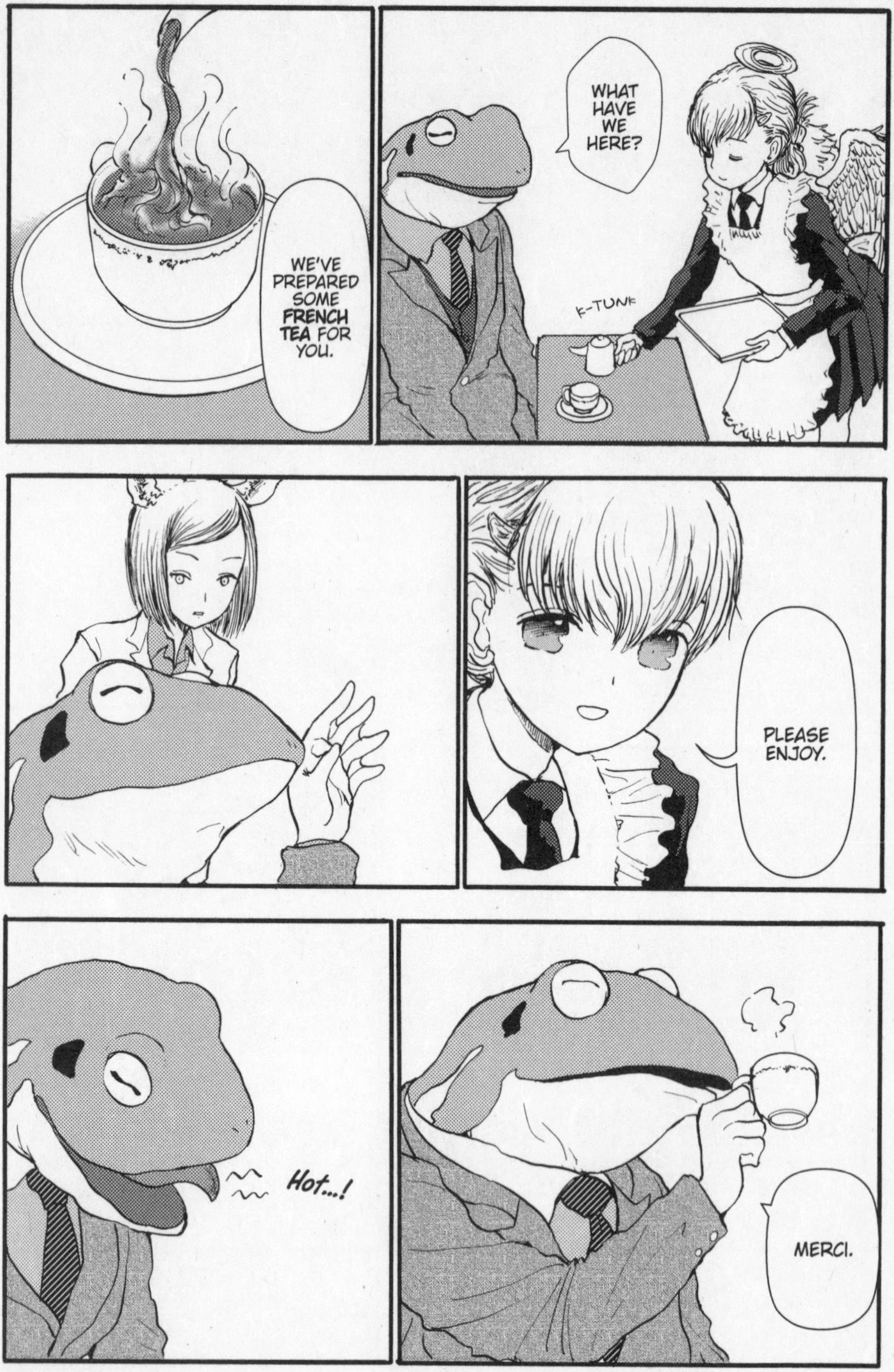

WHAT HAVE WE HERE?
K-TUNK
WE'VE PREPARED SOME FRENCH TEA FOR YOU.
PLEASE ENJOY.
MERCI.
Hot...!

A Centaur's Life

GENETICS MADE EASY: LESSON 4
MIXED RACES

IN RARE CASES (WHICH STILL AMOUNTS TO ABOUT ONE IN TWENTY INDIVIDUALS), A PERSON WILL INHERIT THE RACIAL TRAITS OF *BOTH* PARENTS, PRODUCING A HYBRID. WHAT'S TO EXPLAIN THIS PHENOMENON? WELL, THE POSSIBILITIES ARE A) THAT FOR SOME REASON, THE OFFSPRING'S RACE-DETERMINING GENES HAVE TURNED INTO SOMETHING THAT CANNOT FUNCTION CORRECTLY, OR B) THAT THERE'S NO PROBLEM WITH THE OFFSPRING'S GENES THEMSELVES, BUT THAT FOR SOME REASON THE REGULATION PROCESS CARRIED OUT BY THE RACE-DETERMINING GENES IS DEFECTIVE OR INCOMPLETE.

GENES ON THEIR OWN ARE NOTHING MORE THAN SIMPLE CODES; IN ORDER FOR THEM TO BE ACTIVATED, THE DNA MUST BE TRANSCRIBED INTO RNA (USED IN THE TEMPORARY COPYING OF GENETIC INFORMATION), WHICH THEN GENERATES PROTEIN, WHICH MUST THEN PERFORM ITS OWN FUNCTION. IF ANY PROBLEM OCCURS ALONG THAT PATH, EVEN GOOD GENES WON'T FUNCTION PROPERLY. ONE WELL-KNOWN CASE IS THAT OF TERATOGENESIS (LIMB DEFORMATION) CAUSED BY THALIDOMIDE, A DRUG WHICH WAS USED AS A SLEEPING AID. IN THIS CASE, THE DRUG WAS NOT AFFECTING THE GENES, BUT WAS DEACTIVATING THE PROTEINS RESPONSIBLE FOR LIMB GROWTH. OF COURSE THE ABNORMALITY IN THIS CASE WAS CAUSED BY USE OF MEDICATION, BUT NO TWO ORGANISMS ARE BORN EXACTLY ALIKE, BE THEY THE SAME RACE OR EVEN SIBLINGS, SO THE UNEXPECTED CAN OCCUR EVEN IN A CREATURE BORN IN AN ENVIRONMENT WITHOUT THE INFLUENCE OF DRUGS OR OTHER FOREIGN SUBSTANCES. THESE ARE EXCEPTIONAL CASES, TO BE SURE, BUT THE OCCURRENCE OF A HYBRID IS A RELATIVELY COMMON ONE AMONG THEM.

IT IS FAIRLY COMMON FOR A HYBRID TO INHERIT THE RACIAL TRAITS OF BOTH PARENTS, BUT IN RARER CASES, THE RACIAL TRAITS OF A GRANDPARENT OR EVEN MORE DISTANT ANCESTOR WILL EMERGE.

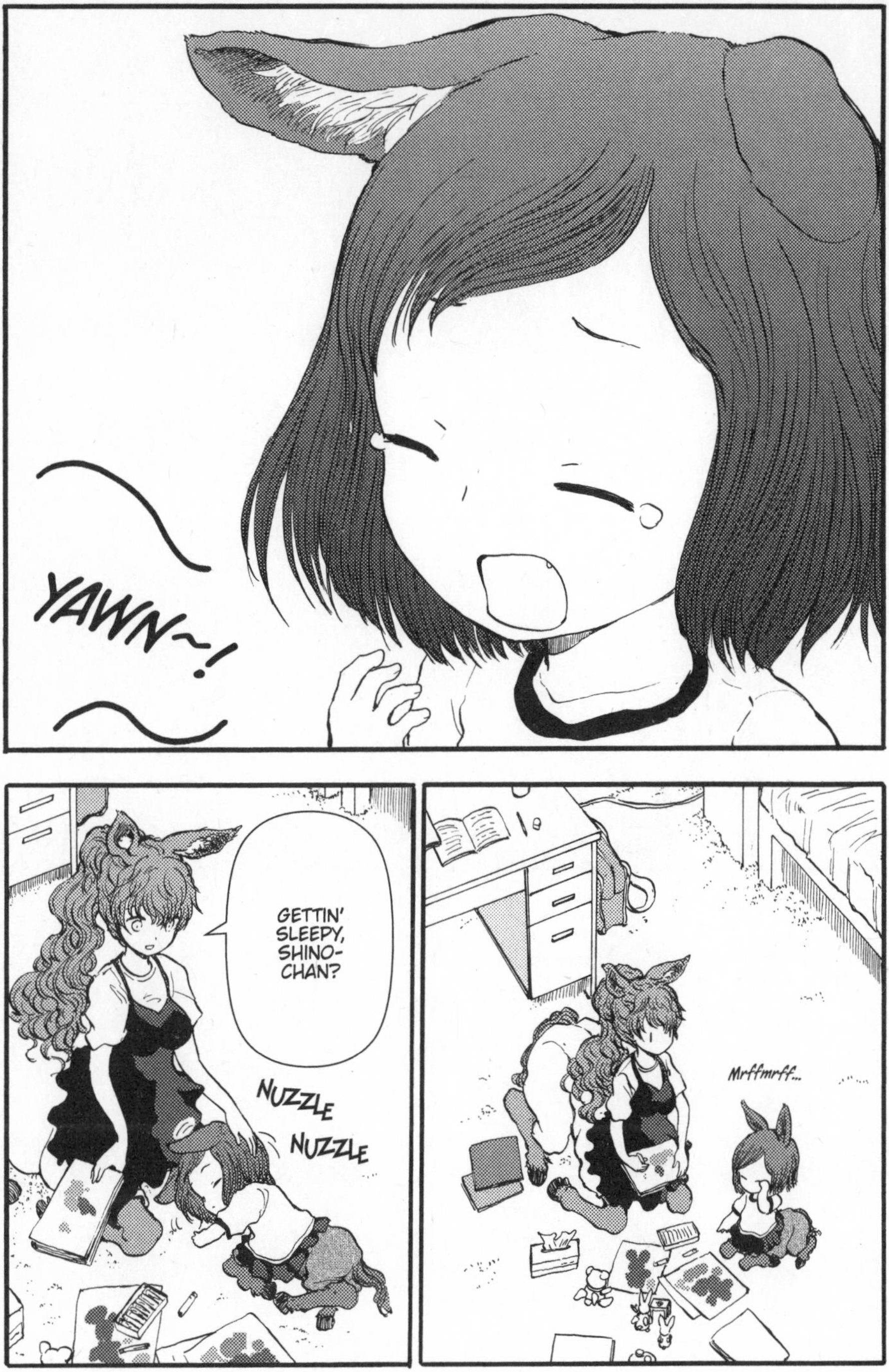
YAWN~!
Mrffmrff...
GETTIN' SLEEPY, SHINO-CHAN?
NUZZLE
NUZZLE

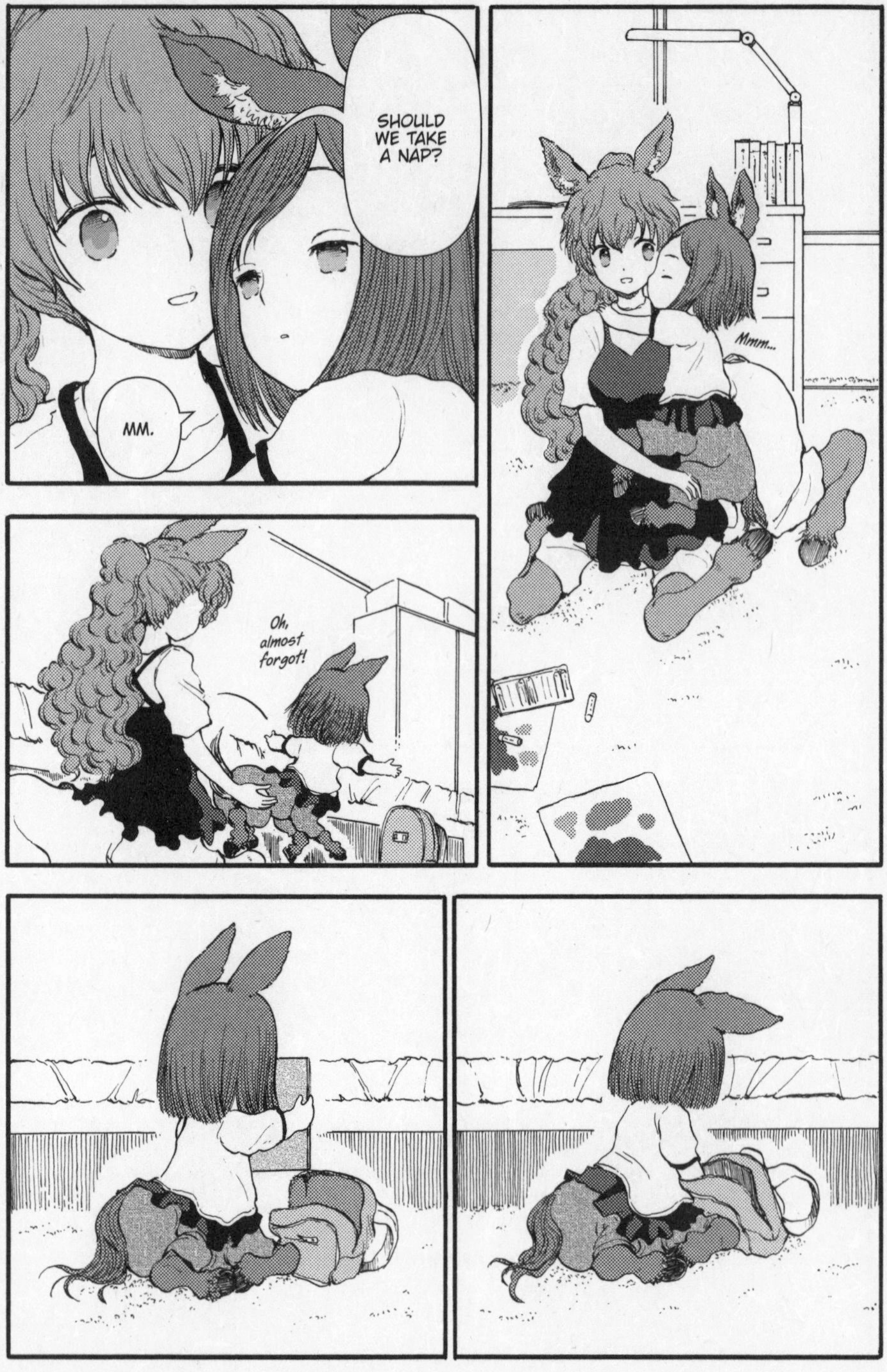
Mmm...
SHOULD WE TAKE A NAP?
MM.
Oh, almost forgot!

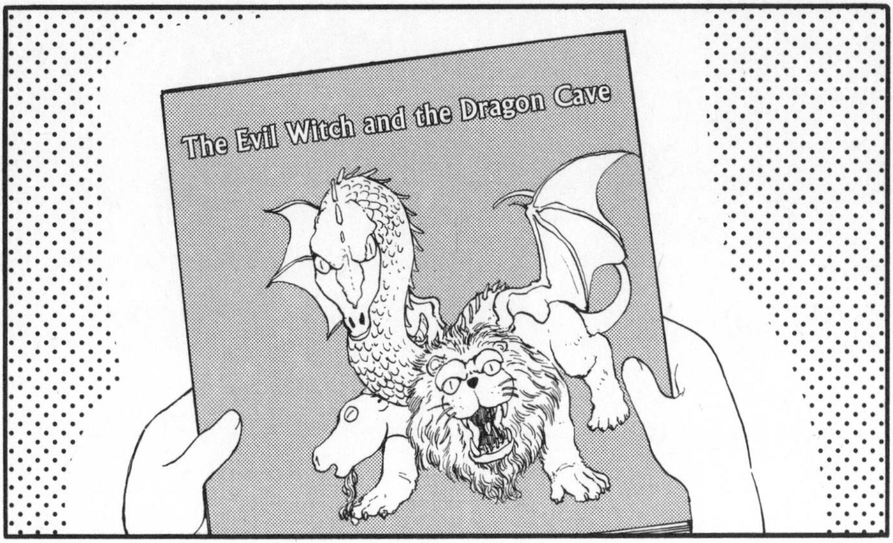
The Evil Witch and the Dragon Cave

CHAPTER 34

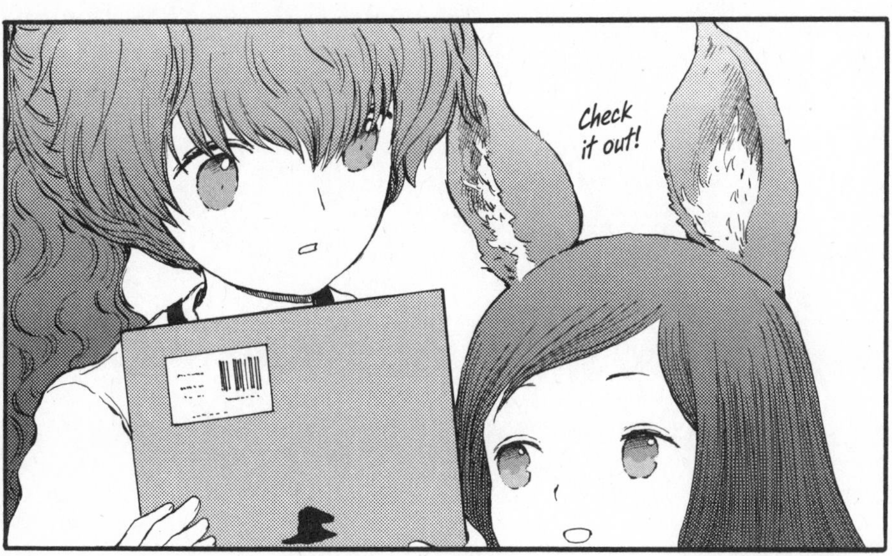
Check it out!

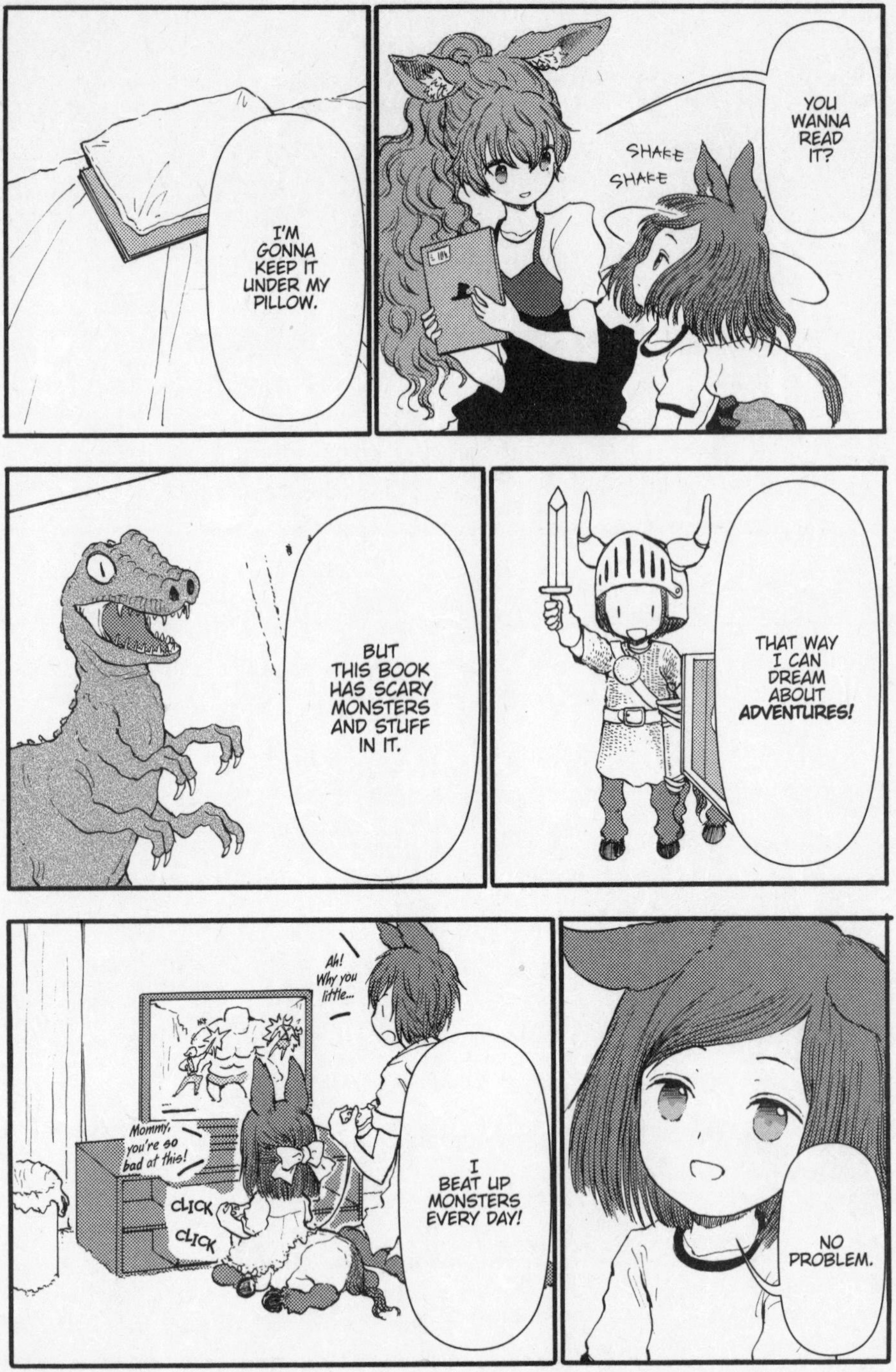
YOU WANNA READ IT?
SHAKE
SHAKE
I'M GONNA KEEP IT UNDER MY PILLOW.
THAT WAY I CAN DREAM ABOUT **ADVENTURES!**
BUT THIS BOOK HAS SCARY MONSTERS AND STUFF IN IT.
NO PROBLEM.
I BEAT UP MONSTERS EVERY DAY!
Ah! Why you little...
Mommy, you're so bad at this!
CLICK
CLICK

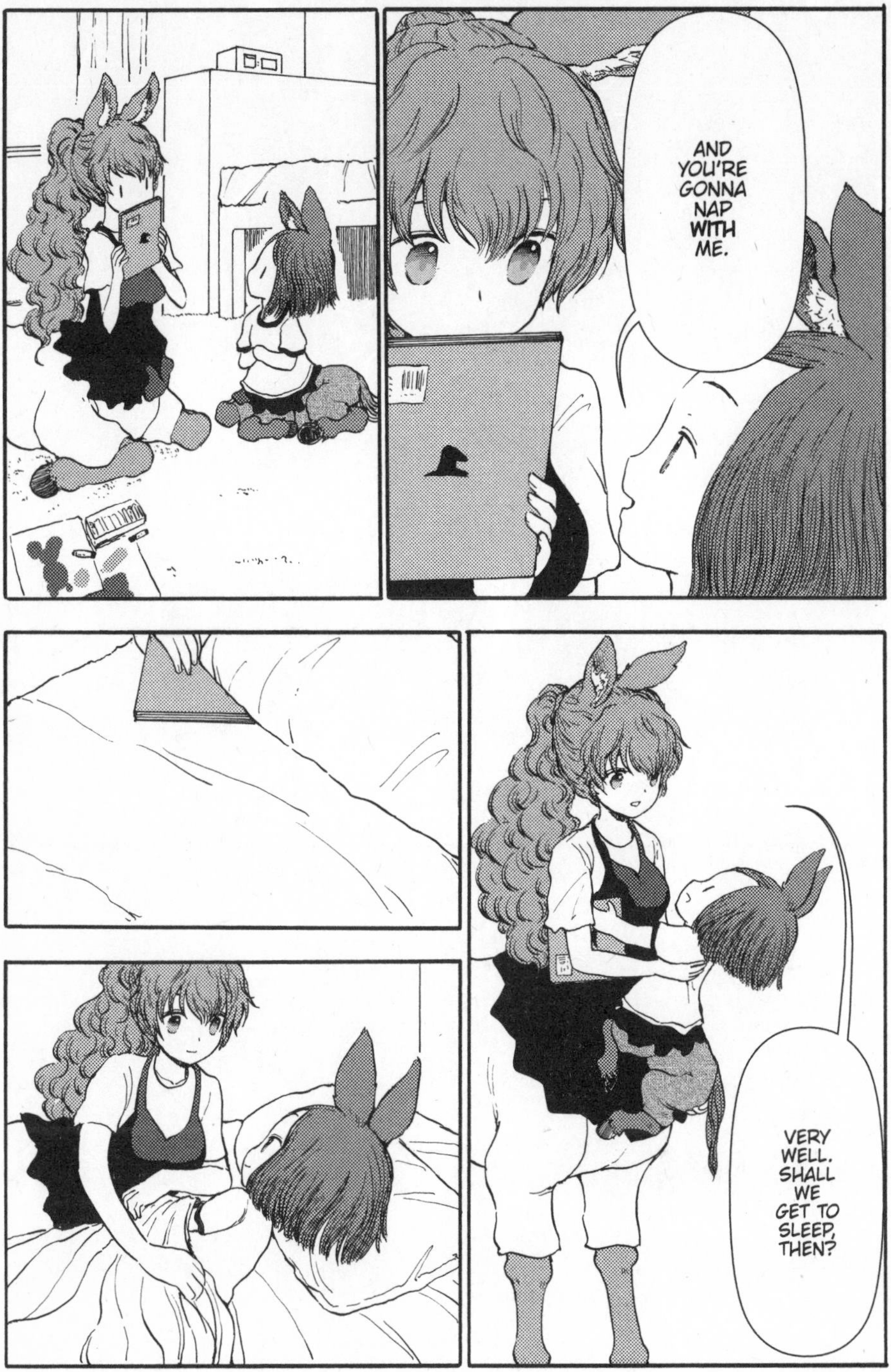
AND YOU'RE GONNA NAP WITH ME.
VERY WELL. SHALL WE GET TO SLEEP, THEN?

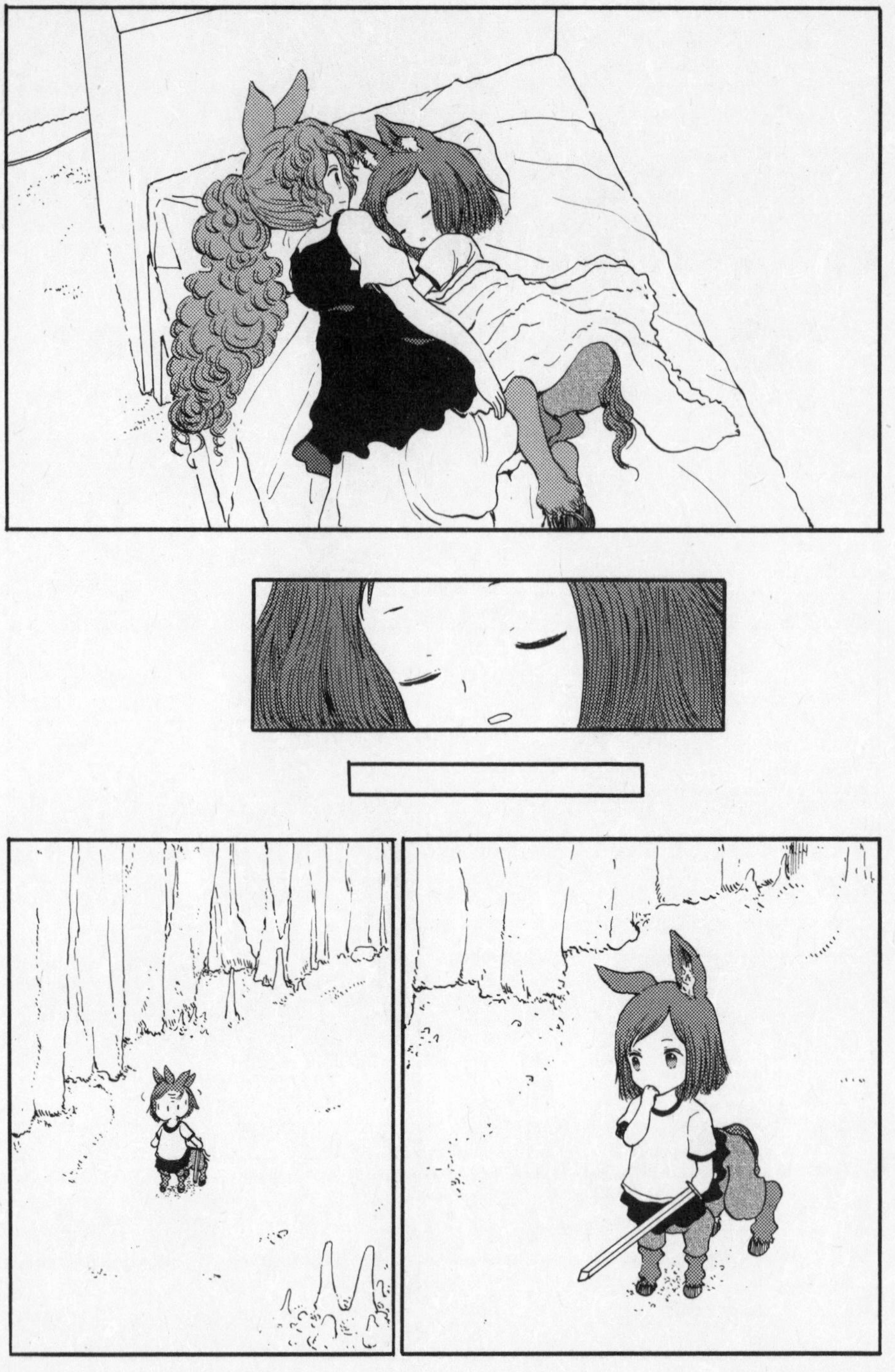

BIG SISTER?

PLINK

ROLL
ROLL

Big sister's not here...

WHUD

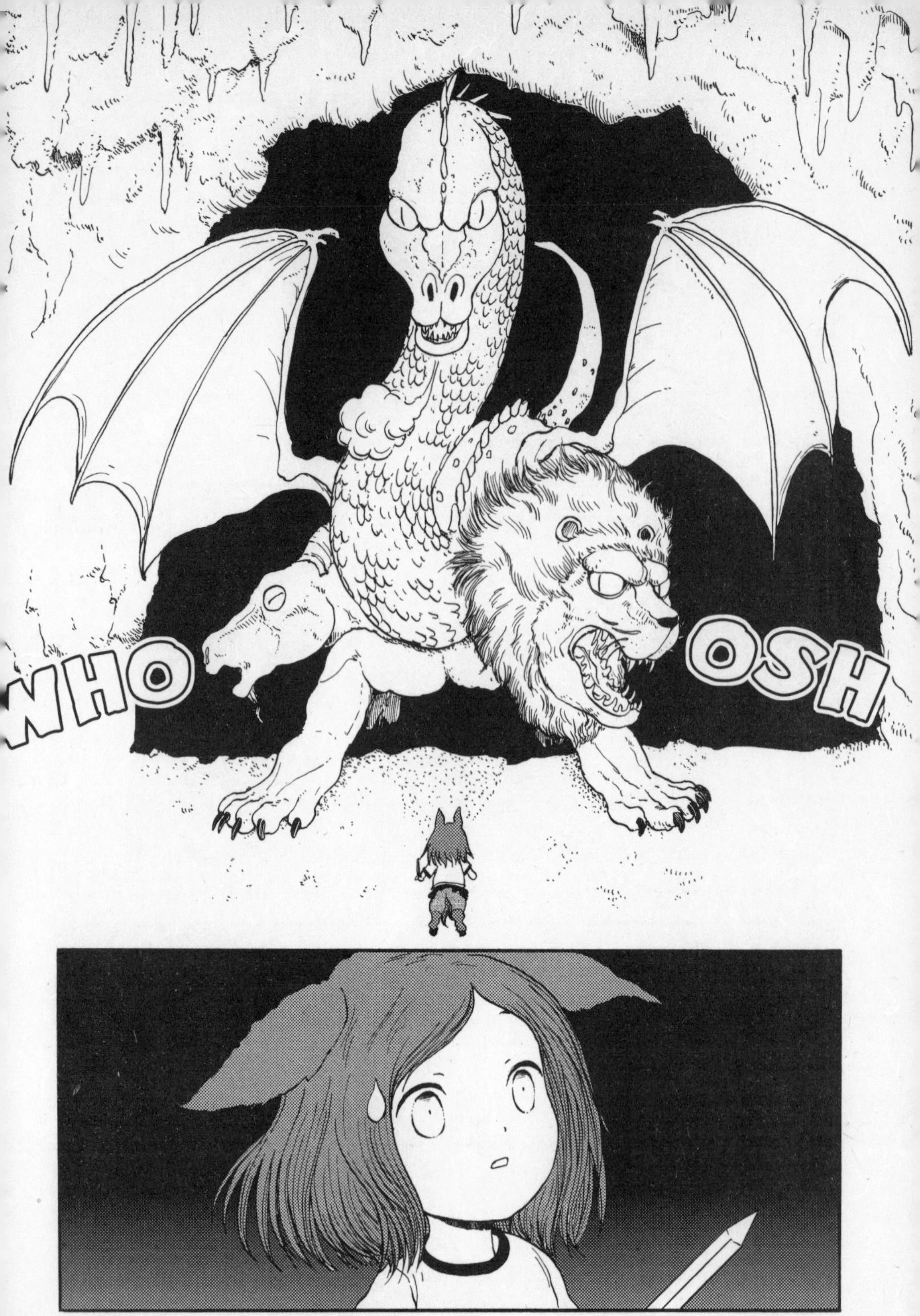
WHO OSH

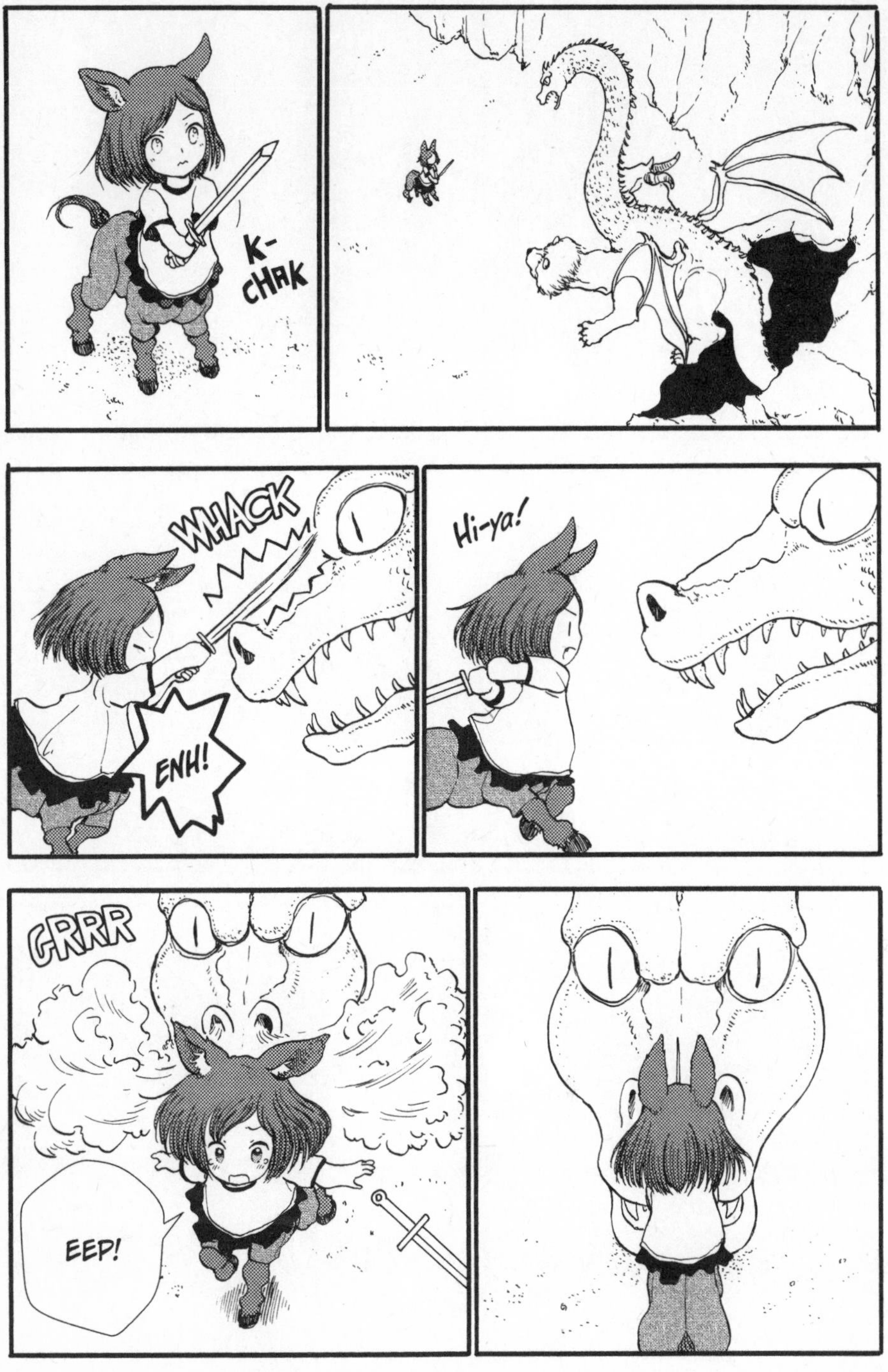
K-
CHAK
Hi-ya!
WHACK
ENH!
GRRR
EEP!

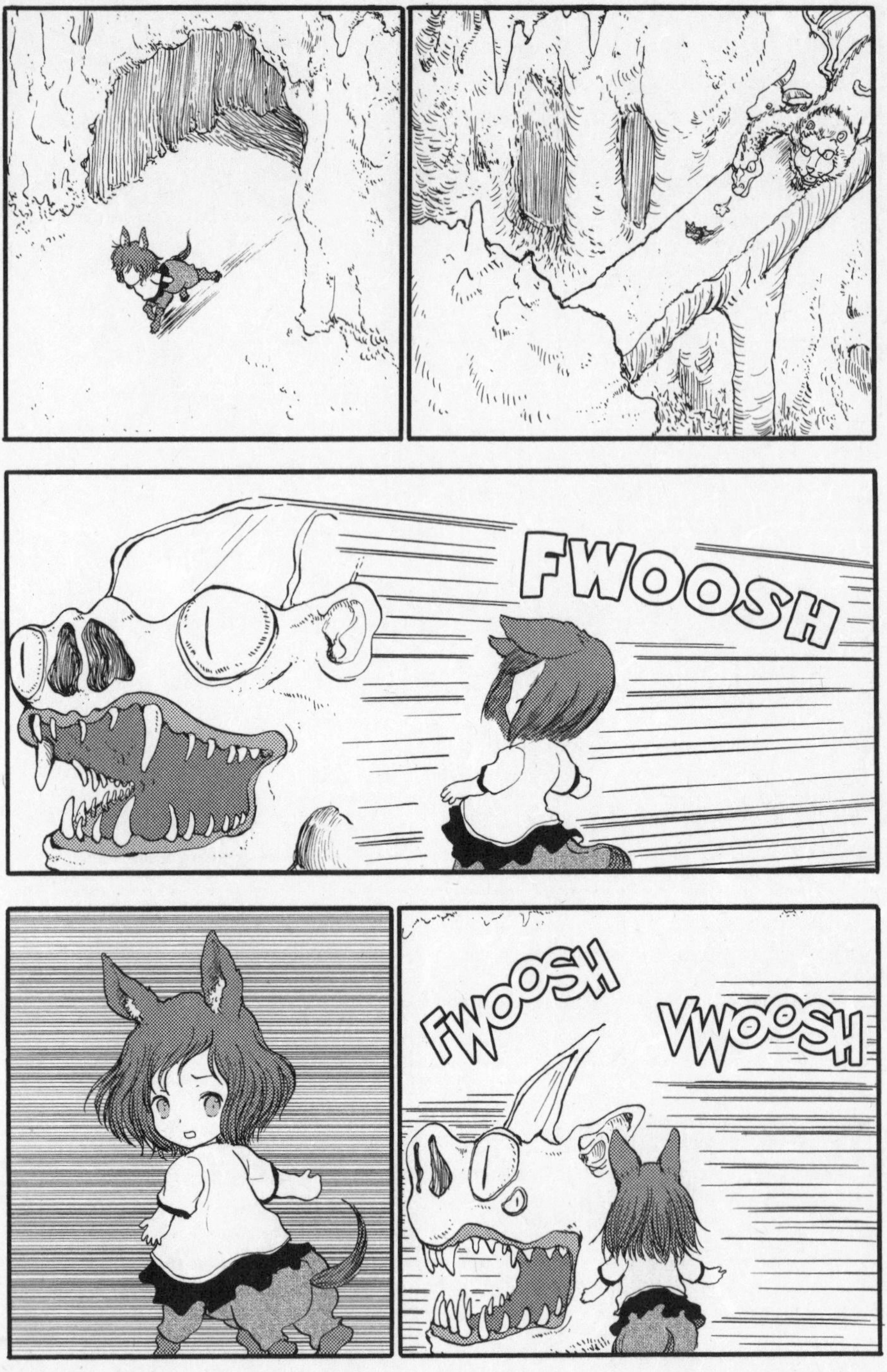
FWOOSH
VWOOSH
FWOOSH

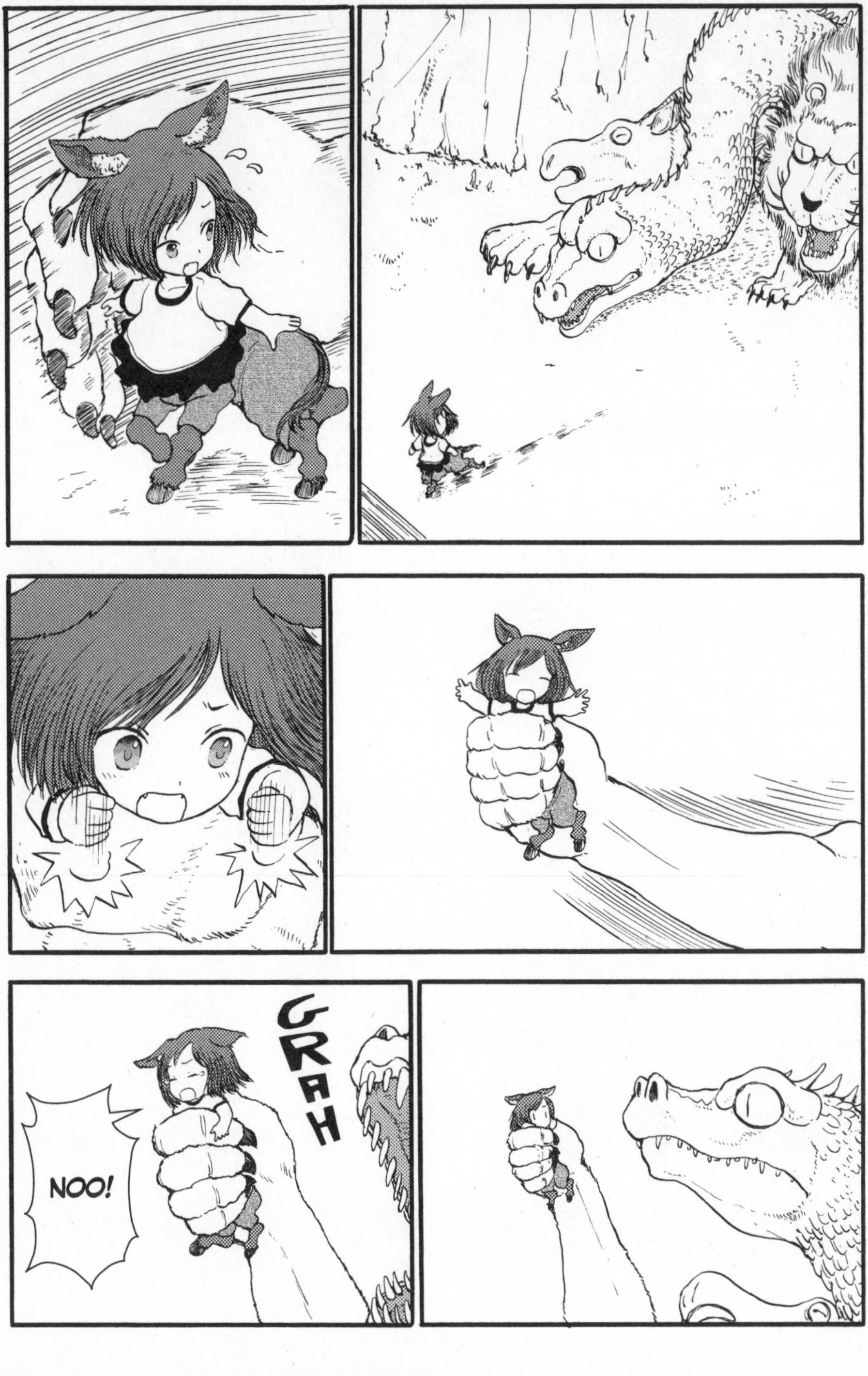
GRAH
NOO!

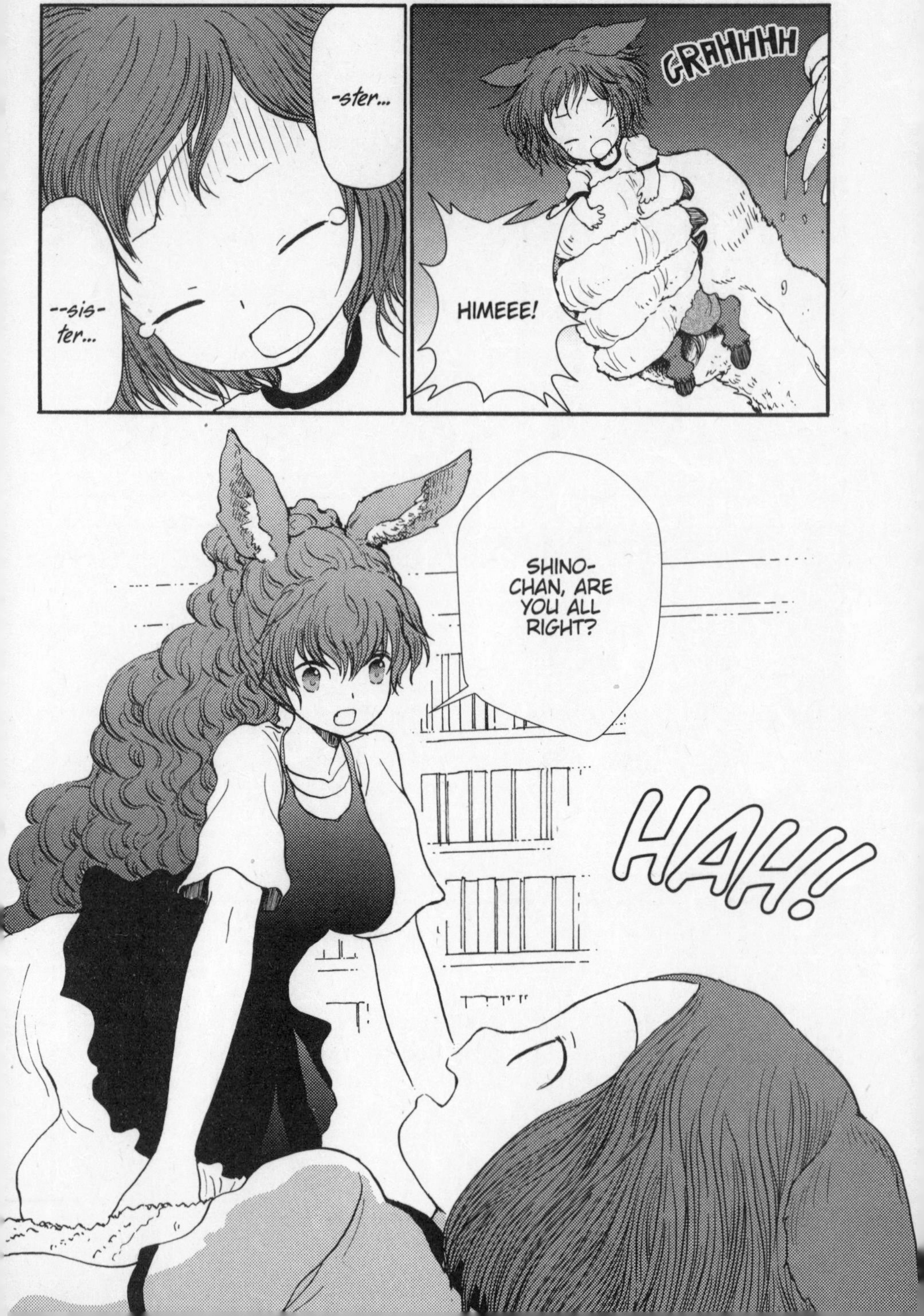
GRAHHHH
HIMEEE!
-ster...
--sis-
ter...
SHINO-
CHAN, ARE
YOU ALL
RIGHT?
HAH!!

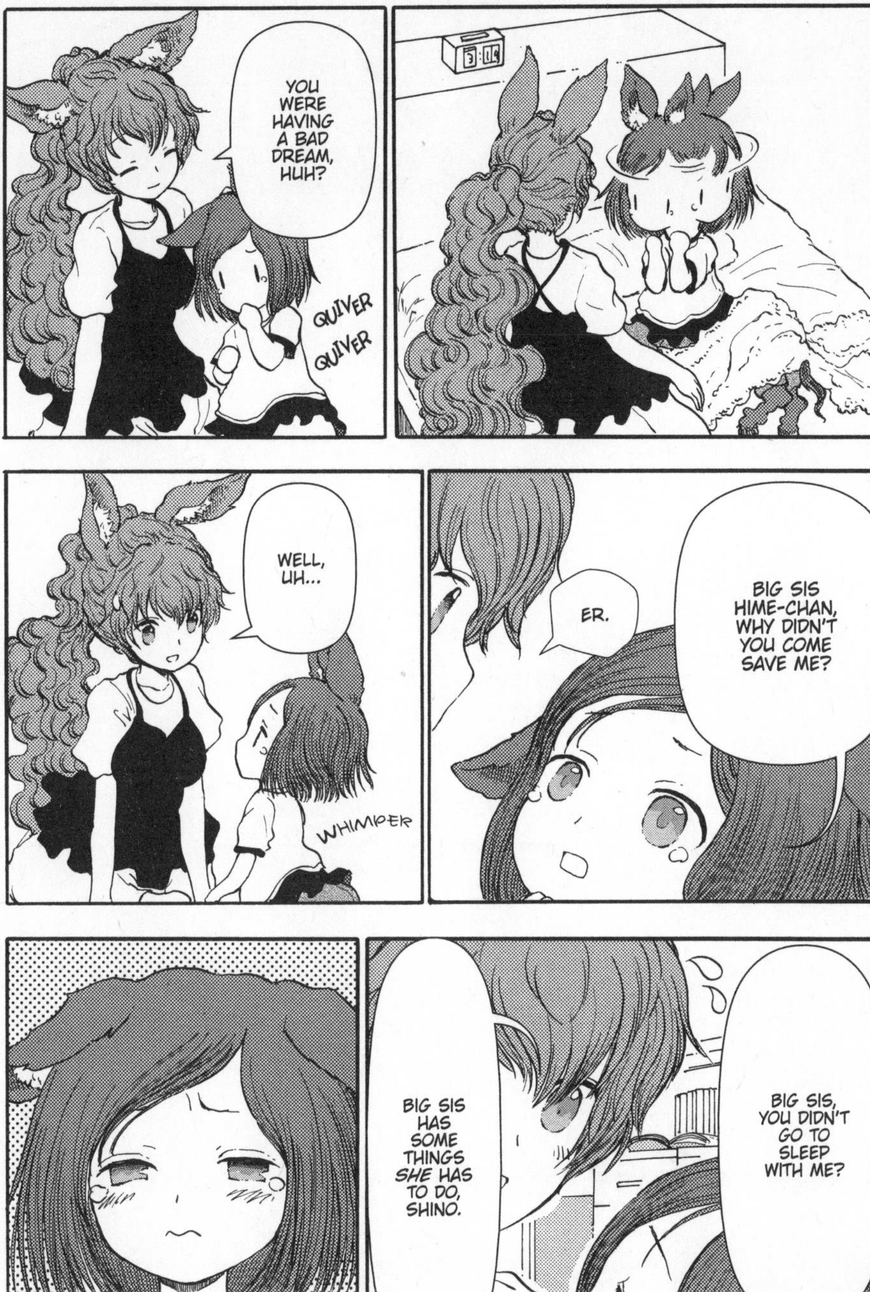
YOU WERE HAVING A BAD DREAM, HUH?
QUIVER QUIVER
BIG SIS HIME-CHAN, WHY DIDN'T YOU COME SAVE ME?
ER.
WELL, UH...
WHIMPER
BIG SIS, YOU DIDN'T GO TO SLEEP WITH ME?
BIG SIS HAS SOME THINGS *SHE* HAS TO DO, SHINO.

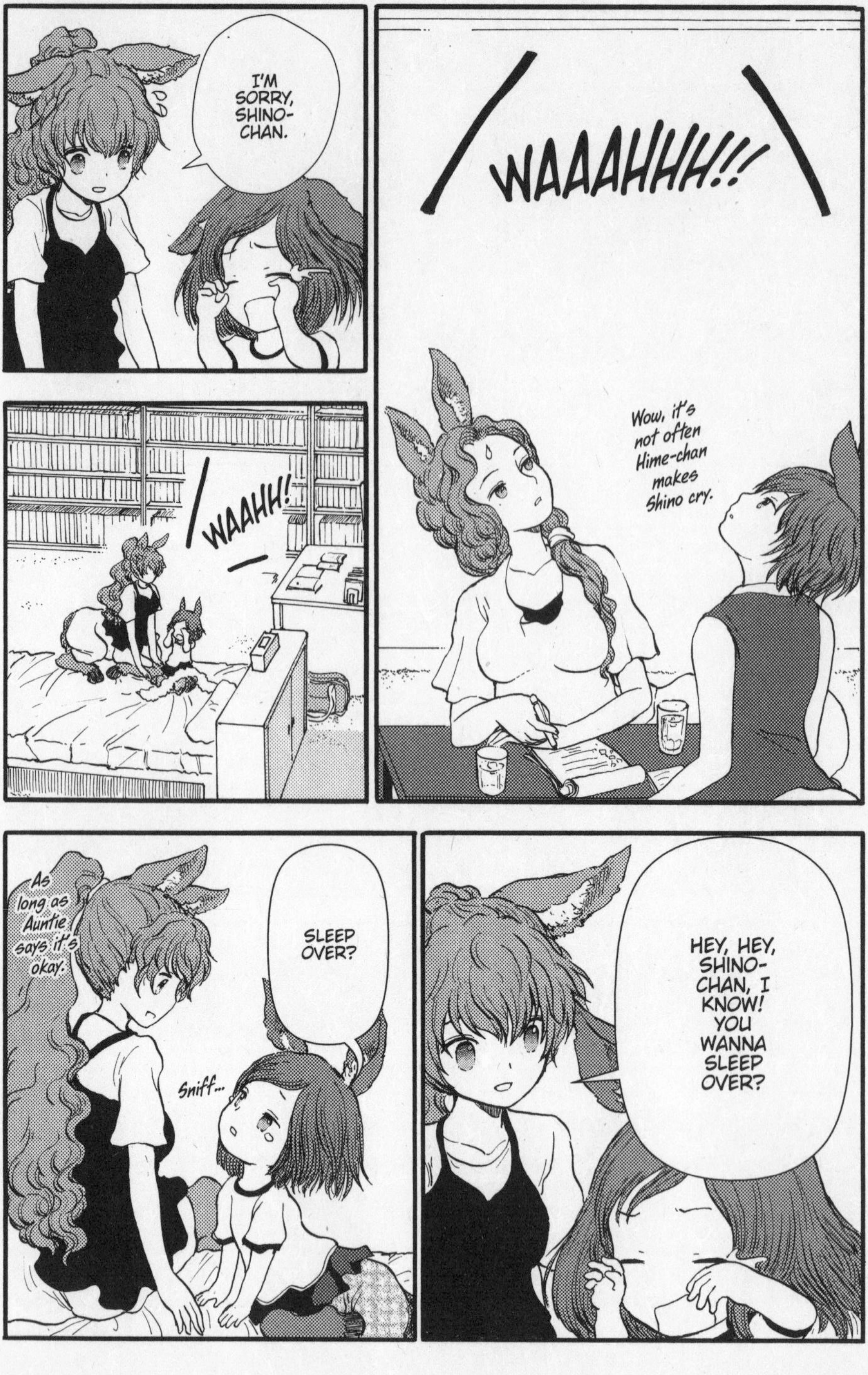
WAAAHHH!!
Wow, it's not often Hime-chan makes Shino cry.
I'M SORRY, SHINO-CHAN.
WAAHH!
HEY, HEY, SHINO-CHAN, I KNOW! YOU WANNA SLEEP OVER?
SLEEP OVER?
As long as Auntie says it's okay.
Sniff...

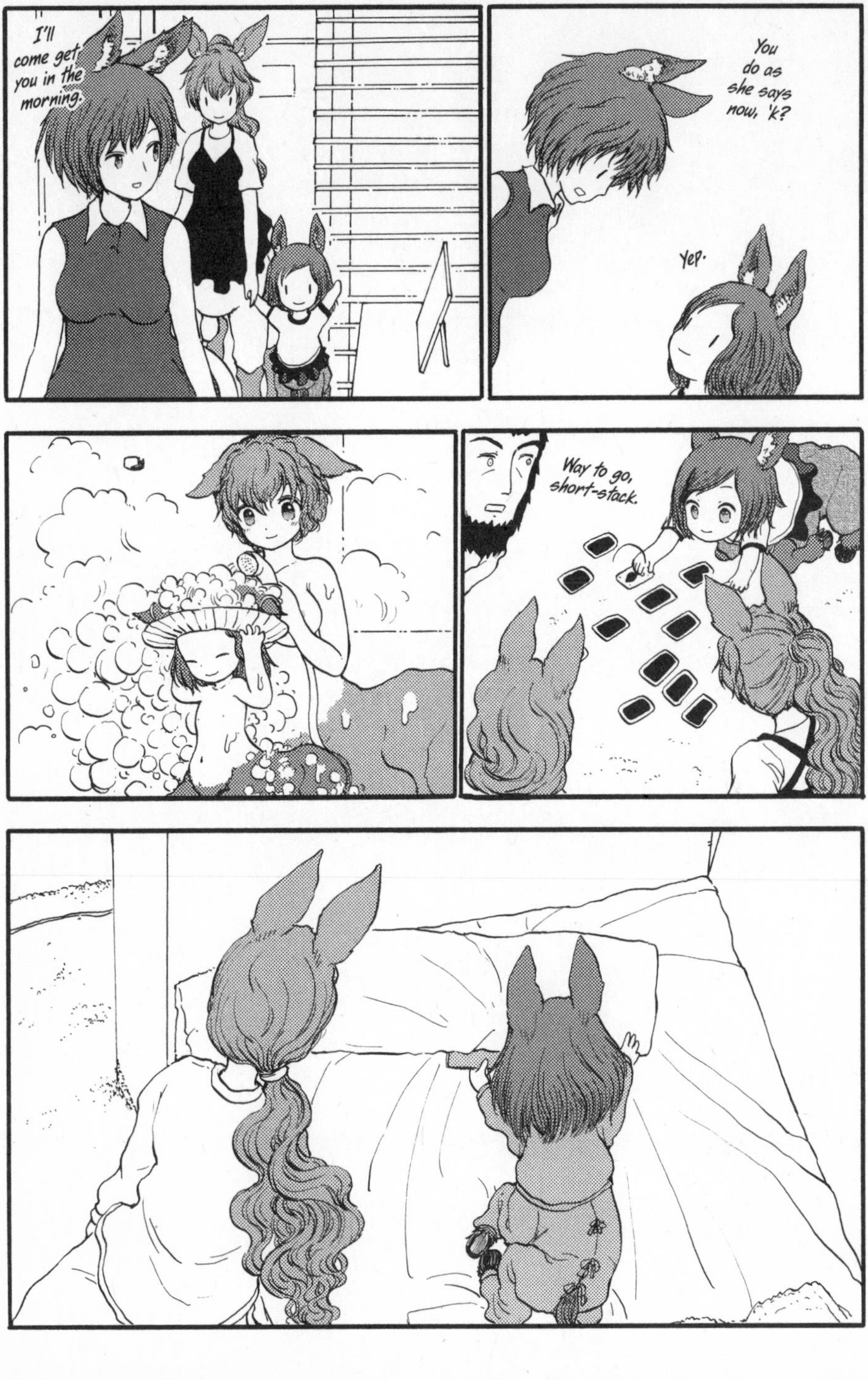
You do as she says now, 'k?
Yep.
I'll come get you in the morning.
Way to go, short-stack.

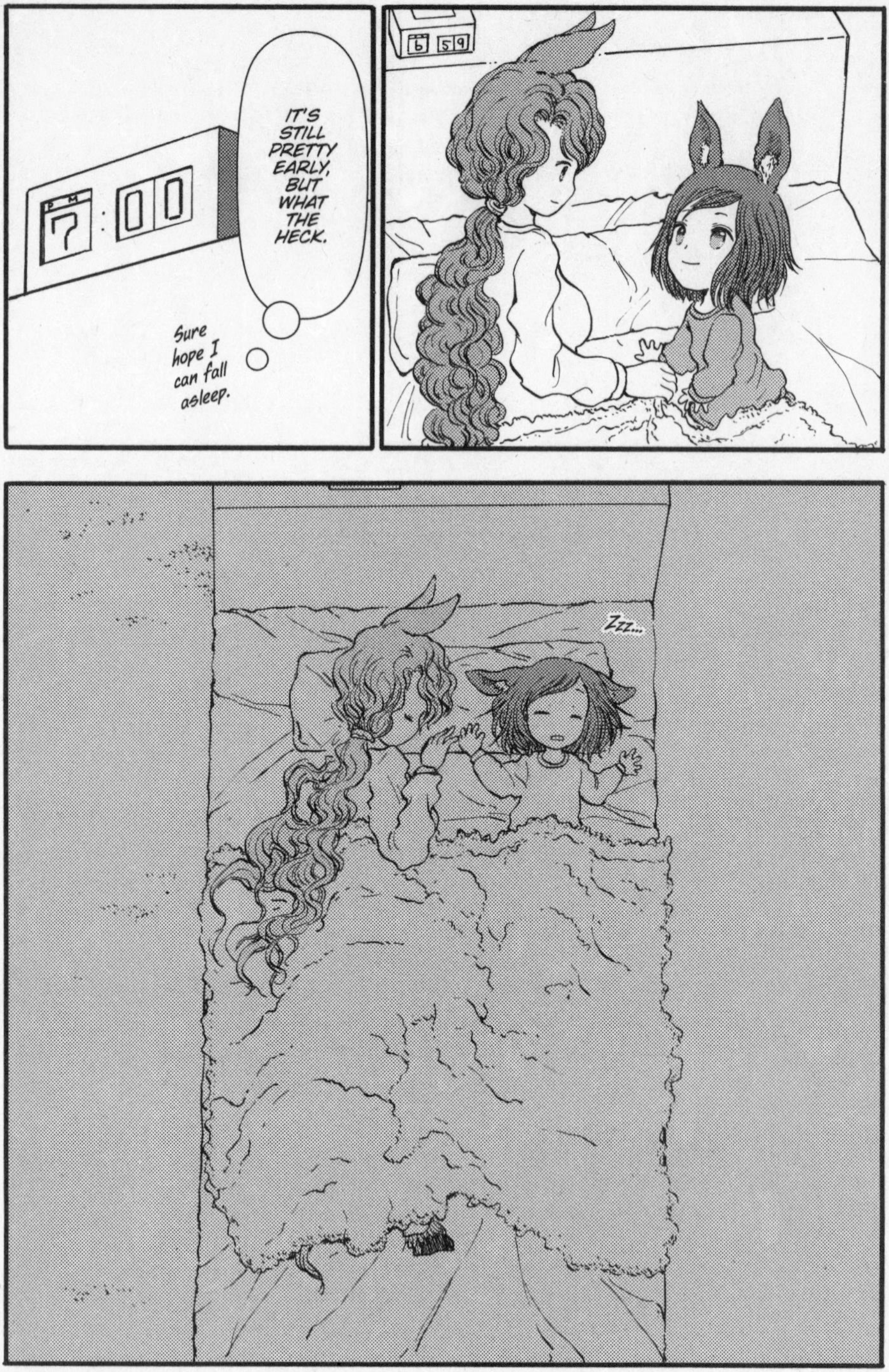
IT'S STILL PRETTY EARLY, BUT WHAT THE HECK.
Sure hope I can fall asleep.
Zzz...

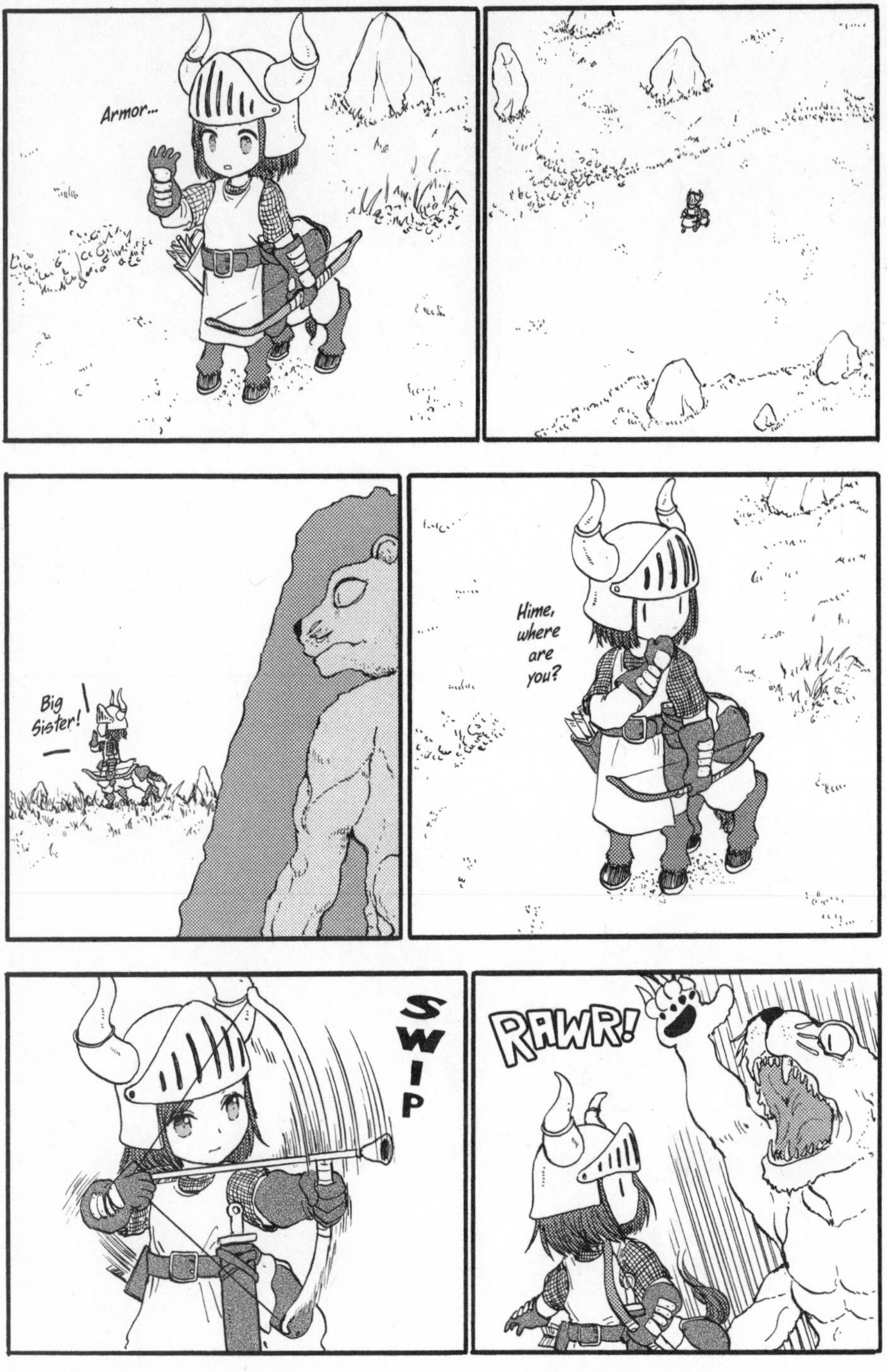
Armor...
Hime, where are you?
Big Sister!
RAWR!
SWIP

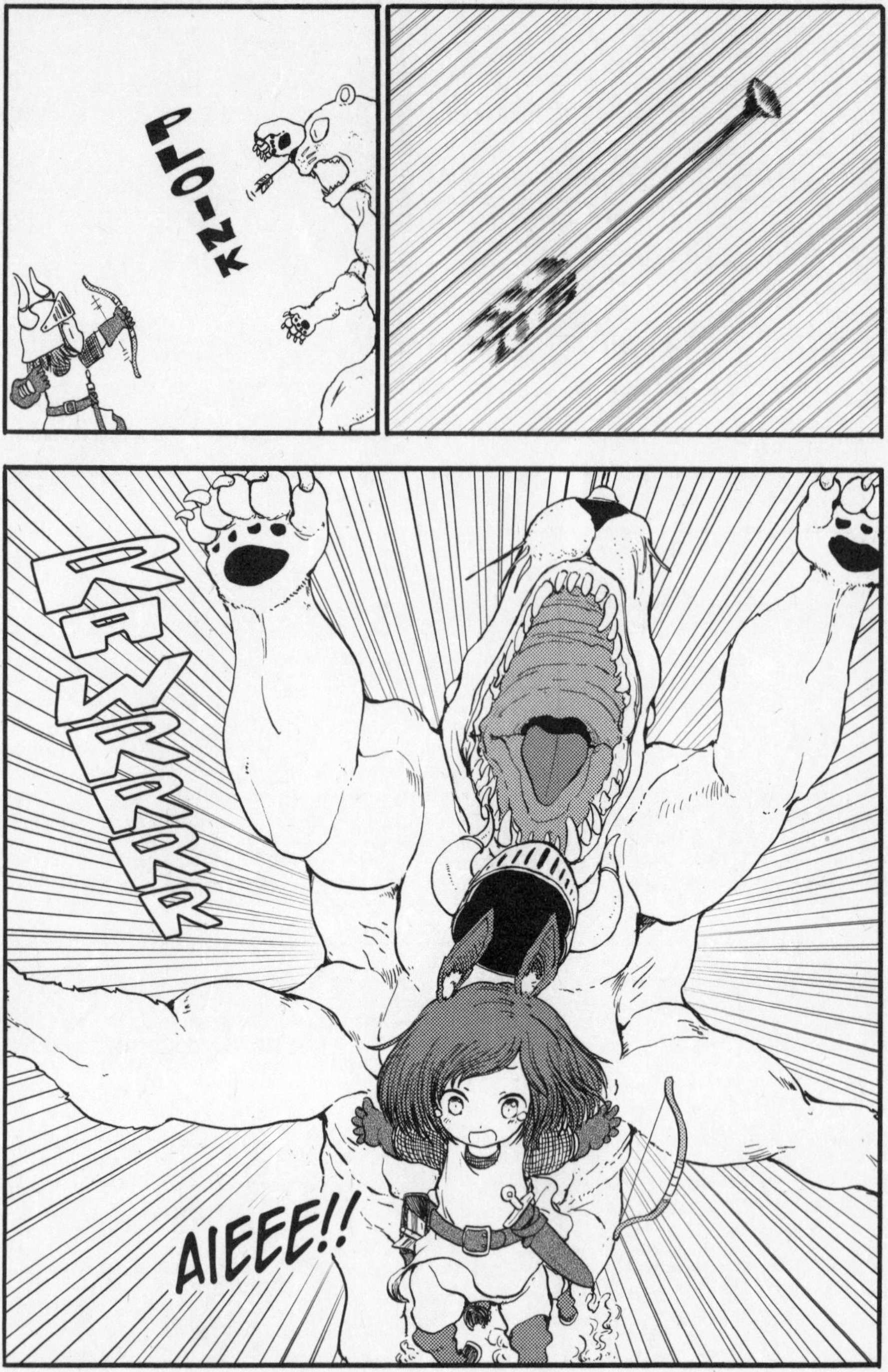
PLOINK
RAWRRRR
AIEEE!!

HIMEEE, WHERE ARE YOUUU?!

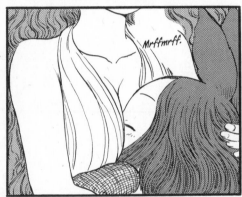

Mrffmrff.

BIG SIS...!

BIG SIS...?!

Mrrf?!

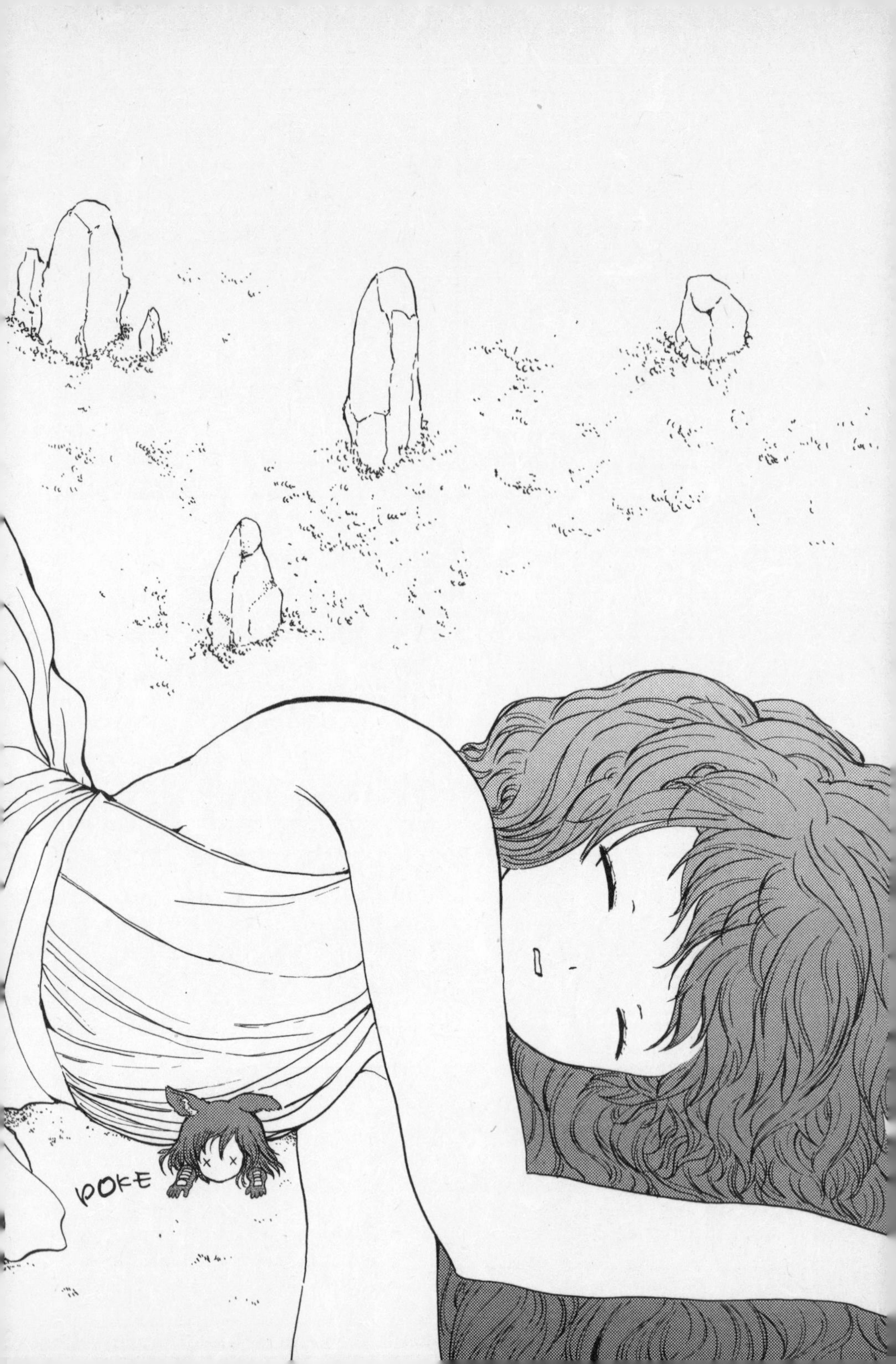
POKE

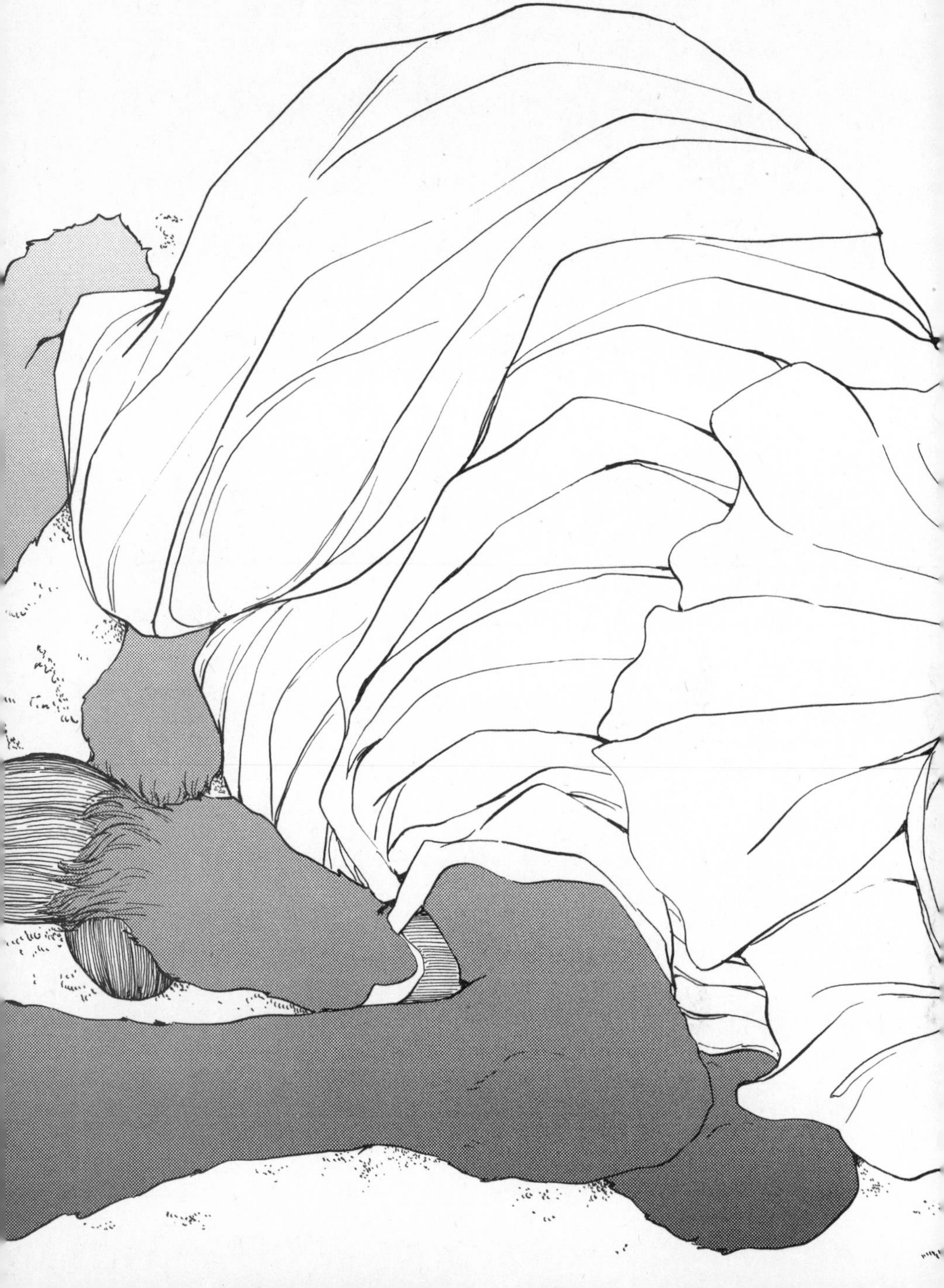

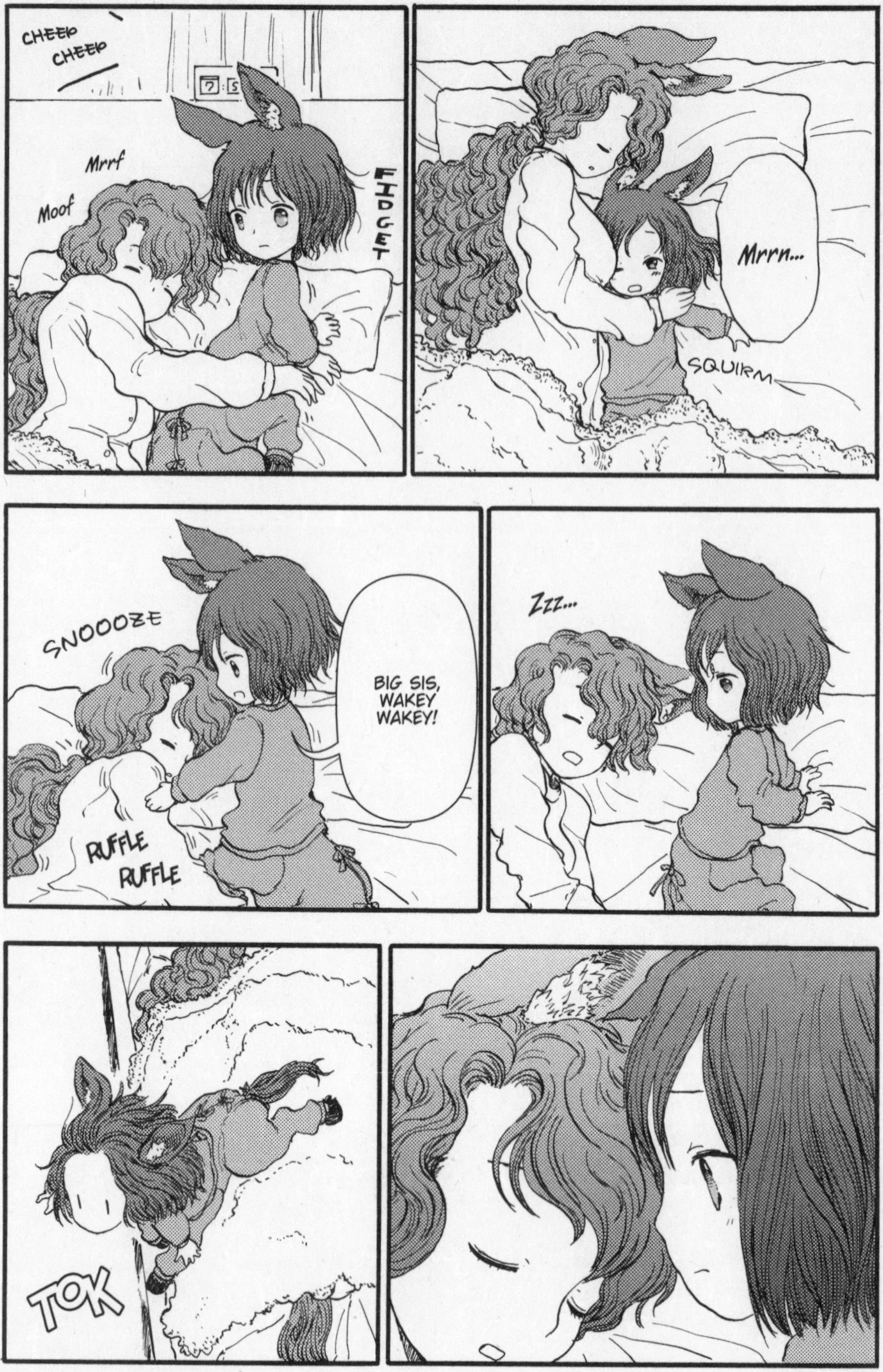
Mrrn...
SQUIRM
CHEEP CHEEP
Mrrf
FIDGET
Moof
Zzz...
BIG SIS, WAKEY WAKEY!
SNOOOZE
RUFFLE RUFFLE
TOK

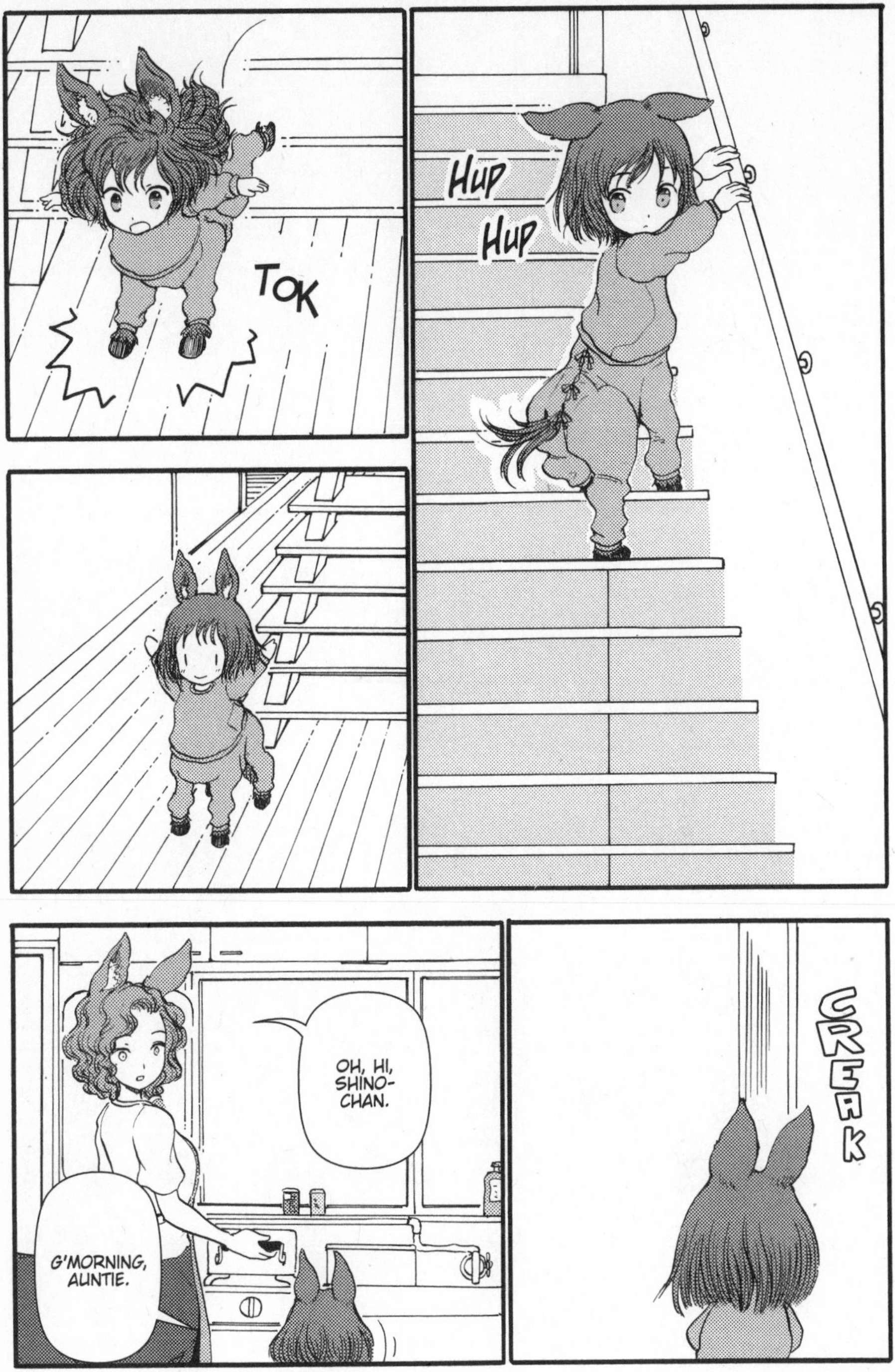
HUP
HUP
TOK
CREAK
OH, HI, SHINO-CHAN.
G'MORNING, AUNTIE.

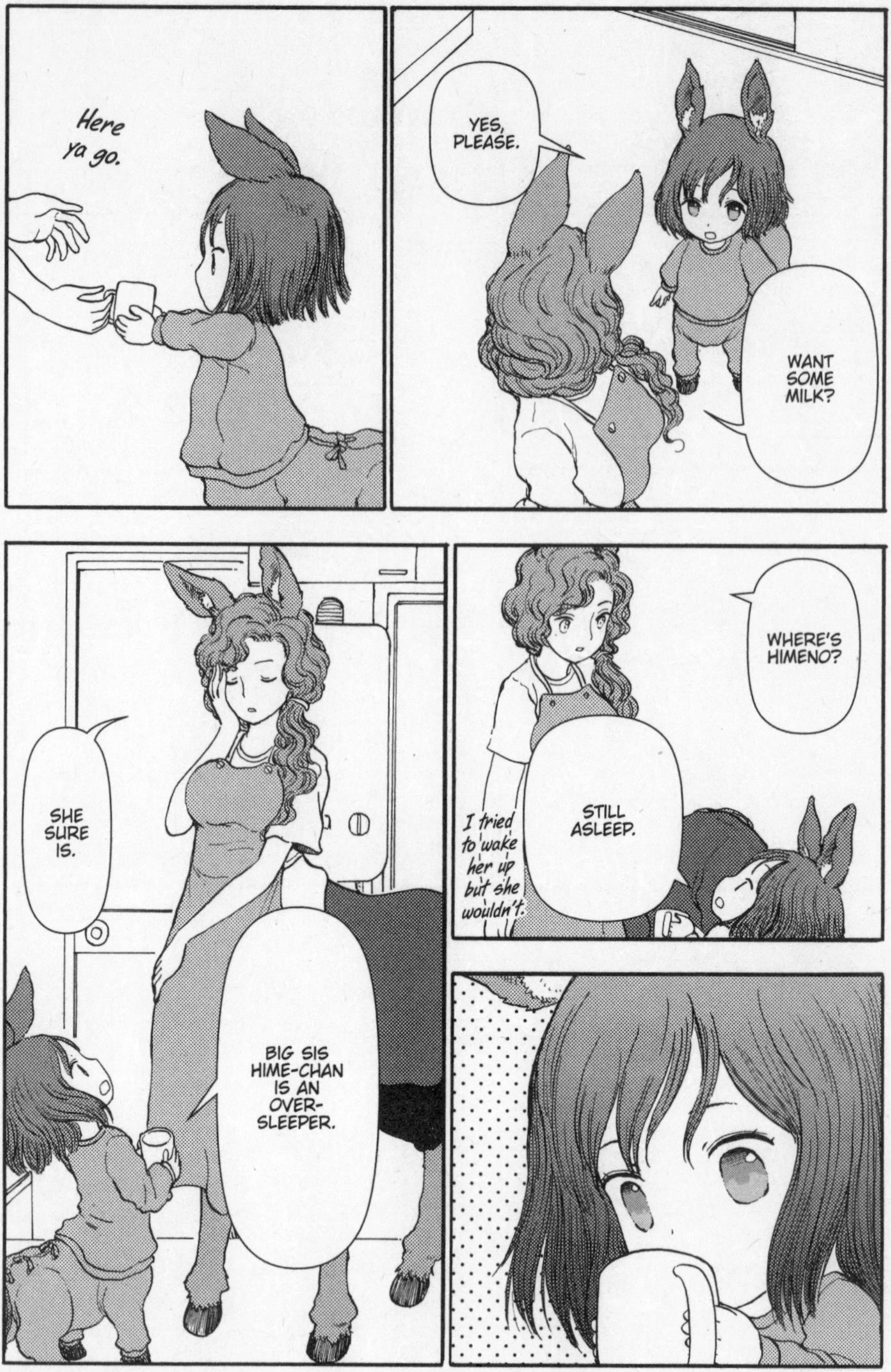
WANT SOME MILK?
YES, PLEASE.
Here ya go.
WHERE'S HIMENO?
STILL ASLEEP.
I tried to wake her up but she wouldn't.
BIG SIS HIME-CHAN IS AN OVER-SLEEPER.
SHE SURE IS.

A Centaur's Life

GENETICS MADE EASY: LESSON 5
NO PERFECT GENES,
NO PERFECT PEOPLE

IT'S IMPORTANT TO REMAIN WARY OF THE ATTITUDES ONCE HELD
IN CERTAIN REGIONS THAT WOULD ELEVATE HYBRIDS AS "SPECIAL,"
OR CONVERSELY THOSE THAT WOULD LOOK DOWN UPON THEM AS
"INCOMPLETE." IN REALITY, THERE ISN'T A SINGLE PERSON WHOSE
GENES ARE COMPLETELY "NORMAL." BY AND LARGE, EVEN THOSE
WHO LOOK COMPLETELY NORMAL AT A GLANCE HAVE SOME KIND
OF UNSEEN ERROR IN THEIR GENES THAT HAS NO IMPACT ON THEIR
ABILITY TO LEAD A HEALTHY AND NORMAL LIFE. IN THE CASE OF
HYBRIDS, THE ERROR SIMPLY HAPPENS TO MANIFEST IN A WAY
THAT IS VISIBLE TO THE EYE. IF YOU SHOULD WITNESS THE USE
OF DISCRIMINATORY LANGUAGE TOWARD PEOPLE OF MIXED RACE,
BE SURE TO CONTACT YOUR LOCAL POLICE OFFICER, THE INTERNAL
BUREAU OF SOCIAL PRESERVATION, OR THE IDEOLOGICAL SECURITY
BRANCH OF THE NATIONAL DEPARTMENT OF DEFENSE. PROMPT
CORRECTIVE ACTION WILL BE TAKEN.

"MIXED KIDS MUST BE EITHER REALLY SMART OR REALLY DUMB."

"THAT KID'S DAMAGED GOODS."

"A LOT OF THOSE TYPES ARE NUTS."

"SHE SURE FITS THE MOLD OF A SHRINE MAIDEN OR PROPHET OR SOMETHING."

"CLEARLY BORN UNDER A BAD MOON."

ALL ARE NOTHING BUT GROUNDLESS SUPERSTITIONS!
BE IT VERBALLY, ON PAPER, OR OVER THE WEB, MAKING
SUCH ASSERTIONS TOWARDS ANOTHER INDIVIDUAL IS A
SERIOUS CRIME THAT WILL INCUR PUNISHMENT UP TO
AND INCLUDING THE DEATH PENALTY!

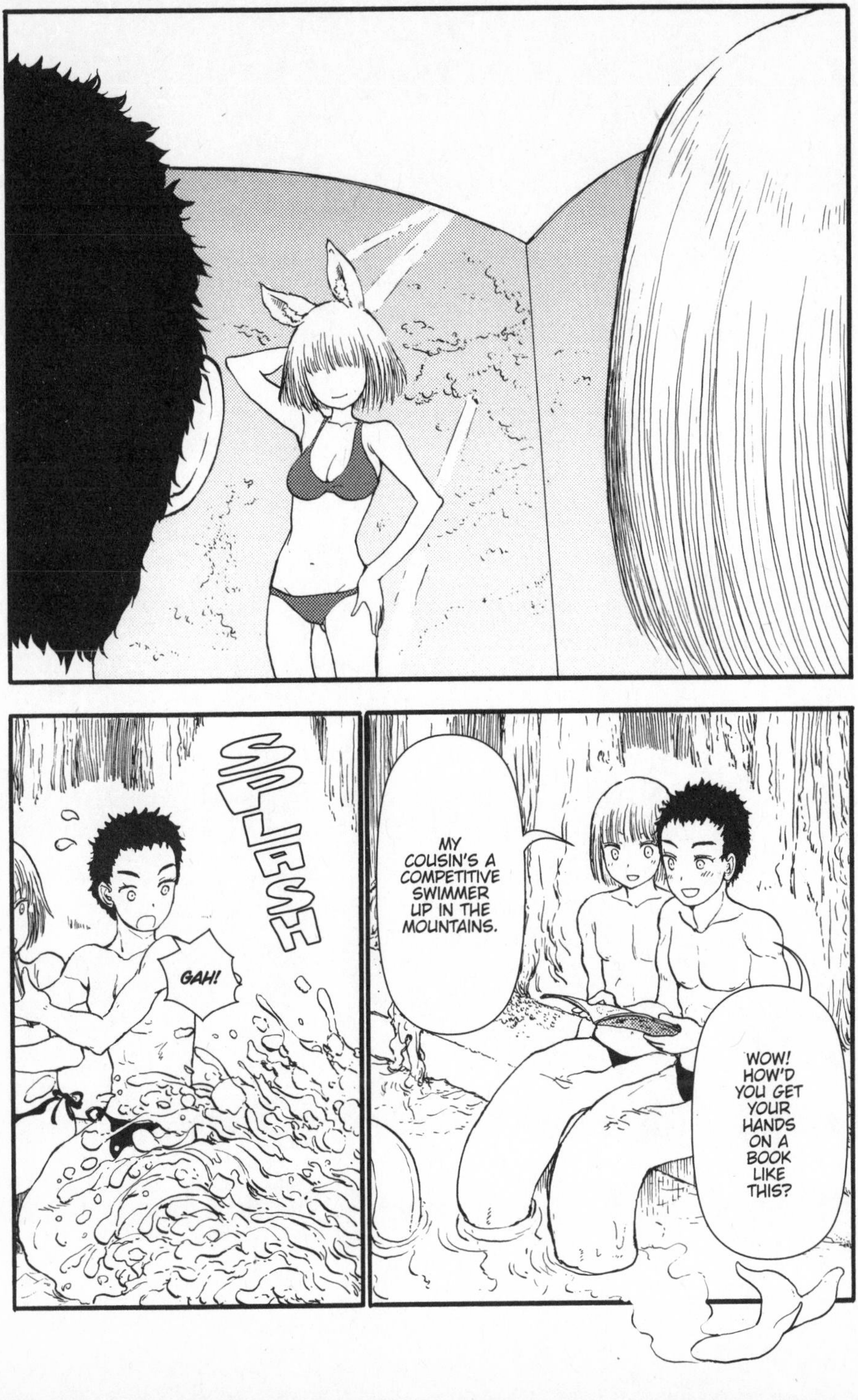
MY COUSIN'S A COMPETITIVE SWIMMER UP IN THE MOUNTAINS.
WOW! HOW'D YOU GET YOUR HANDS ON A BOOK LIKE THIS?
SPLASH
GAH!

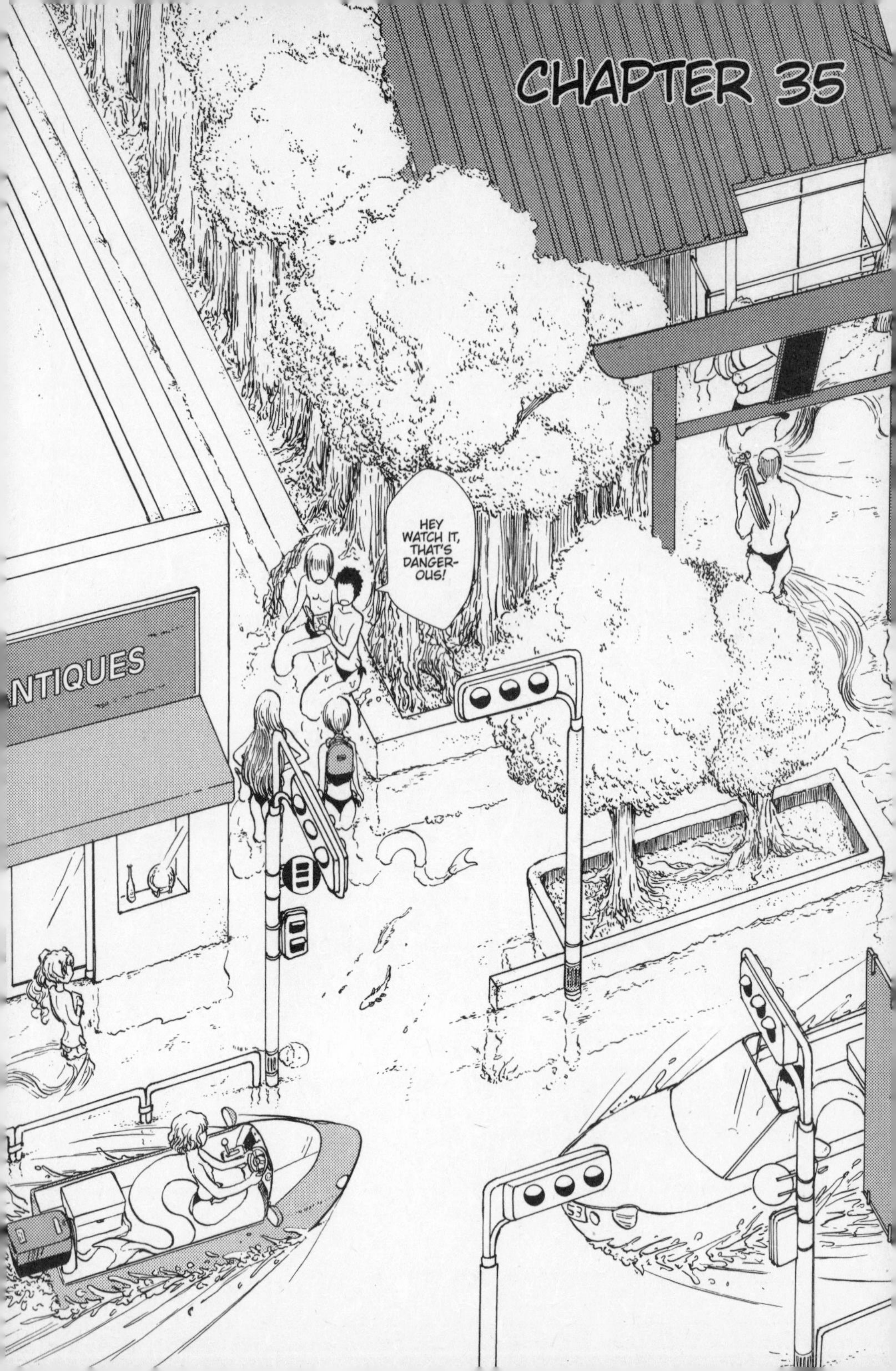
CHAPTER 35
HEY WATCH IT, THAT'S DANGER-OUS!
NTIQUES

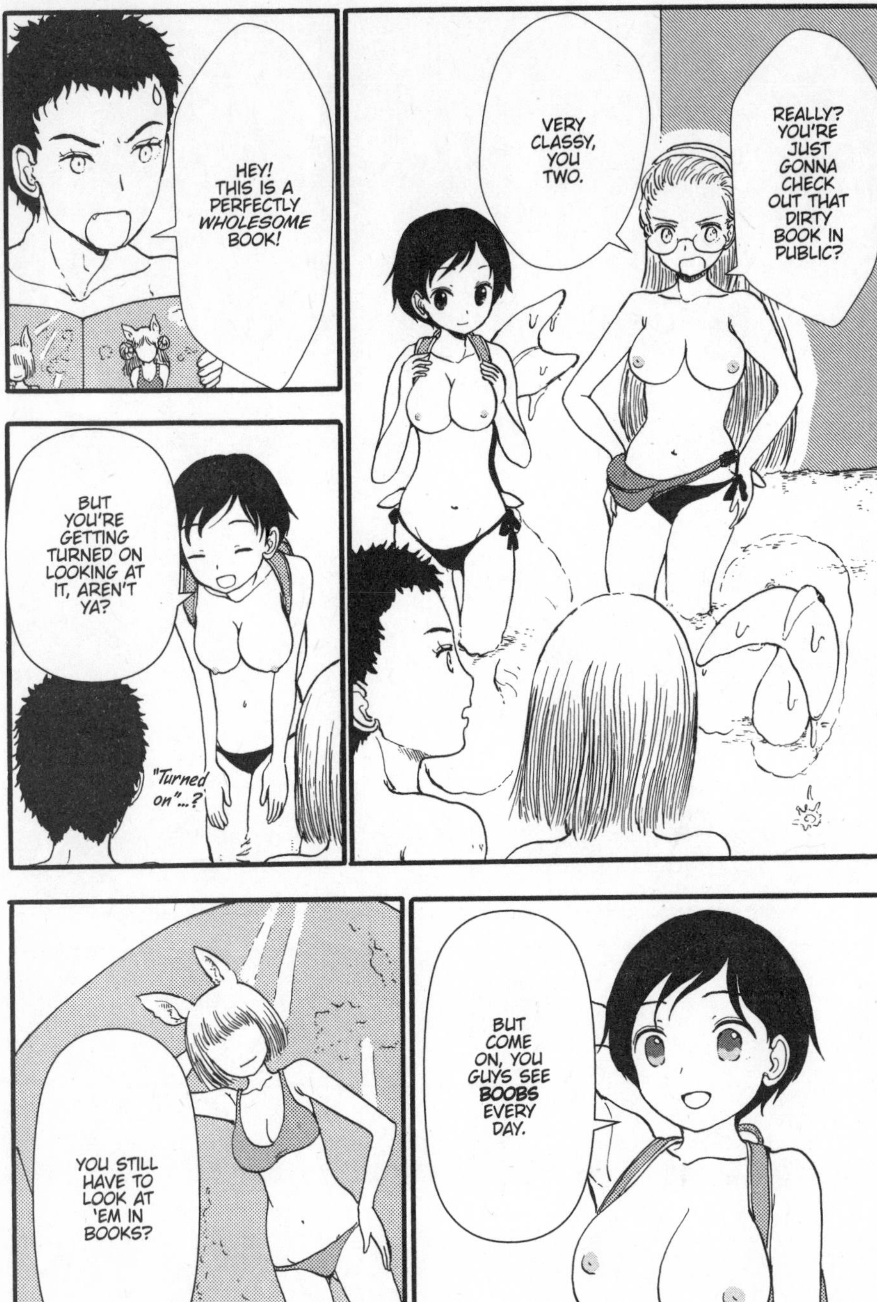
REALLY? YOU'RE JUST GONNA CHECK OUT THAT DIRTY BOOK IN PUBLIC?
VERY CLASSY, YOU TWO.
HEY! THIS IS A PERFECTLY *WHOLESOME* BOOK!
BUT YOU'RE GETTING TURNED ON LOOKING AT IT, AREN'T YA?
"Turned on"...?
BUT COME ON, YOU GUYS SEE **BOOBS** EVERY DAY.
YOU STILL HAVE TO LOOK AT 'EM IN BOOKS?

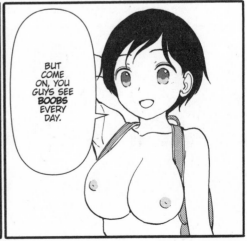

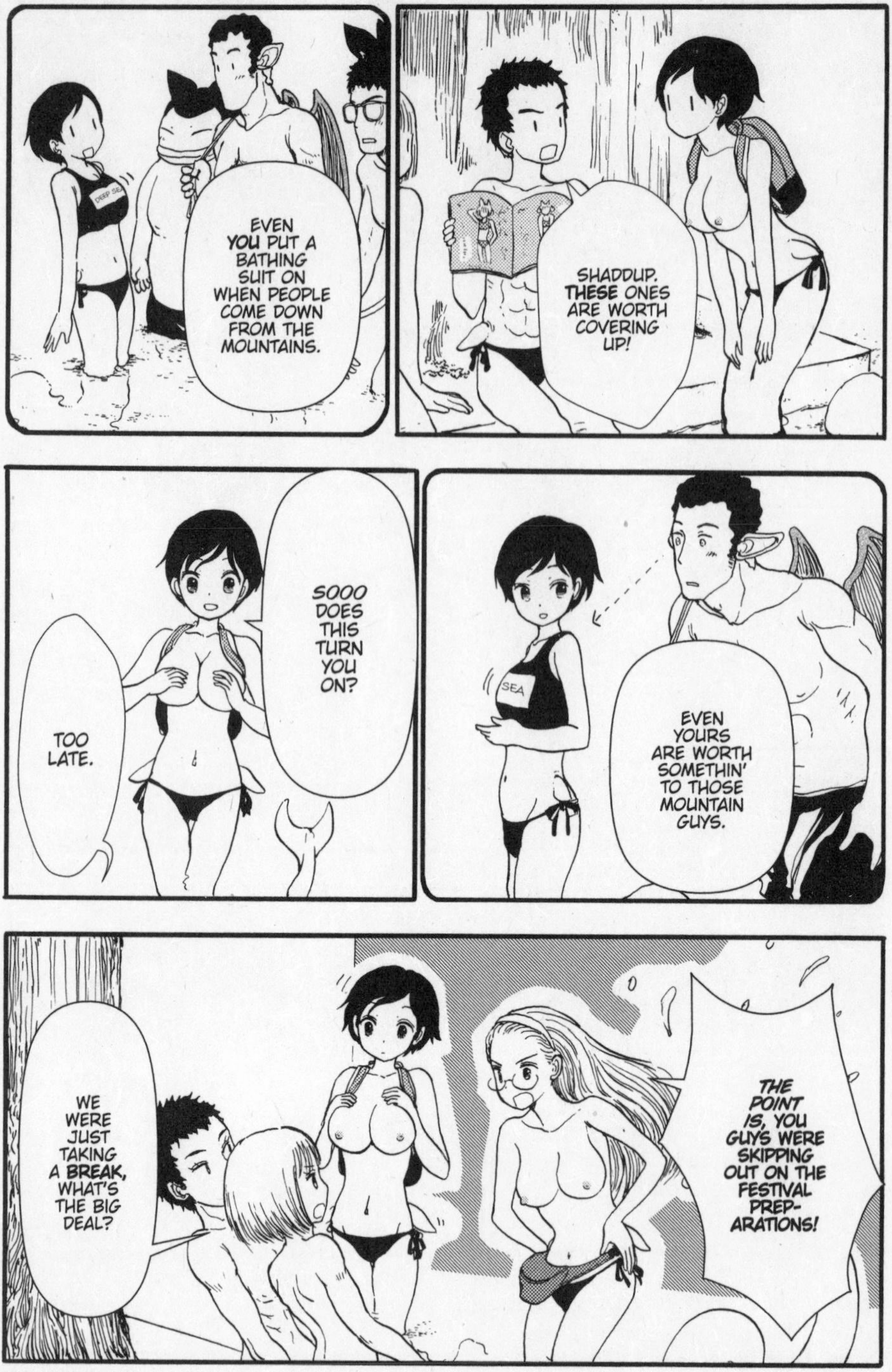
SHADDUP. THESE ONES ARE WORTH COVERING UP!
DEEP SEA
EVEN YOU PUT A BATHING SUIT ON WHEN PEOPLE COME DOWN FROM THE MOUNTAINS.
EVEN YOURS ARE WORTH SOMETHIN' TO THOSE MOUNTAIN GUYS.
SEA
SOOO DOES THIS TURN YOU ON?
TOO LATE.
THE POINT IS, YOU GUYS WERE SKIPPING OUT ON THE FESTIVAL PREP-ARATIONS!
WE WERE JUST TAKING A BREAK, WHAT'S THE BIG DEAL?

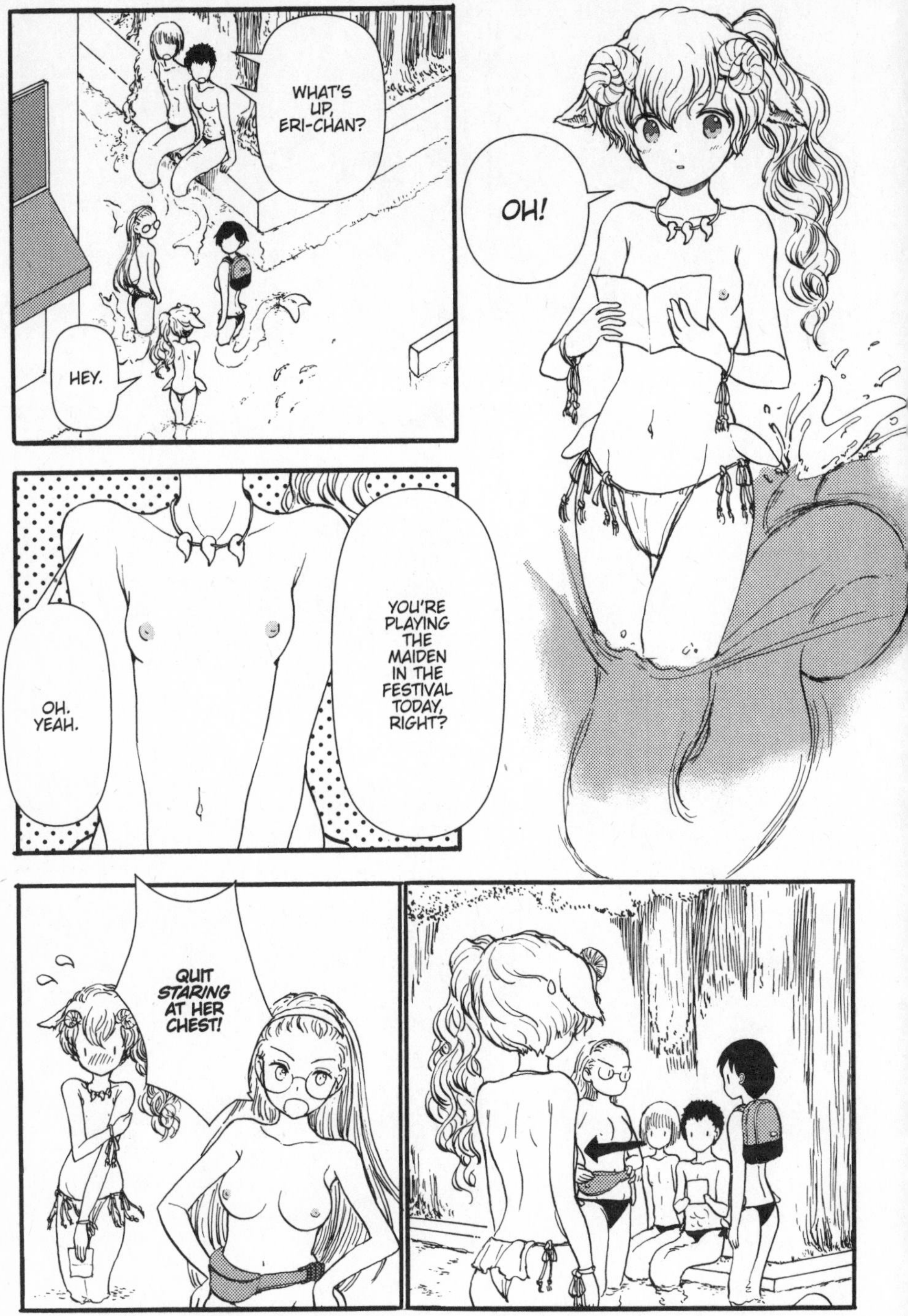
OH!
WHAT'S UP, ERI-CHAN?
HEY.
YOU'RE PLAYING THE MAIDEN IN THE FESTIVAL TODAY, RIGHT?
OH. YEAH.
QUIT *STARING* AT HER CHEST!

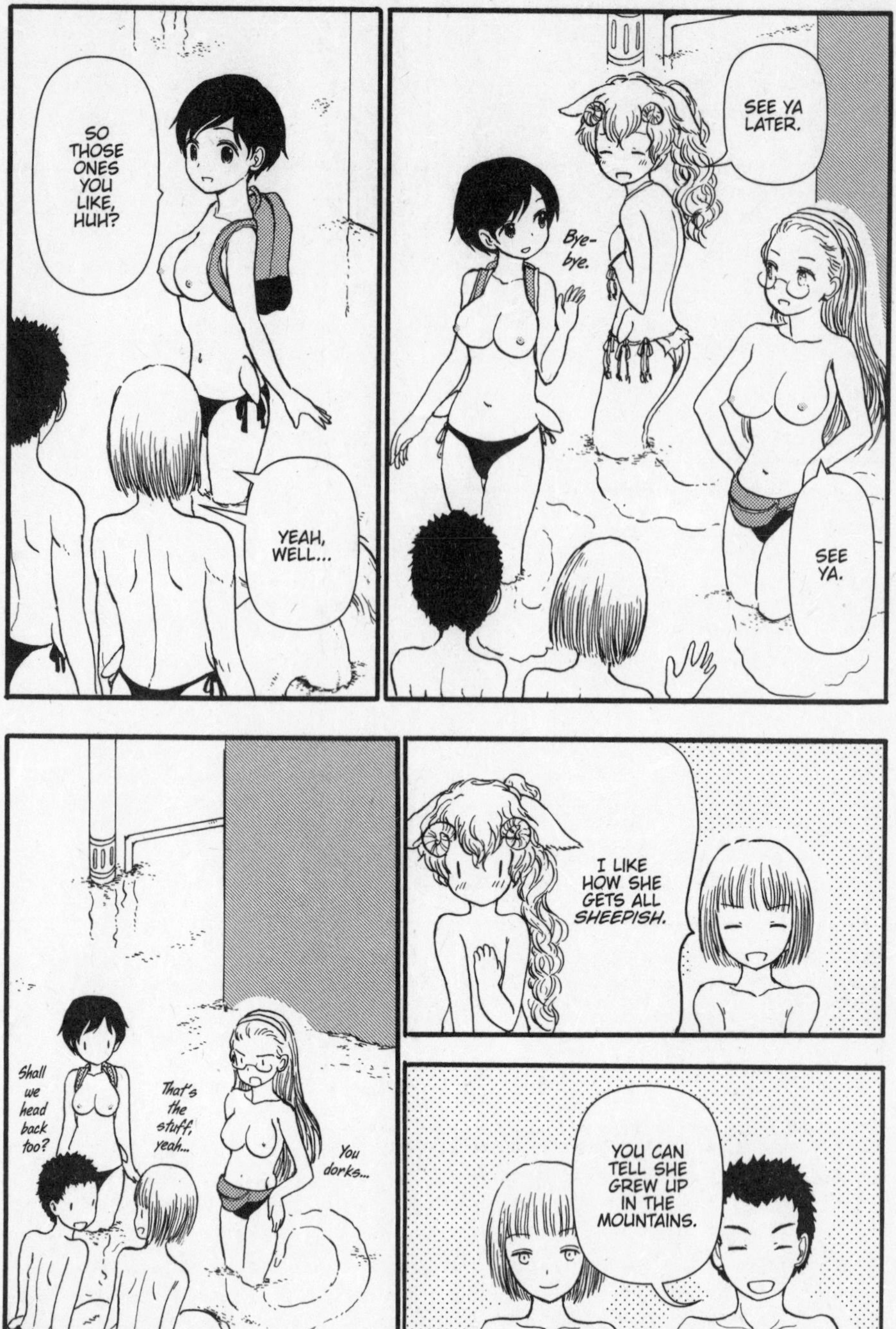
SEE YA LATER.
Bye-bye.
SEE YA.
SO THOSE ONES YOU LIKE, HUH?
YEAH, WELL...
I LIKE HOW SHE GETS ALL SHEEPISH.
YOU CAN TELL SHE GREW UP IN THE MOUNTAINS.
You dorks...
That's the stuff, yeah...
Shall we head back too?

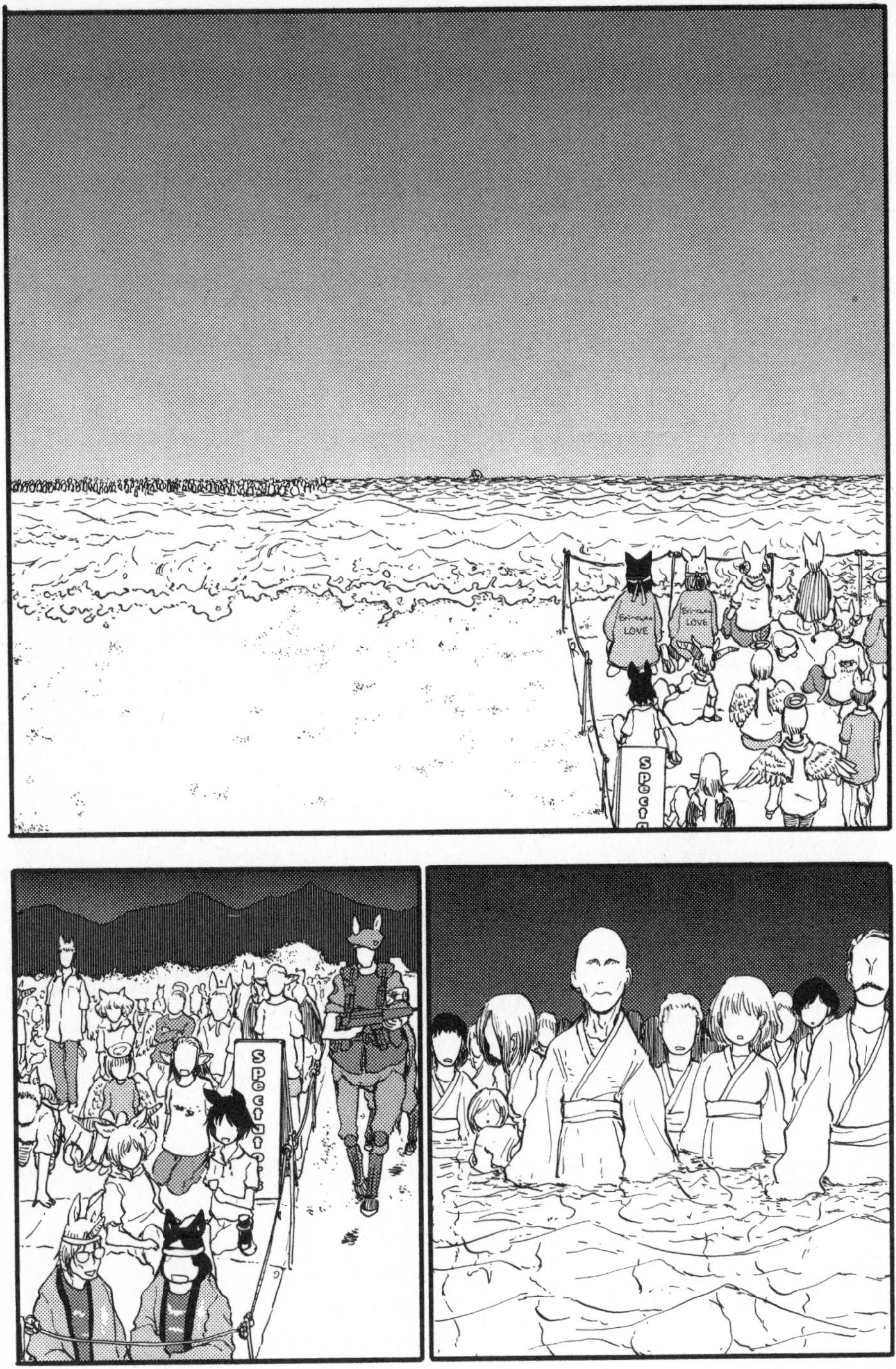
LOVE
LOVE

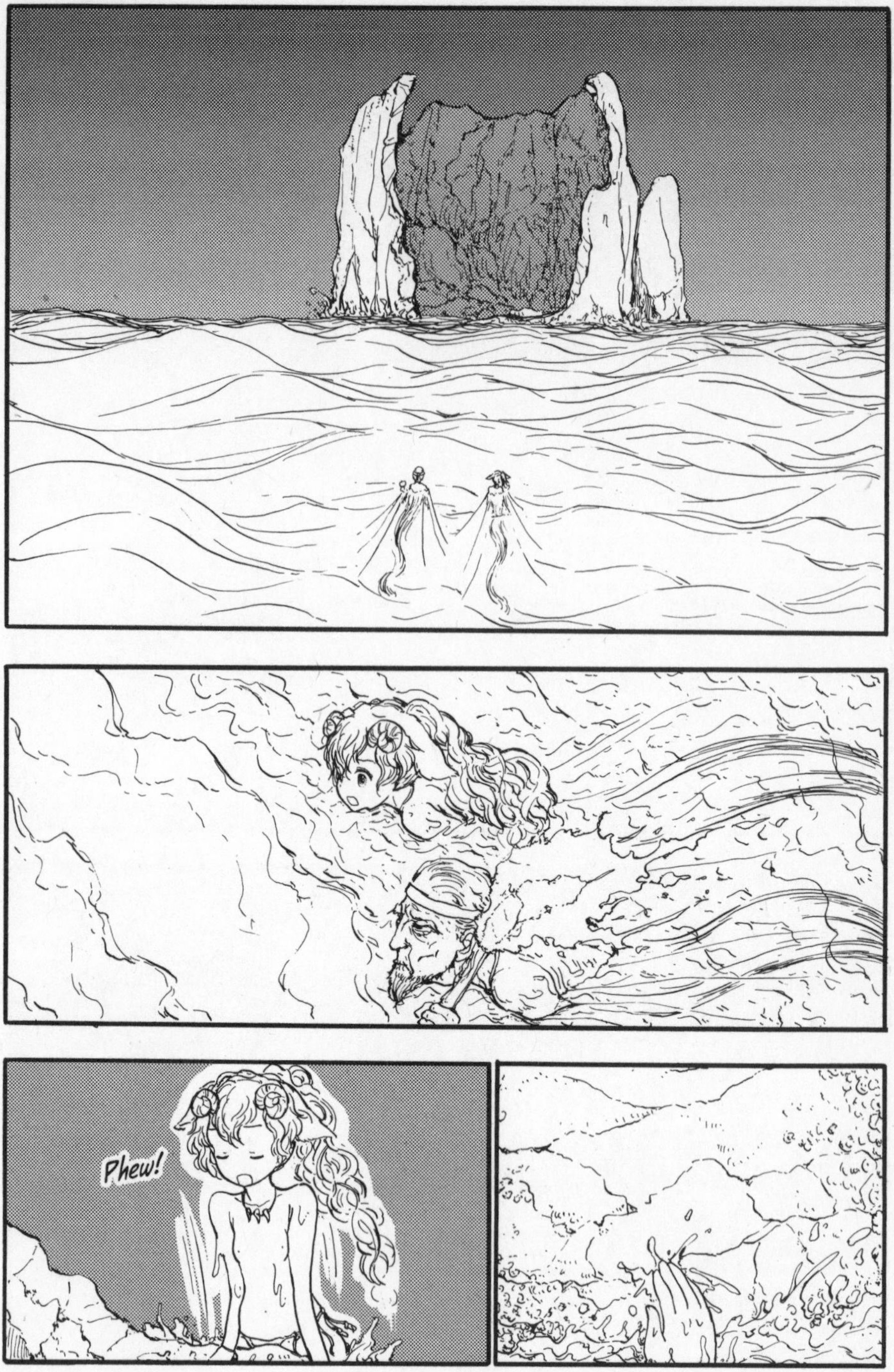
Phew!

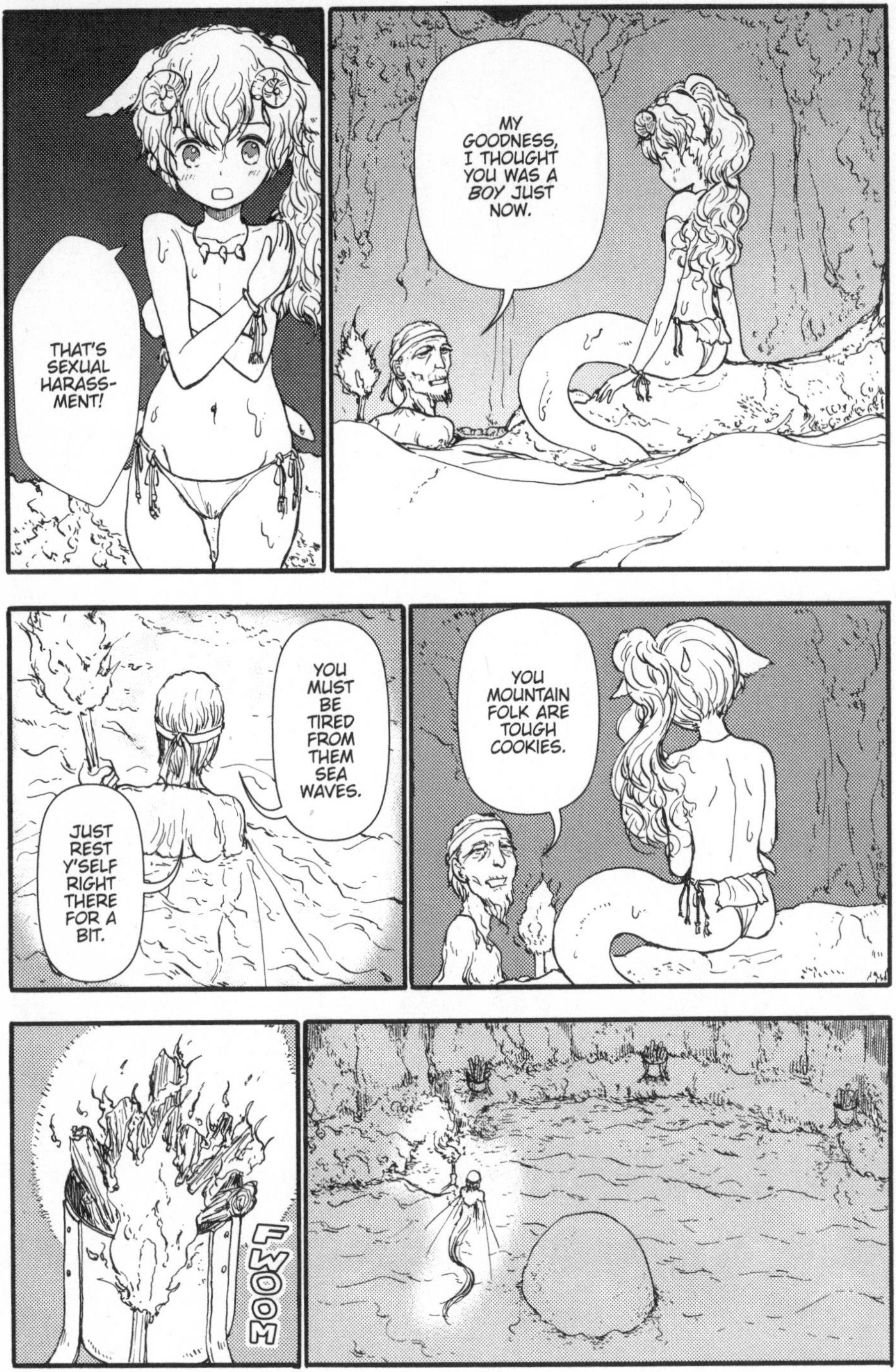
MY GOODNESS, I THOUGHT YOU WAS A BOY JUST NOW.
THAT'S SEXUAL HARASS-MENT!
YOU MOUNTAIN FOLK ARE TOUGH COOKIES.
YOU MUST BE TIRED FROM THEM SEA WAVES.
JUST REST Y'SELF RIGHT THERE FOR A BIT.
FWOOM

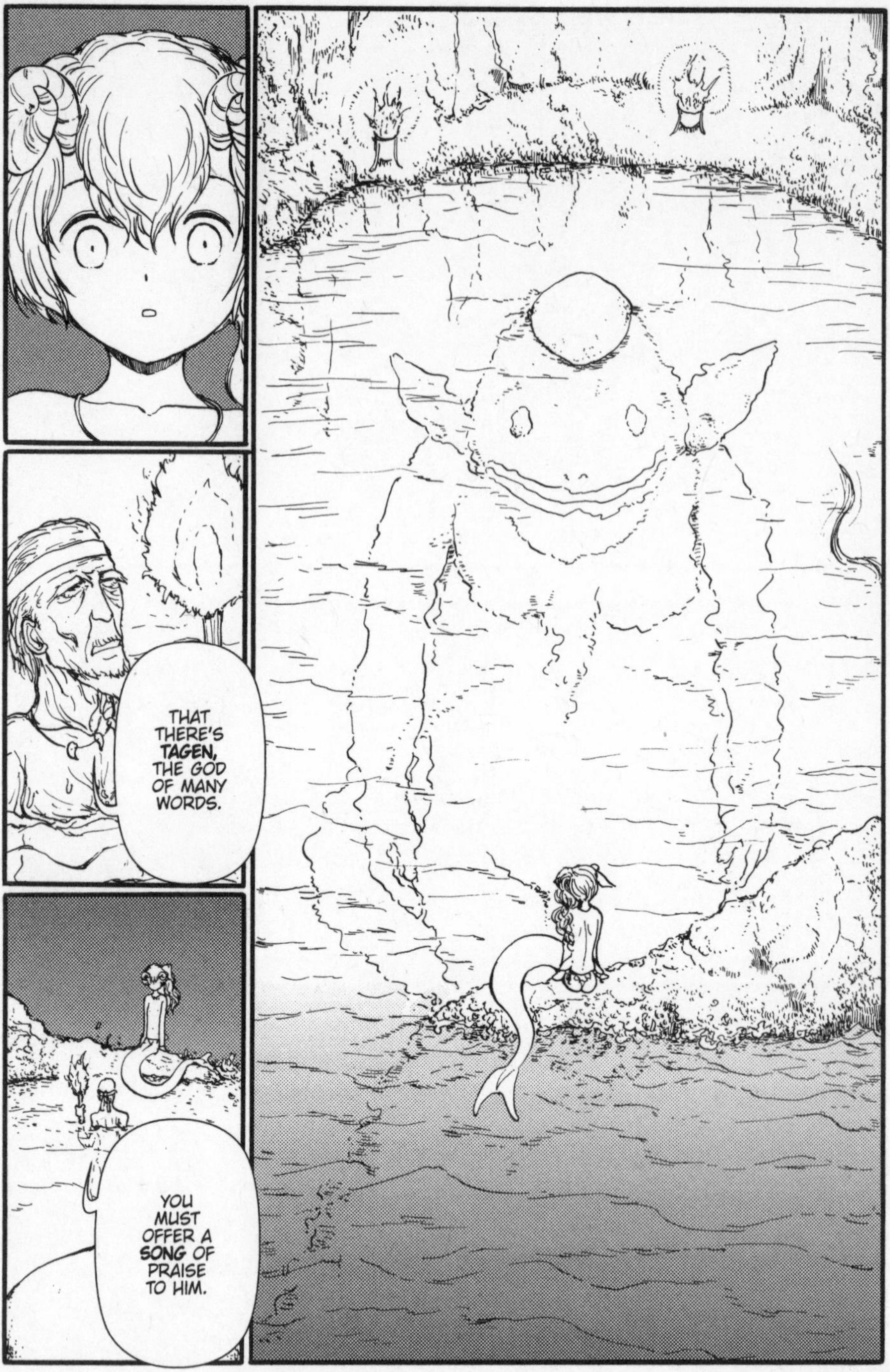
THAT THERE'S **TAGEN,** THE GOD OF MANY WORDS.
YOU MUST OFFER A **SONG** OF PRAISE TO HIM.

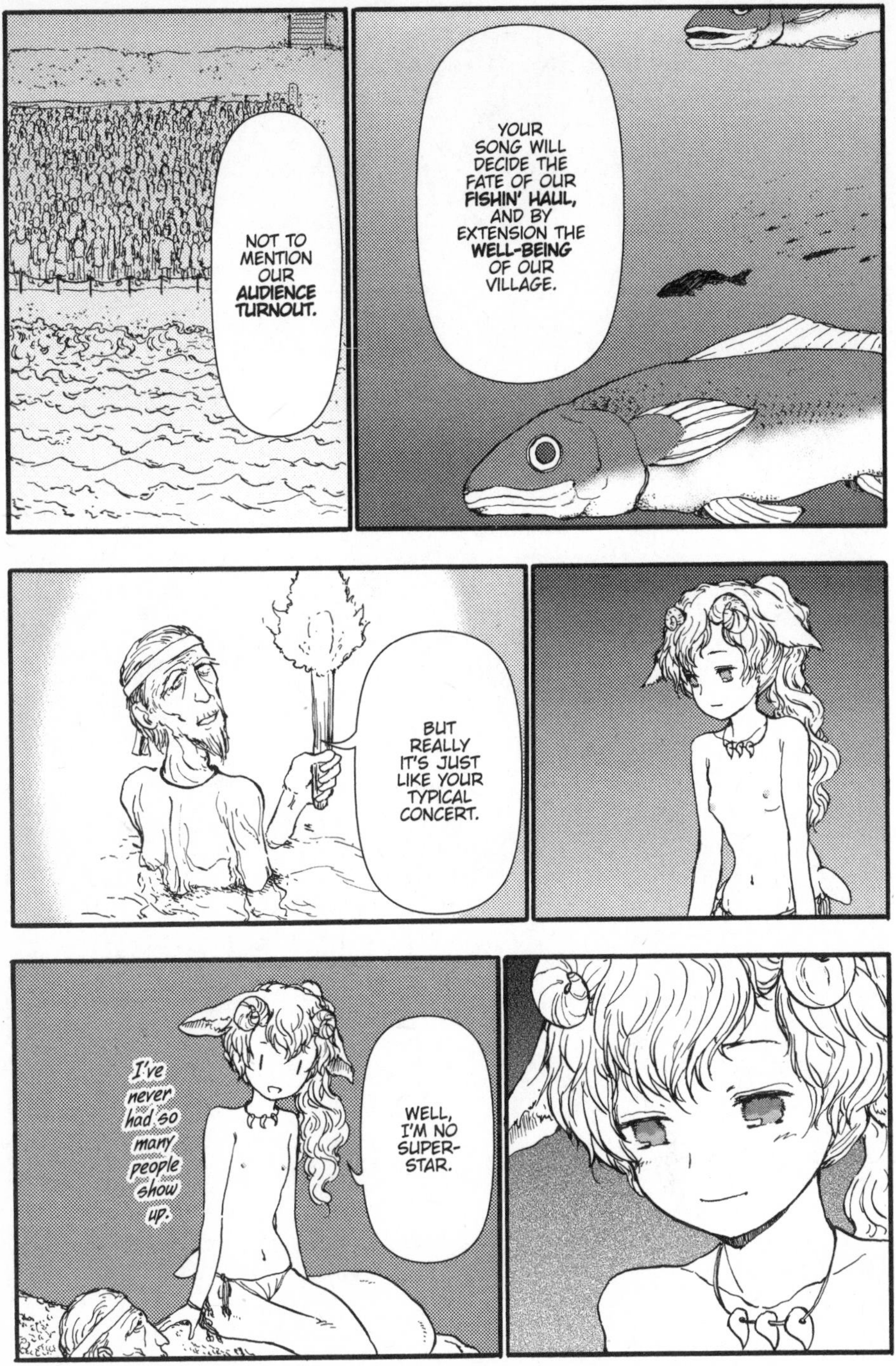
YOUR SONG WILL DECIDE THE FATE OF OUR **FISHIN' HAUL,** AND BY EXTENSION THE **WELL-BEING** OF OUR VILLAGE.
NOT TO MENTION OUR **AUDIENCE TURNOUT.**
BUT REALLY IT'S JUST LIKE YOUR TYPICAL CONCERT.
WELL, I'M NO SUPER-STAR.
I've never had so many people show up.

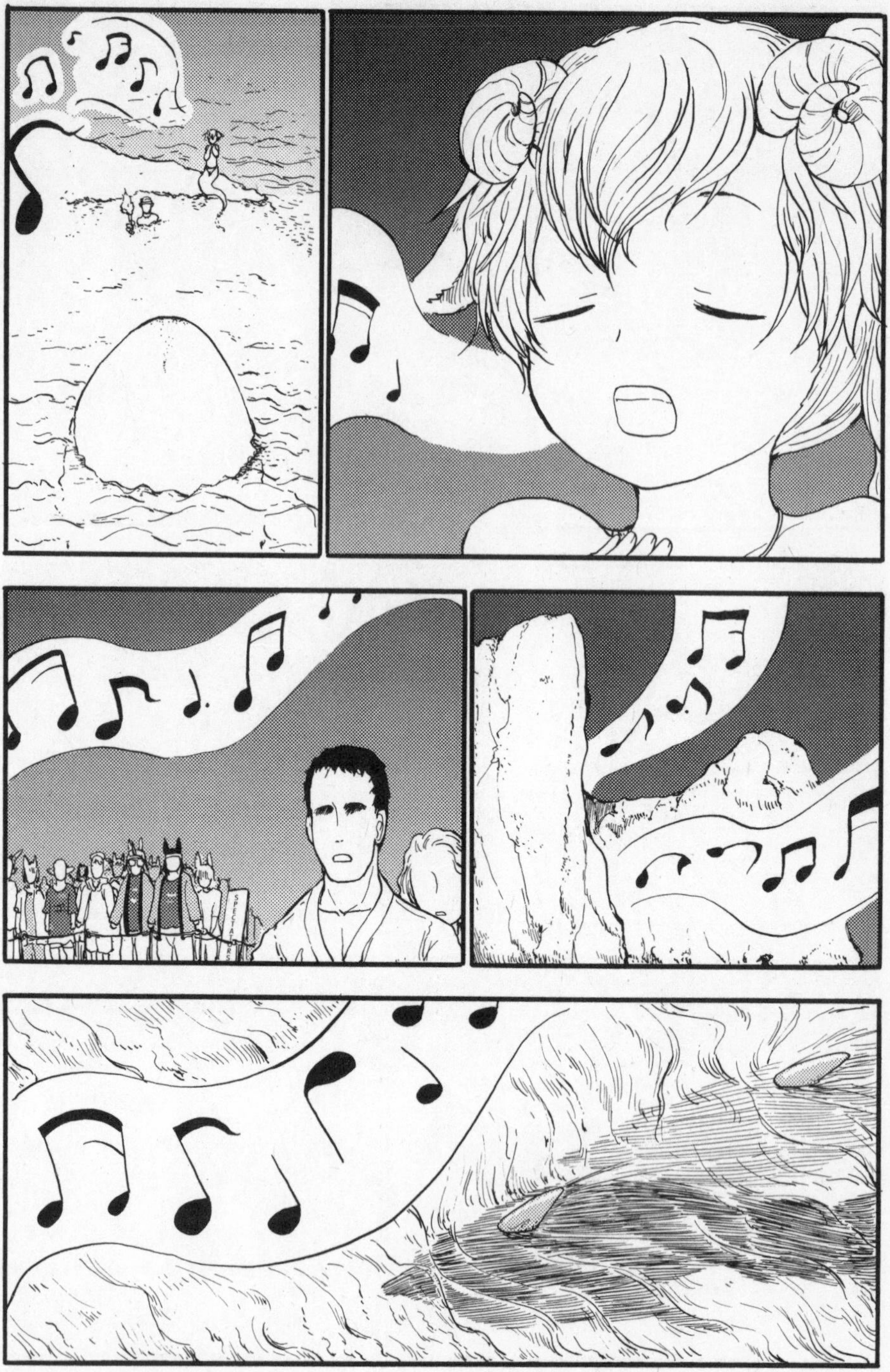
SPECTATORS

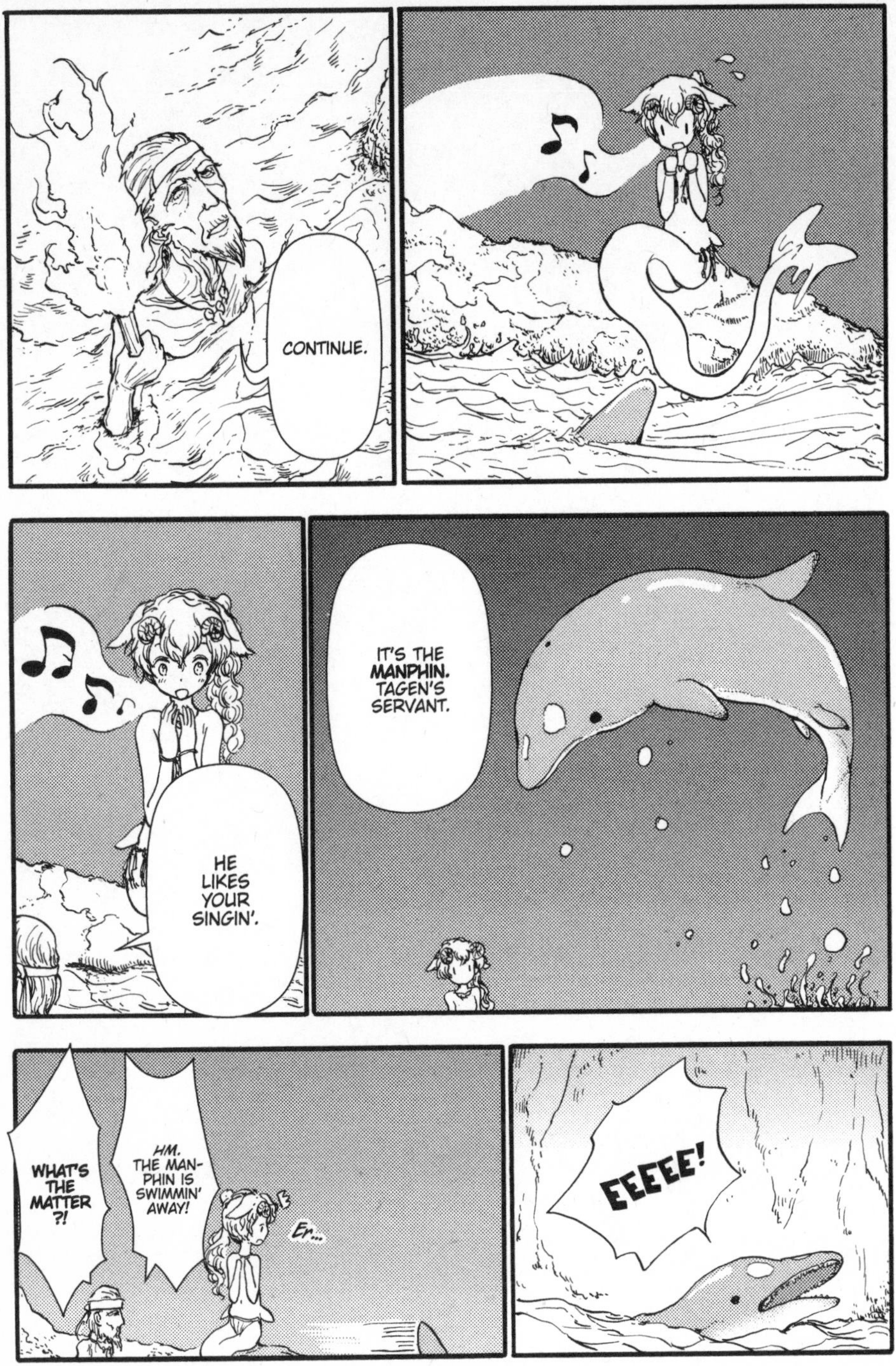
CONTINUE.
IT'S THE MANPHIN. TAGEN'S SERVANT.
HE LIKES YOUR SINGIN'.
EEEEE!
HM. THE MAN-PHIN IS SWIMMIN' AWAY!
WHAT'S THE MATTER ?!
Er...

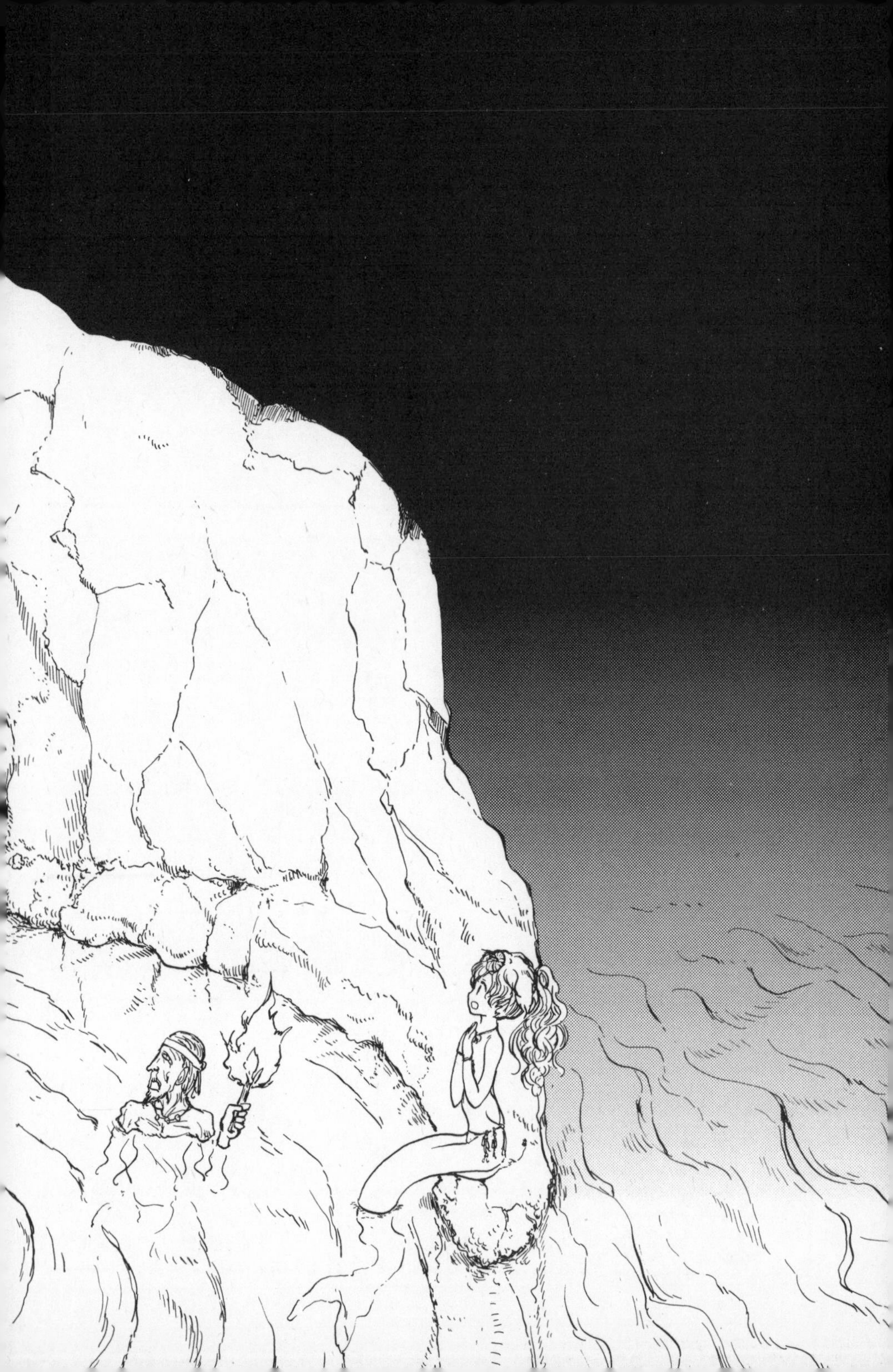

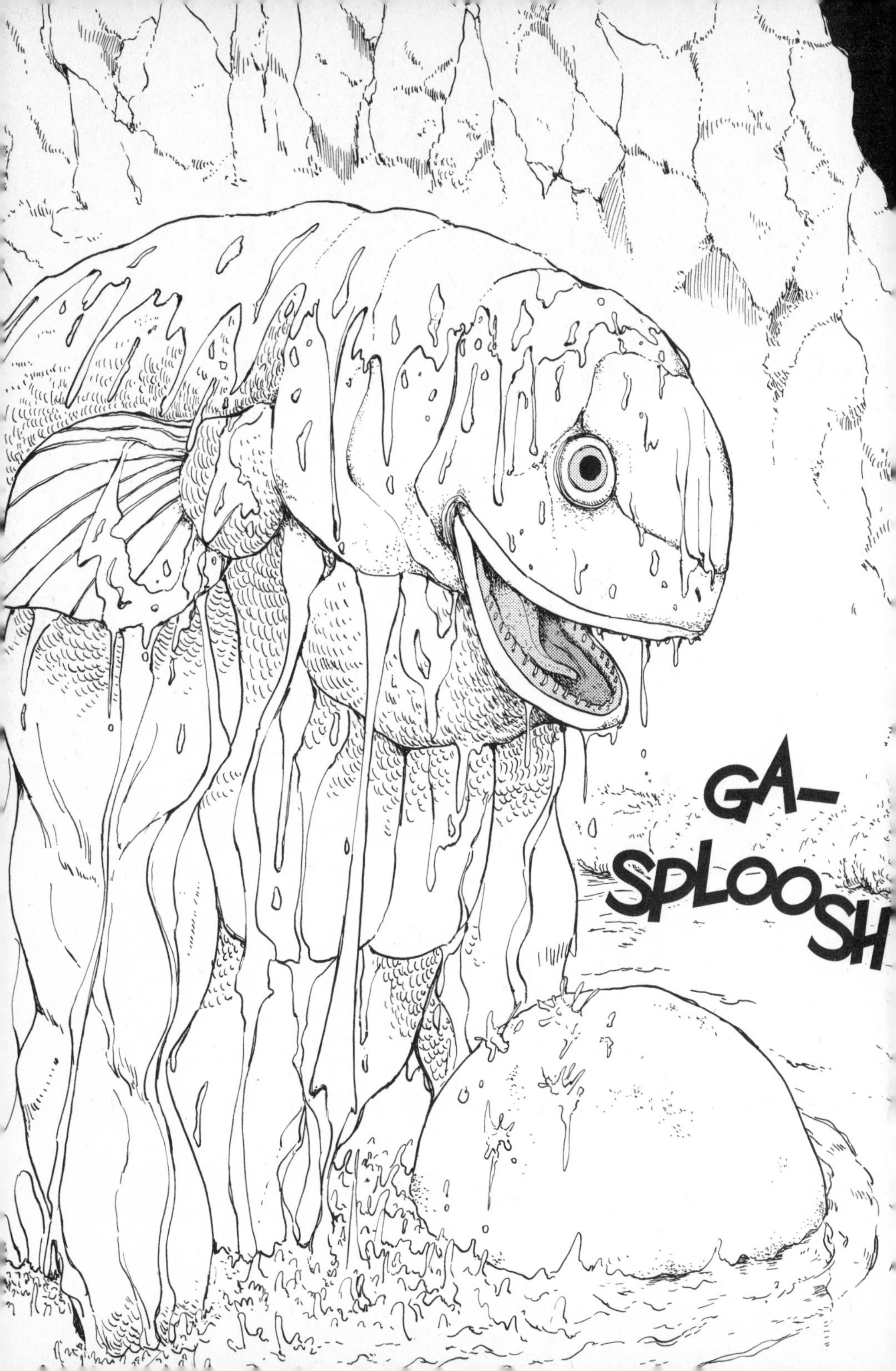
GA-
SPLOOSH

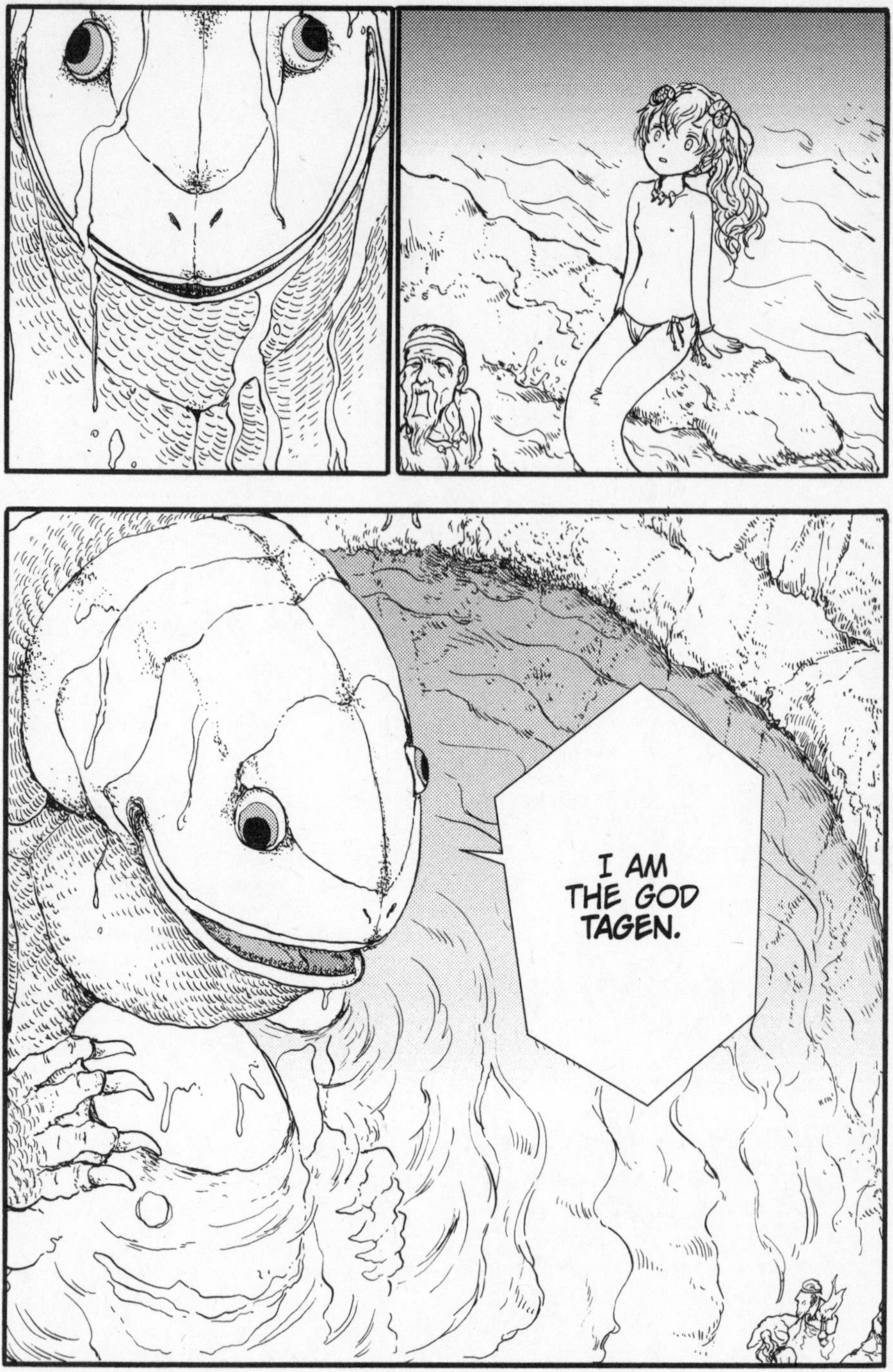
I AM THE GOD TAGEN.

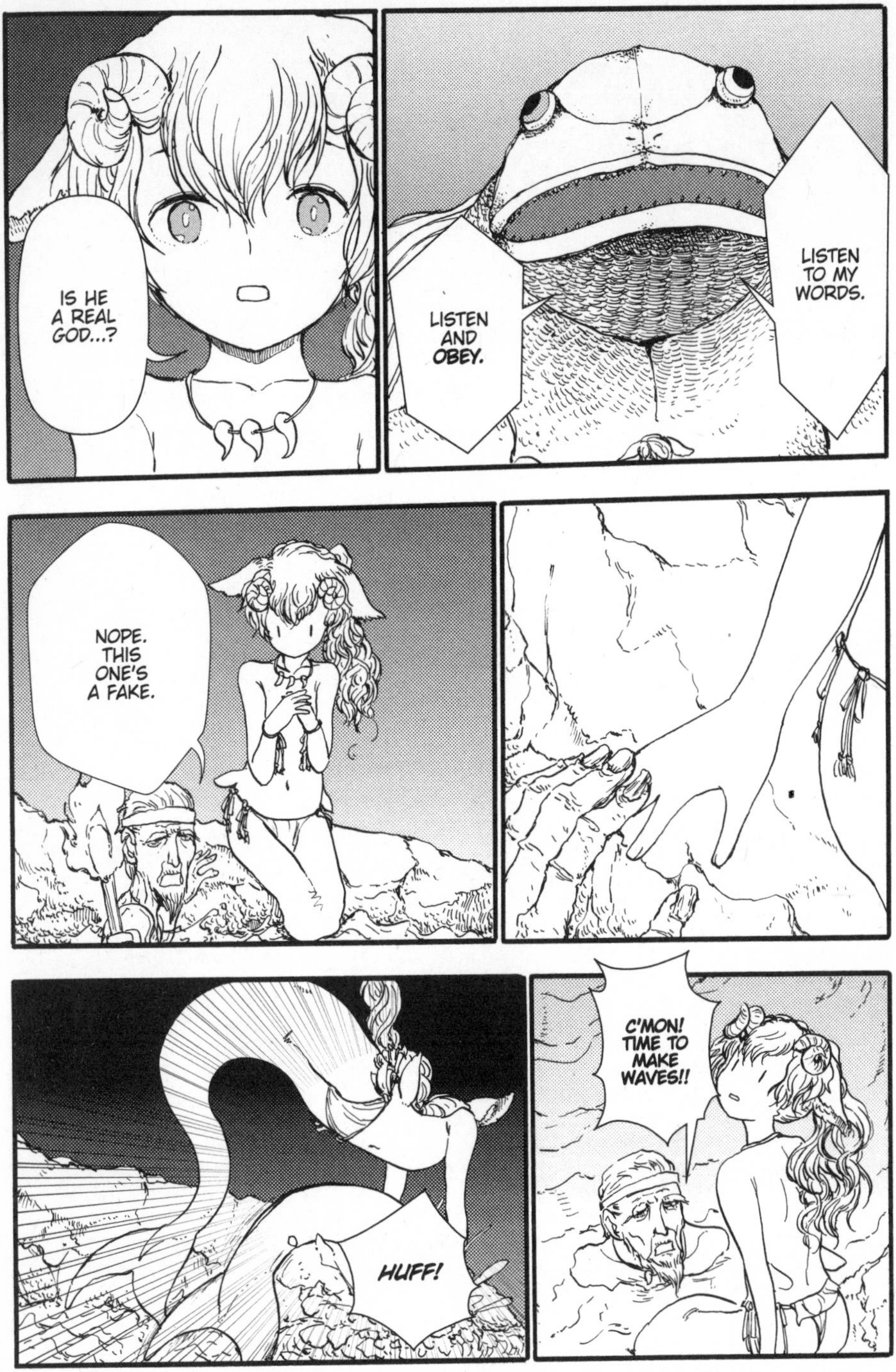
LISTEN TO MY WORDS.
LISTEN AND OBEY.
IS HE A REAL GOD...?
NOPE. THIS ONE'S A FAKE.
C'MON! TIME TO MAKE WAVES!!
HUFF!

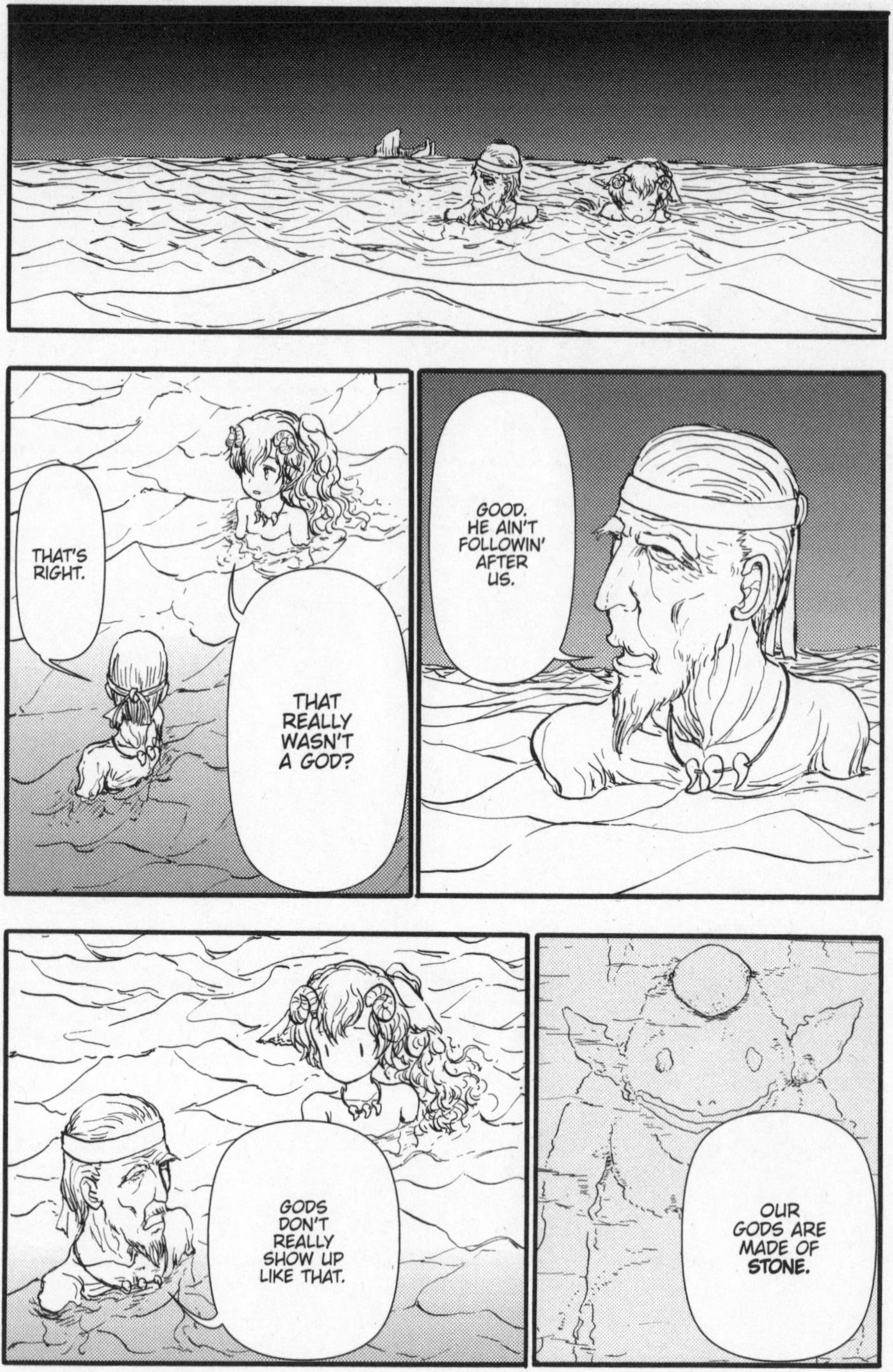
GOOD. HE AIN'T FOLLOWIN' AFTER US.
THAT REALLY WASN'T A GOD?
THAT'S RIGHT.
OUR GODS ARE MADE OF STONE.
GODS DON'T REALLY SHOW UP LIKE THAT.

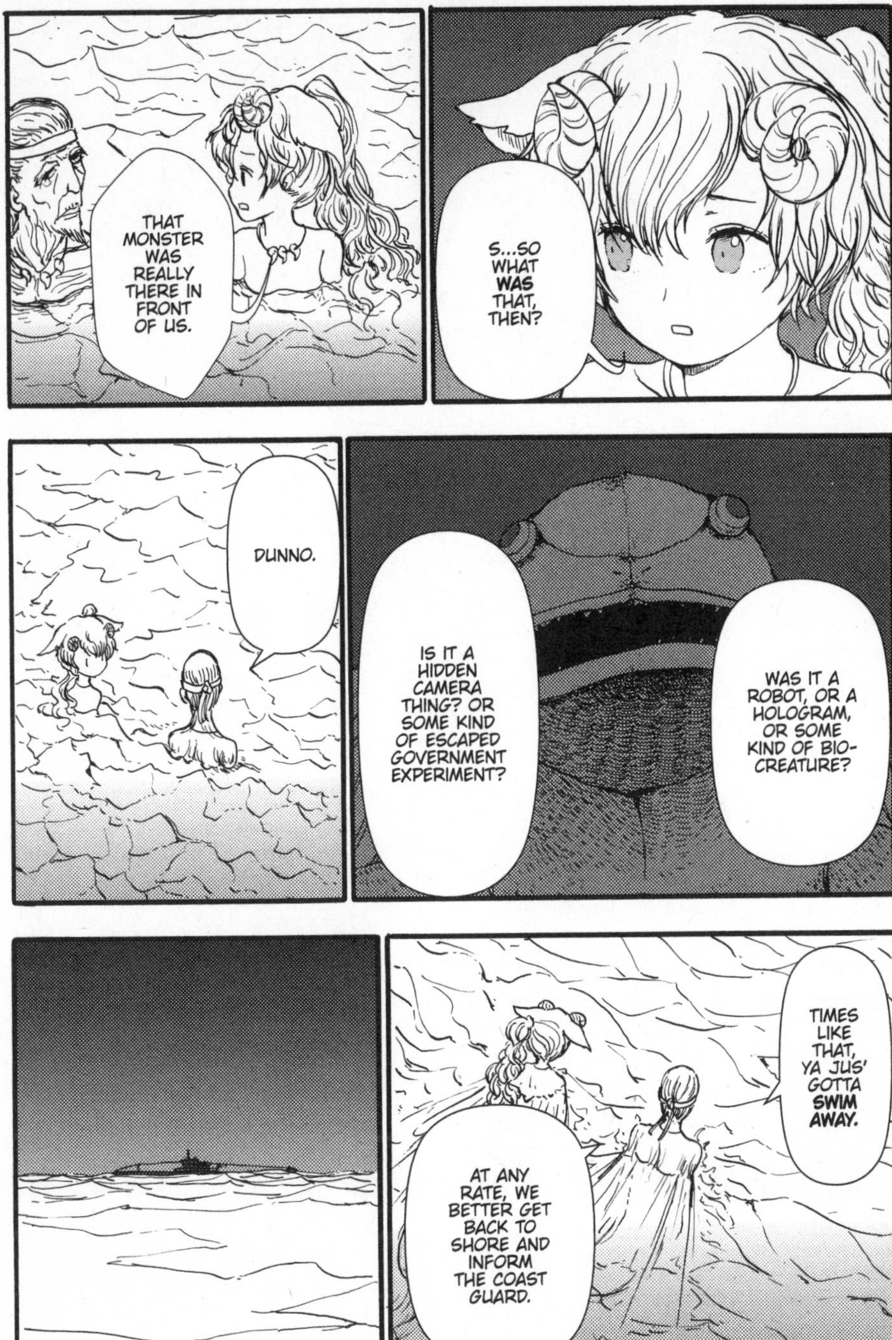
S...SO WHAT **WAS** THAT, THEN?
THAT MONSTER WAS REALLY THERE IN FRONT OF US.
WAS IT A ROBOT, OR A HOLOGRAM, OR SOME KIND OF BIO-CREATURE?
IS IT A HIDDEN CAMERA THING? OR SOME KIND OF ESCAPED GOVERNMENT EXPERIMENT?
DUNNO.
TIMES LIKE THAT, YA JUS' GOTTA **SWIM AWAY.**
AT ANY RATE, WE BETTER GET BACK TO SHORE AND INFORM THE COAST GUARD.

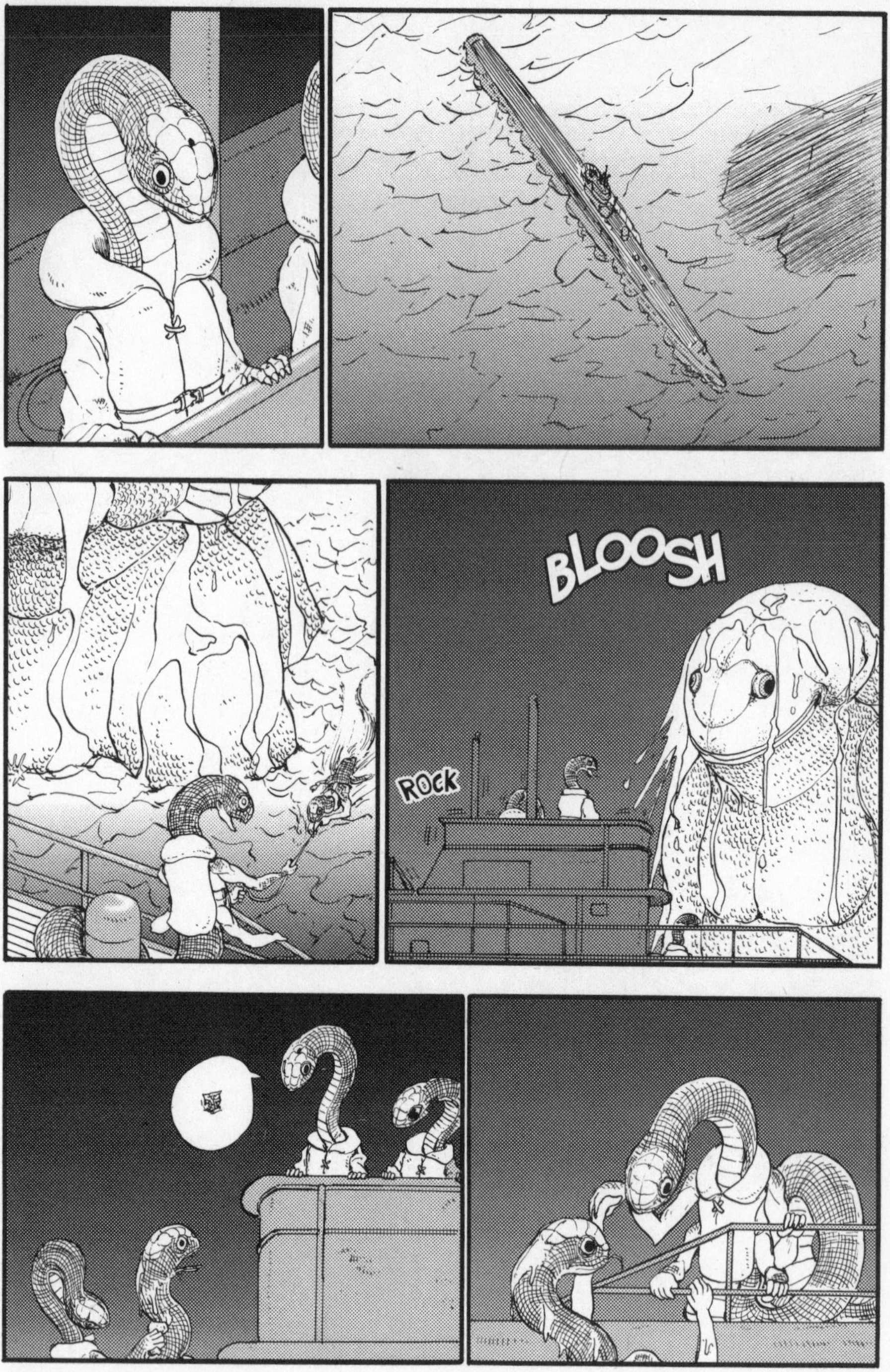
BLOOSH
ROCK

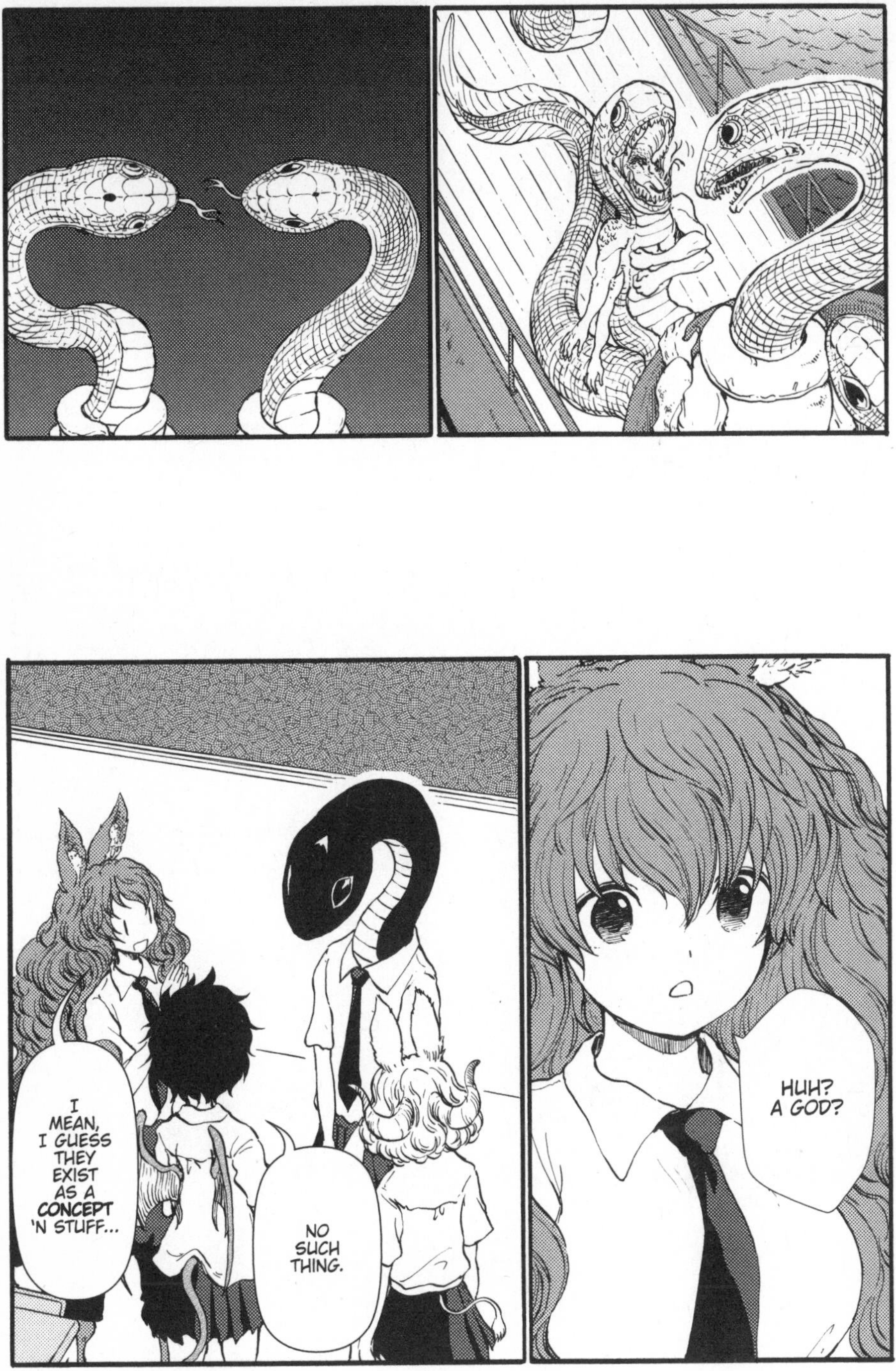
HUH? A GOD?
NO SUCH THING.
I MEAN, I GUESS THEY EXIST AS A **CONCEPT** 'N STUFF...

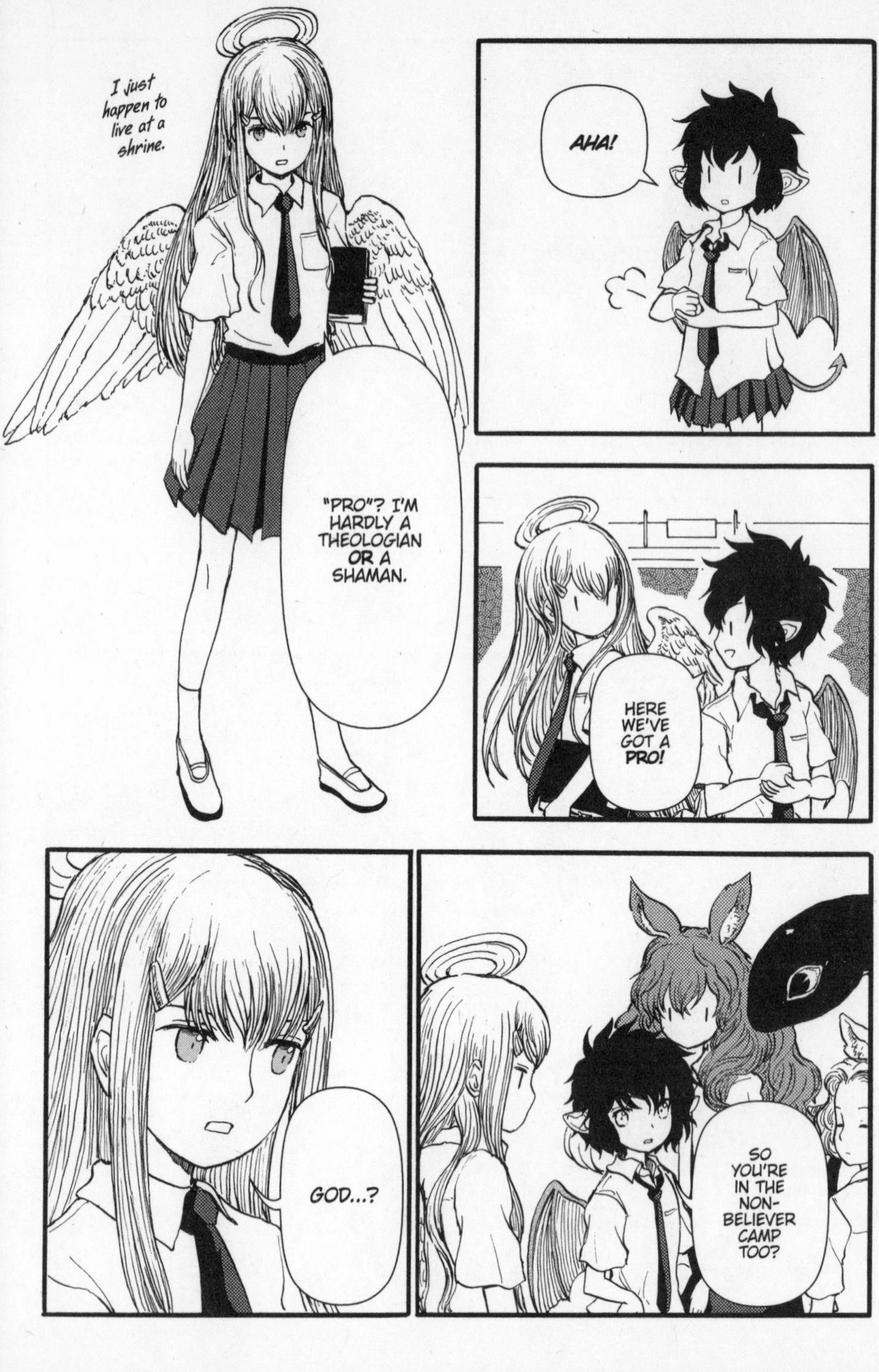
AHA!
HERE WE'VE GOT A PRO!
"PRO"? I'M HARDLY A THEOLOGIAN OR A SHAMAN.
I just happen to live at a shrine.
SO YOU'RE IN THE NON-BELIEVER CAMP TOO?
GOD...?

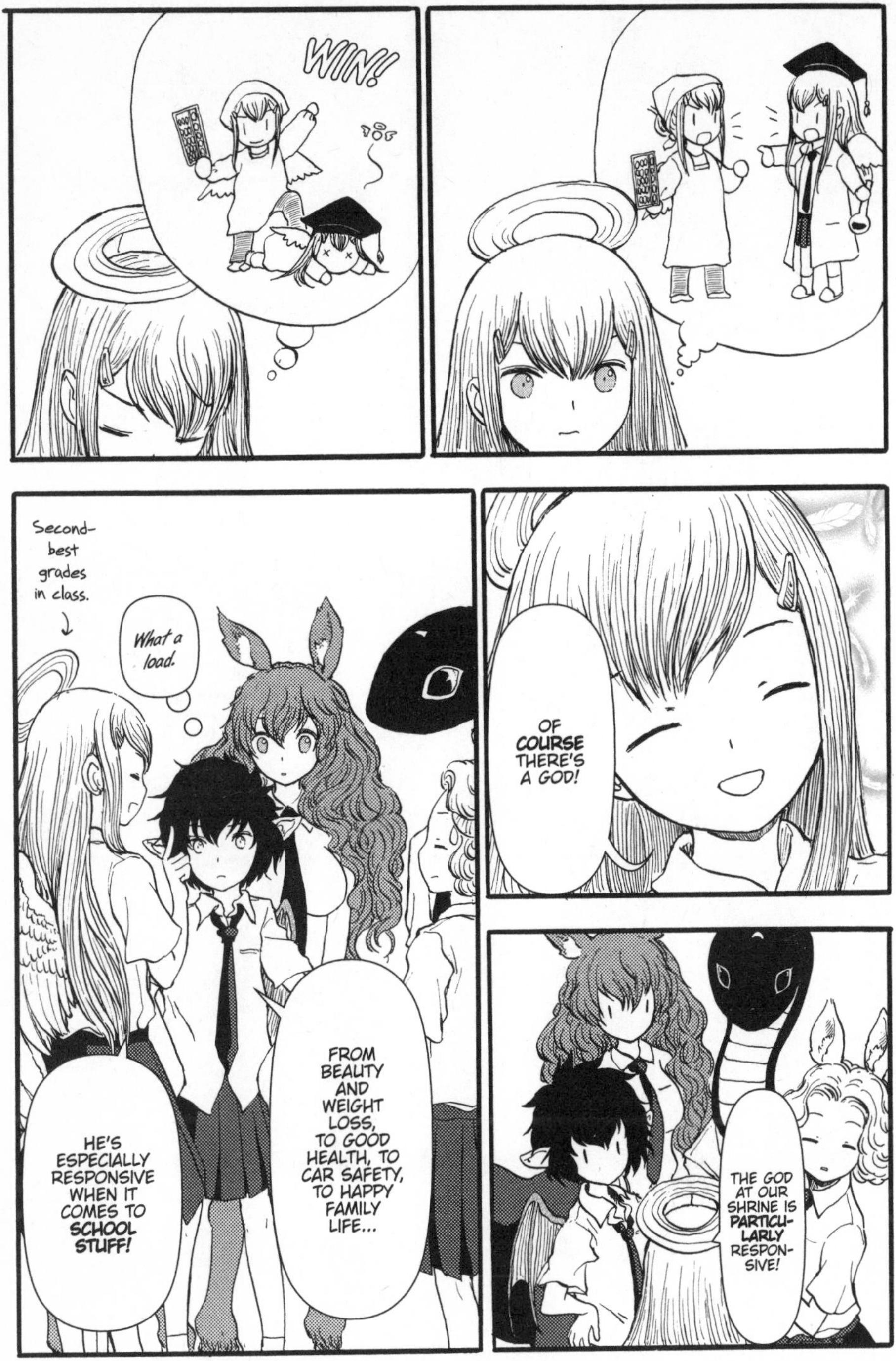
WIN!
OF COURSE THERE'S A GOD!
THE GOD AT OUR SHRINE IS PARTICULARLY RESPONSIVE!
FROM BEAUTY AND WEIGHT LOSS, TO GOOD HEALTH, TO CAR SAFETY, TO HAPPY FAMILY LIFE...
HE'S ESPECIALLY RESPONSIVE WHEN IT COMES TO SCHOOL STUFF!
Second-best grades in class.
What a load.

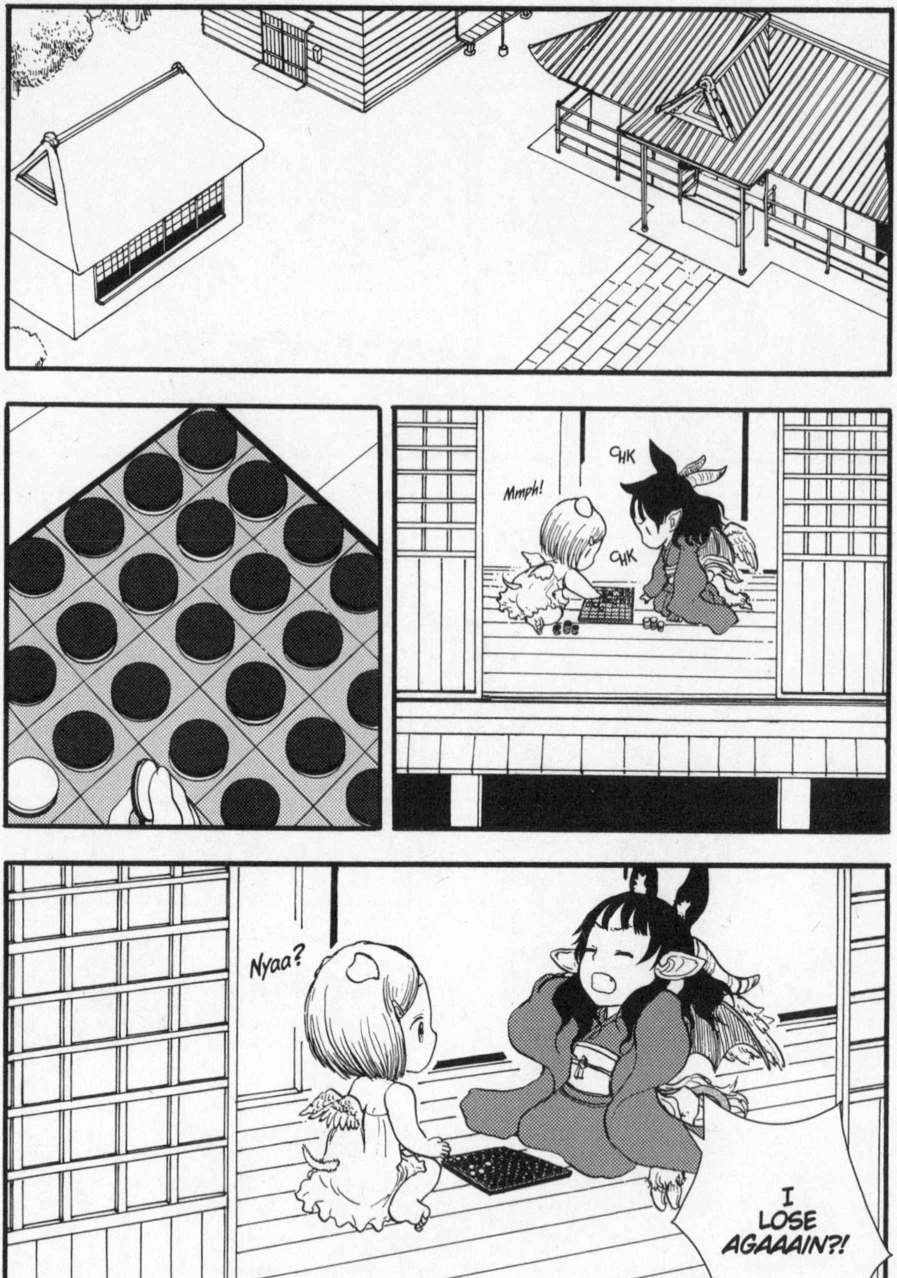
CHK
Mmph!
CHK
I LOSE AGAAAIN?!
Nyaa?

A Centaur's Life

GENETICS MADE EASY: LESSON 6
HUMAN BEINGS HAVE GENES FROM OTHER RACES

ABOUT ONE IN EVERY HUNDRED HYBRID CHILDREN IS BORN WITH TRAITS
FOUND NEITHER IN THE MOTHER NOR FATHER. FOR INSTANCE, THE CHILD
OF AN ANGELFOLK COUPLE MIGHT BE BORN WITH HORNS. THIS PHENOMENON
IS DUE NOT ONLY TO MALFUNCTION OF THE OFFSPRING'S RACE-DETERMINING
GENES, BUT ALSO THE FACT THAT VIRTUALLY ALL PEOPLE POSSESS GENES
CONTAINING INFORMATION ON VIRTUALLY ALL RACES. EVEN IF, FOR EXAMPLE,
YOU HAVE A FAMILY LINE THAT HAD BIRTHED NOTHING BUT CENTAURS FOR
GENERATIONS, A CENTAUR WITH HORNS COULD BE BORN INTO THE FAMILY IF
GOATFOLK BLOOD WERE MIXED IN SOMEWHERE IN THE ANCESTRY. RACIALLY
MIXED BLOODLINES MEAN THAT HORNLESS PARENTS COULD POTENTIALLY
GIVE BIRTH TO HORNED OFFSPRING, OR WINGLESS PARENTS TO WINGED
ONES (THIS IS KNOWN AS "ATAVISTIC" HEREDITY).

IN CENTAURS, THE OCCURRENCE OF HYBRIDISM
IS RELATIVELY RARE ACROSS THE GLOBE DUE TO
THEIR HISTORICAL BACKGROUND. NEVERTHELESS,
THEY POSSESS THE GENES OF VIRTUALLY ALL
OTHER RACES. IT IS THOUGHT, HOWEVER, THAT
MERFOLK GENES ARE UNCOMMON IN PEOPLE LIVING
IN LANDLOCKED REGIONS OF NORTH AMERICA AND
EUROPE (WHILE VIRTUALLY ALL JAPANESE HAVE
MERFOLK GENES).

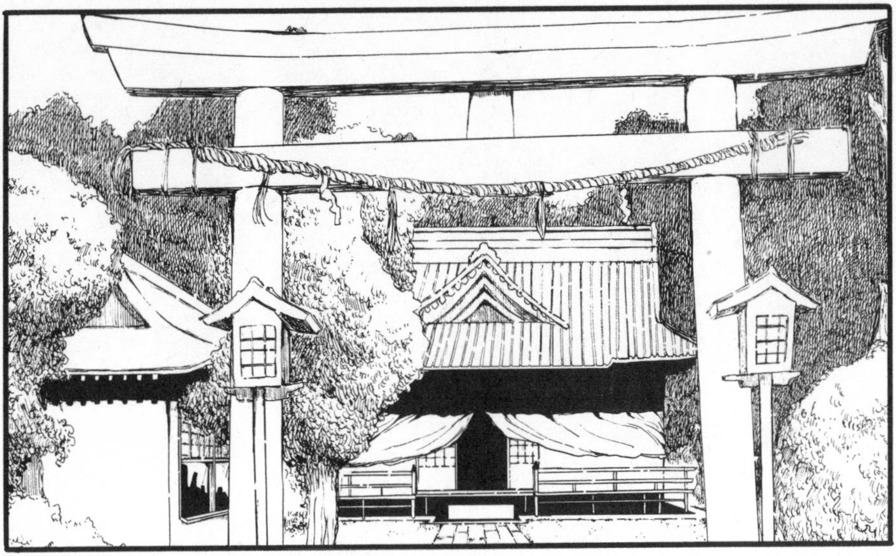

CHAPTER 36

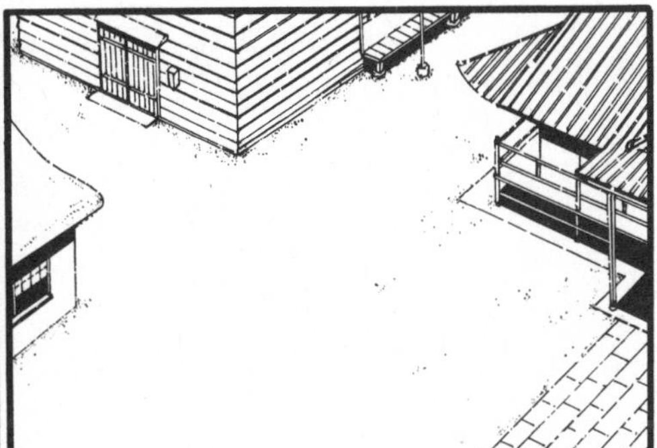

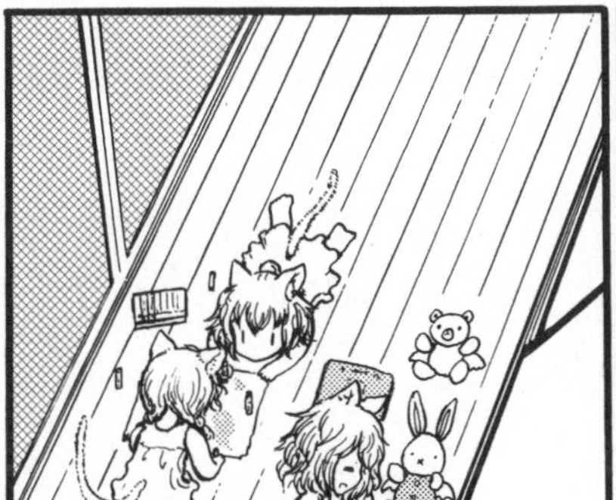

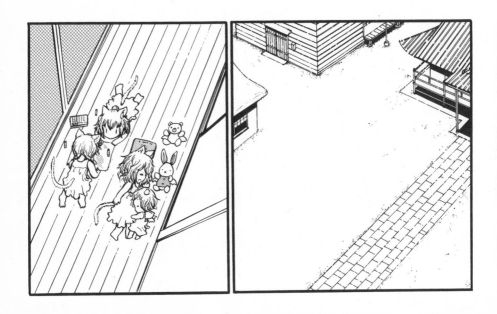

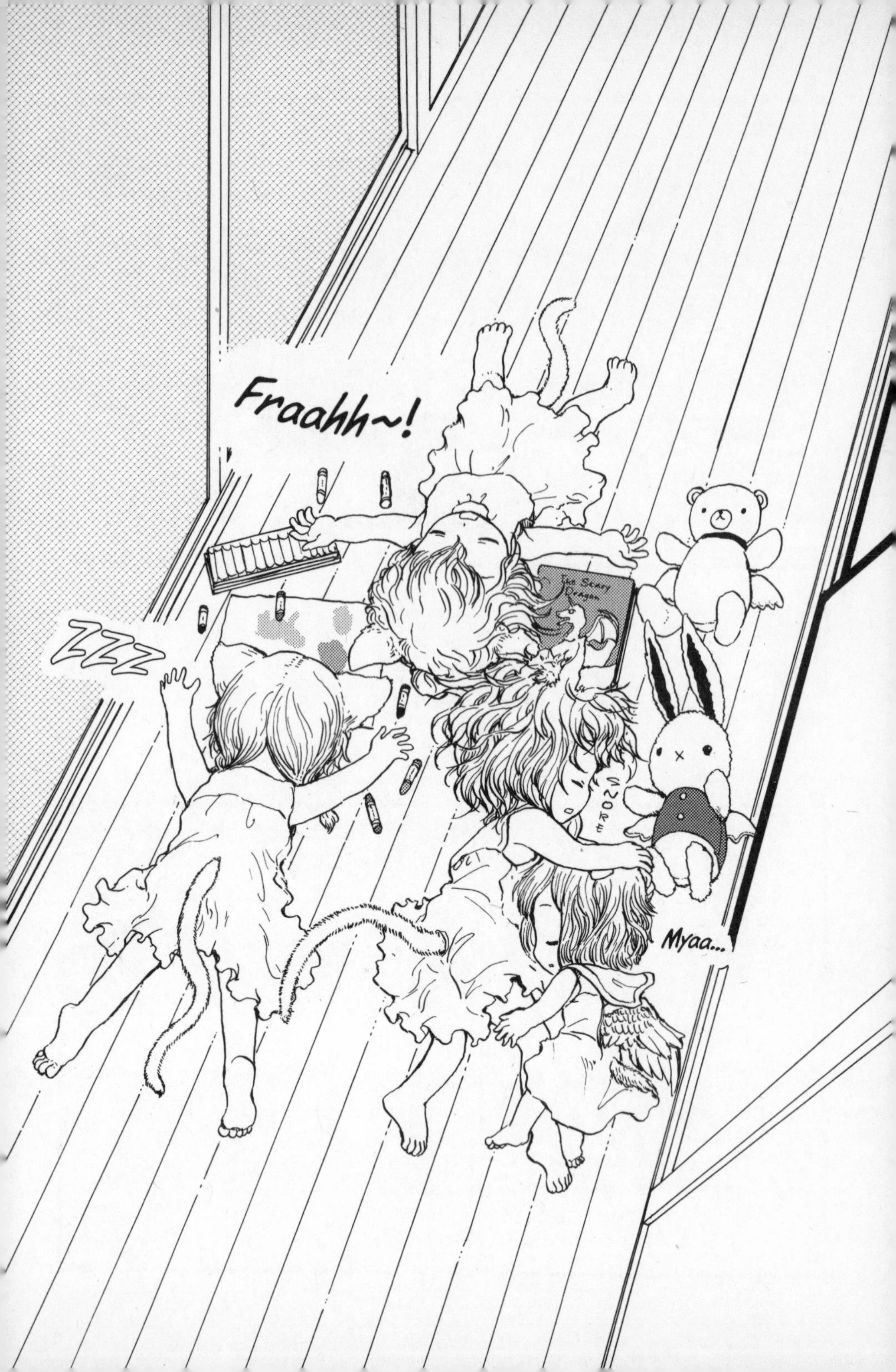
Fraahh~!
The Scary Dragon
ZZZ
SNORE
Myaa...

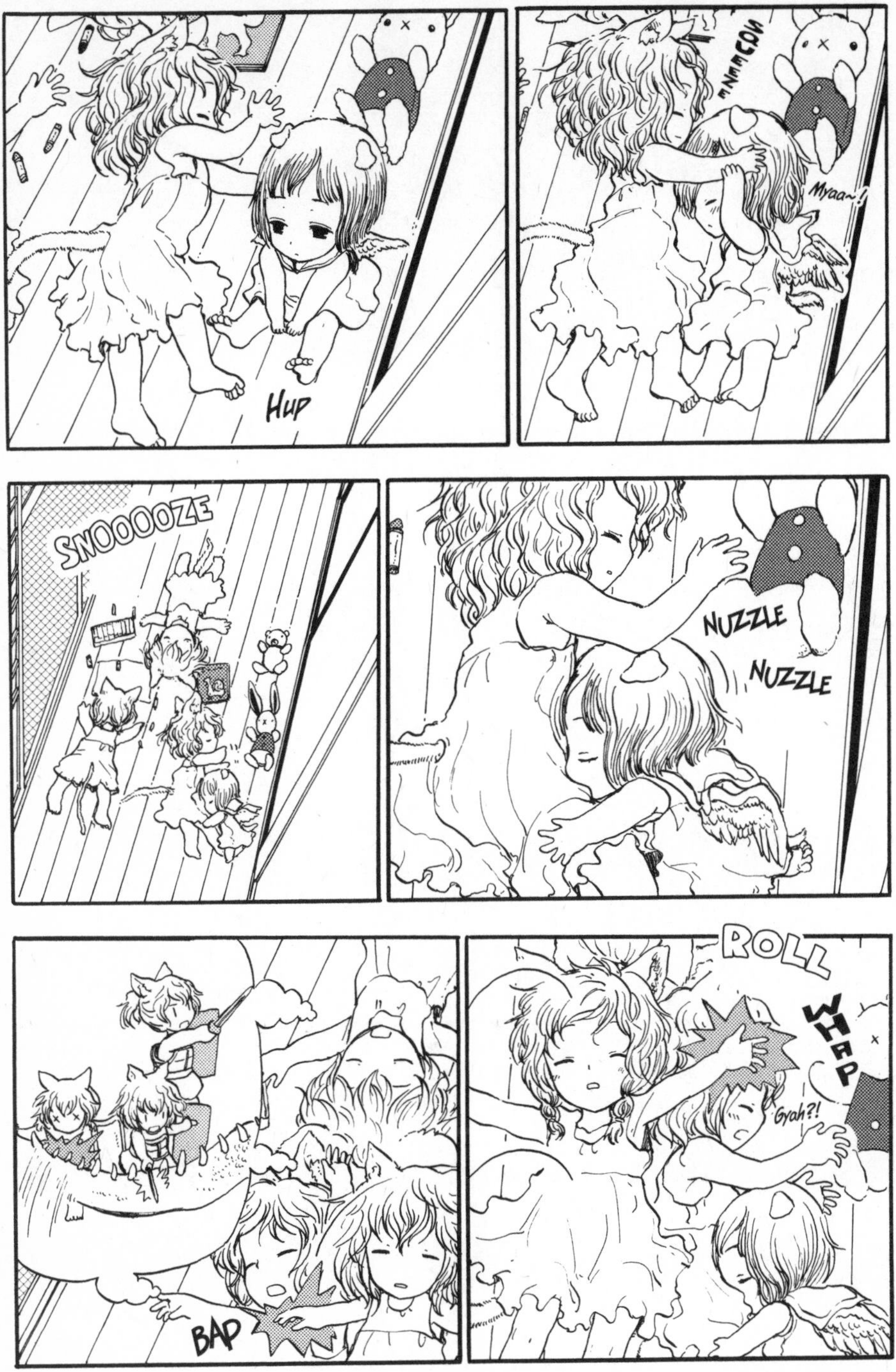
MNMMCOW
Myaa~!
Hup
NUZZLE
NUZZLE
SNOOOOZE
ROLL
WHAP
Gyah?!
BAP

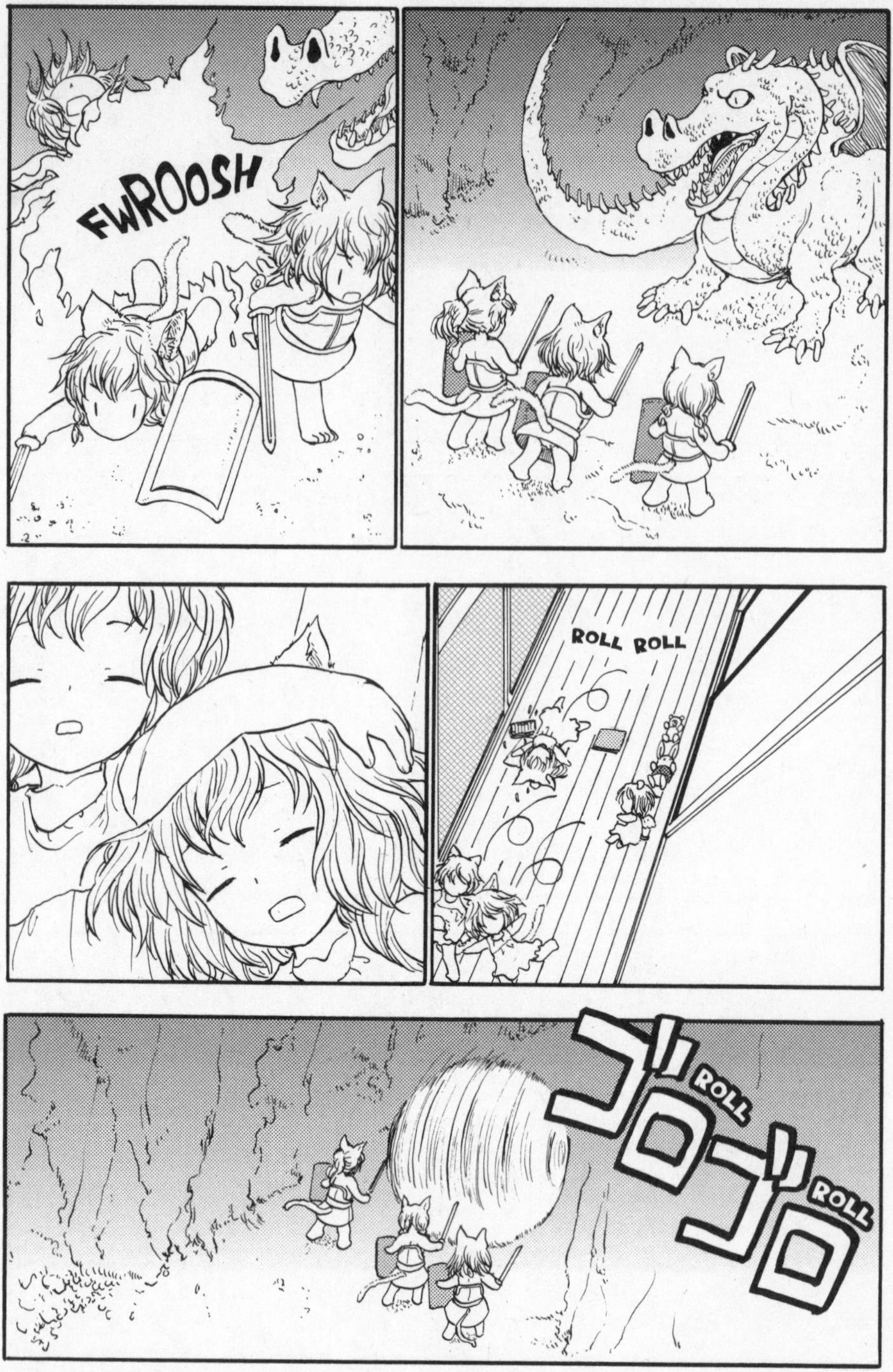
FWROOSH
ROLL ROLL
ゴロゴロ
ROLL
ROLL

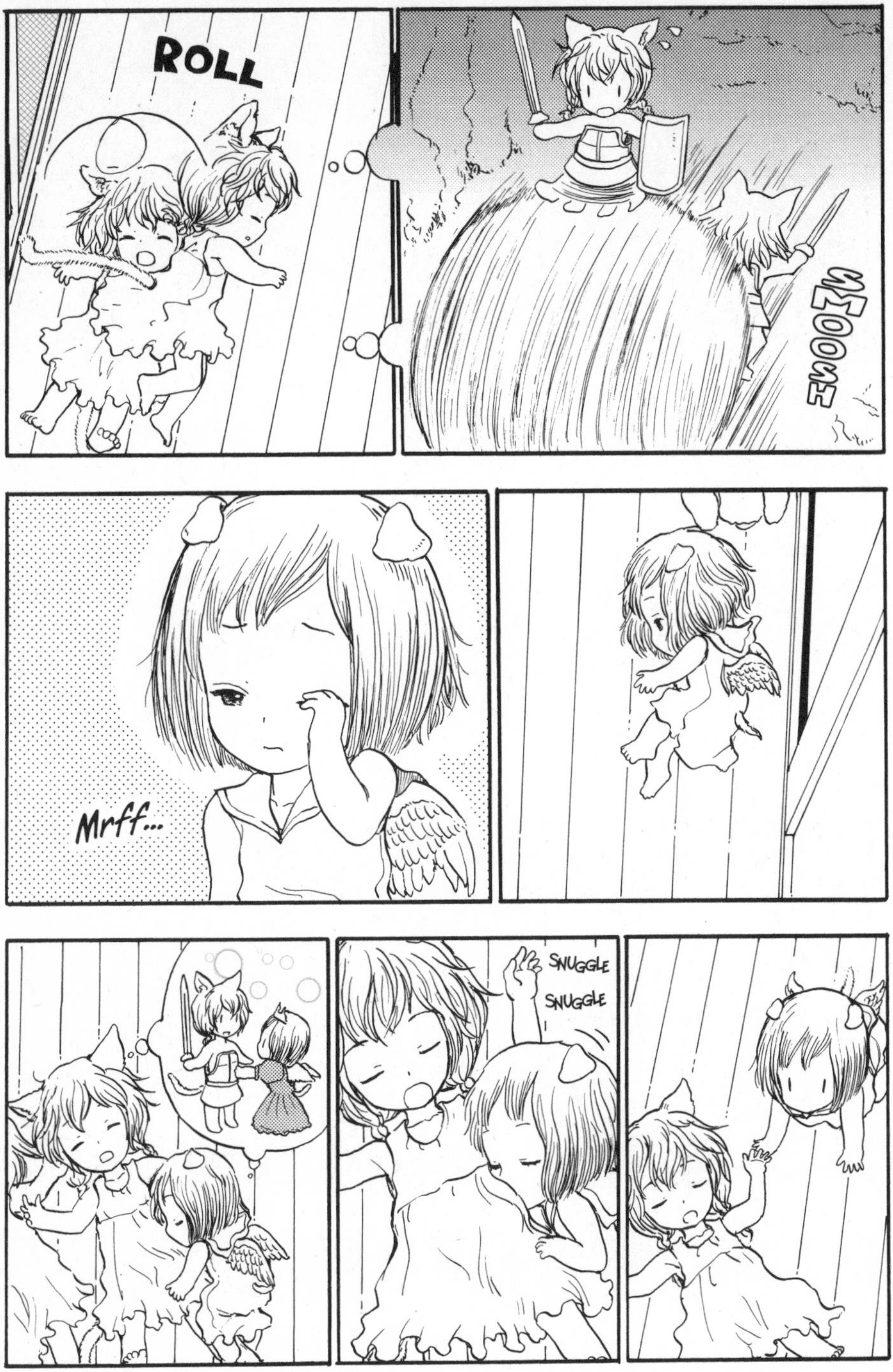
SWOOSH
ROLL
Mrff...
SNUGGLE
SNUGGLE

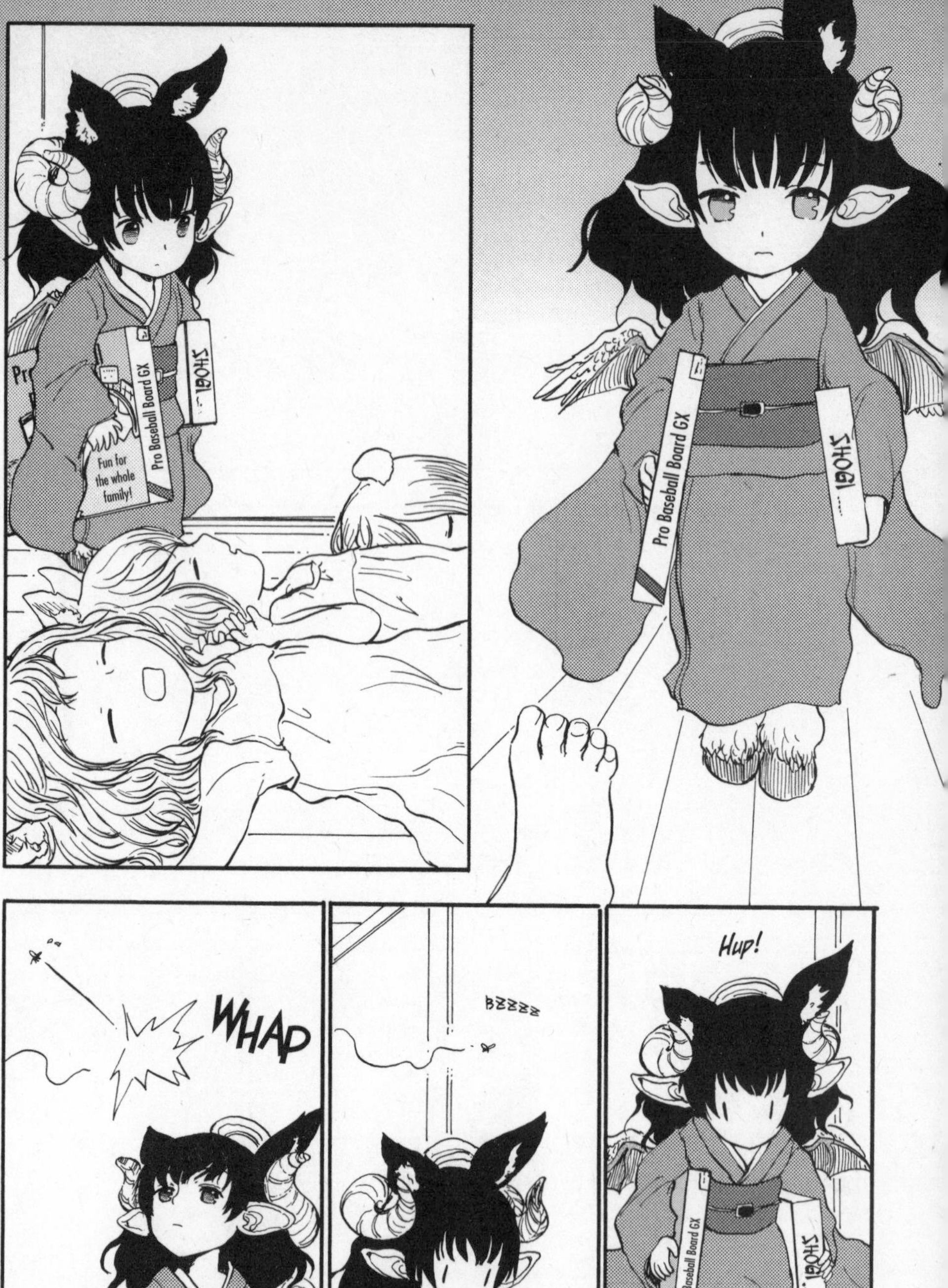

Pro Baseball Board GX
SHOGI...
Pro Baseball Board GX
SHOGI...
Fun for the whole family!
Hup!
Pro Baseball Board GX
SHOGI...
BZZZZ
WHAP

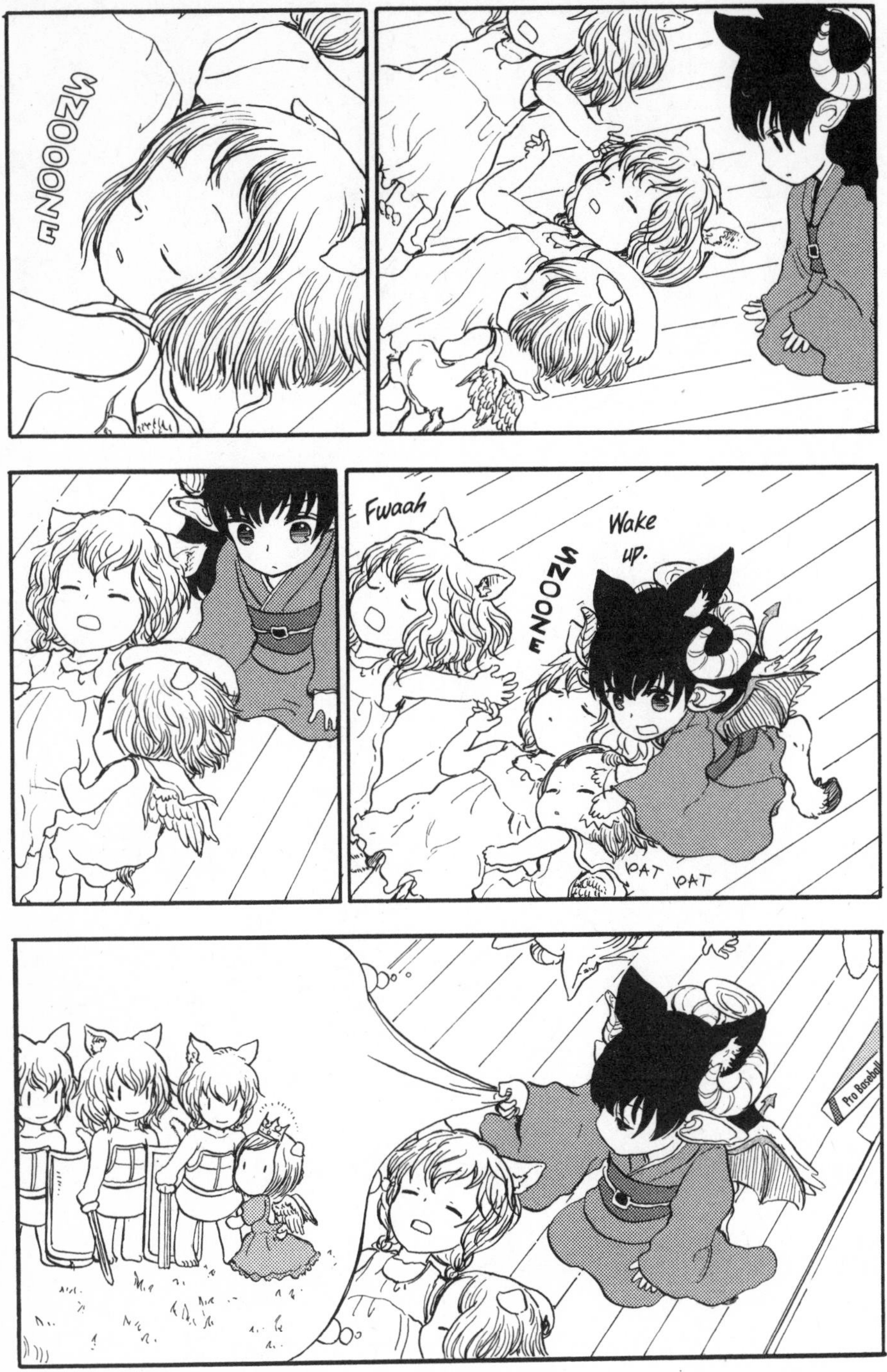
SNOOOZE
Wake up.
SNOOZE
Fwaah
PAT PAT
Pro Baseball

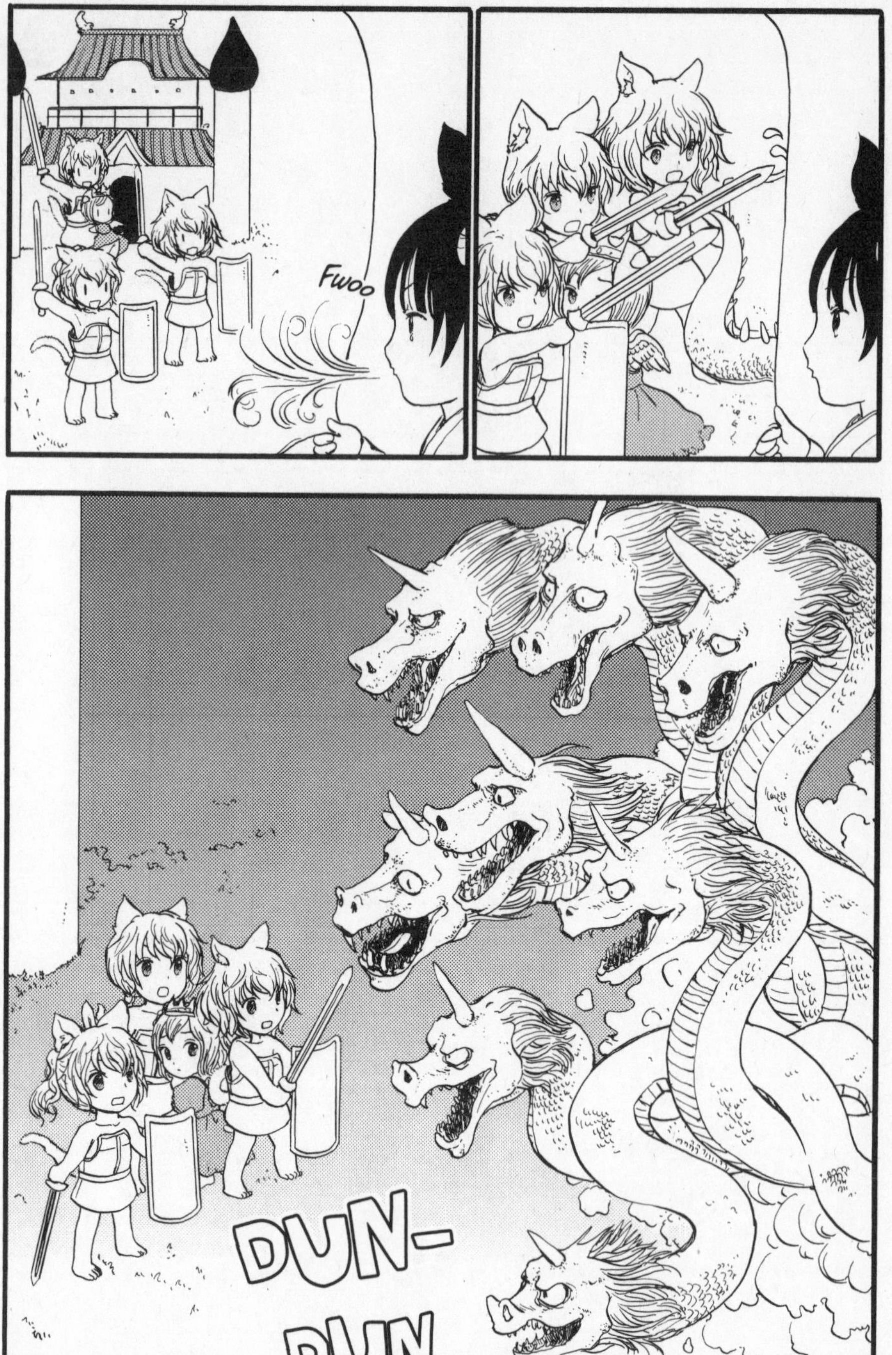
Fwoo
DUN-
DUN

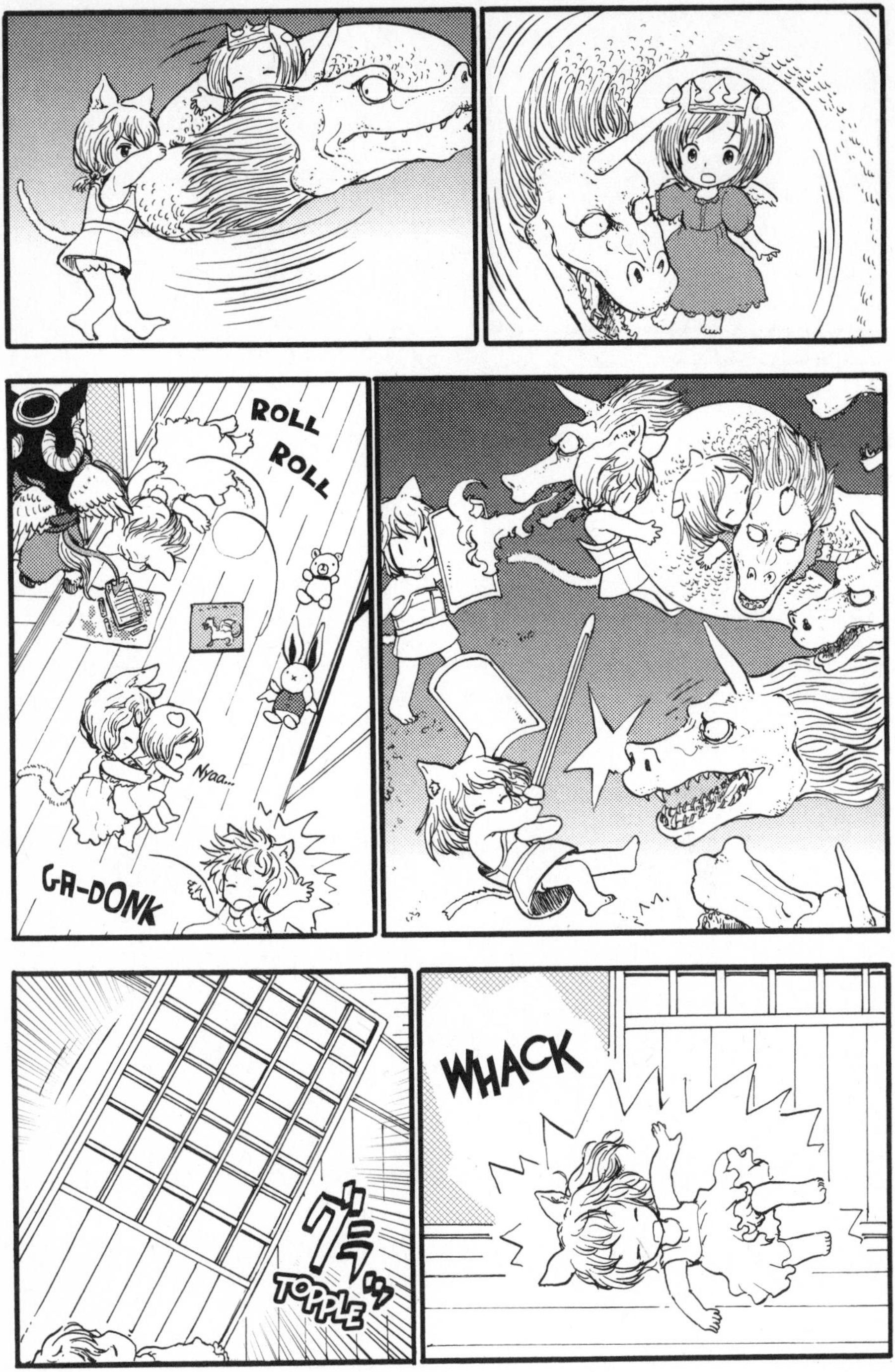
ROLL ROLL
Nyaa...
GA-DONK
WHACK
グラ…
TOPPLE

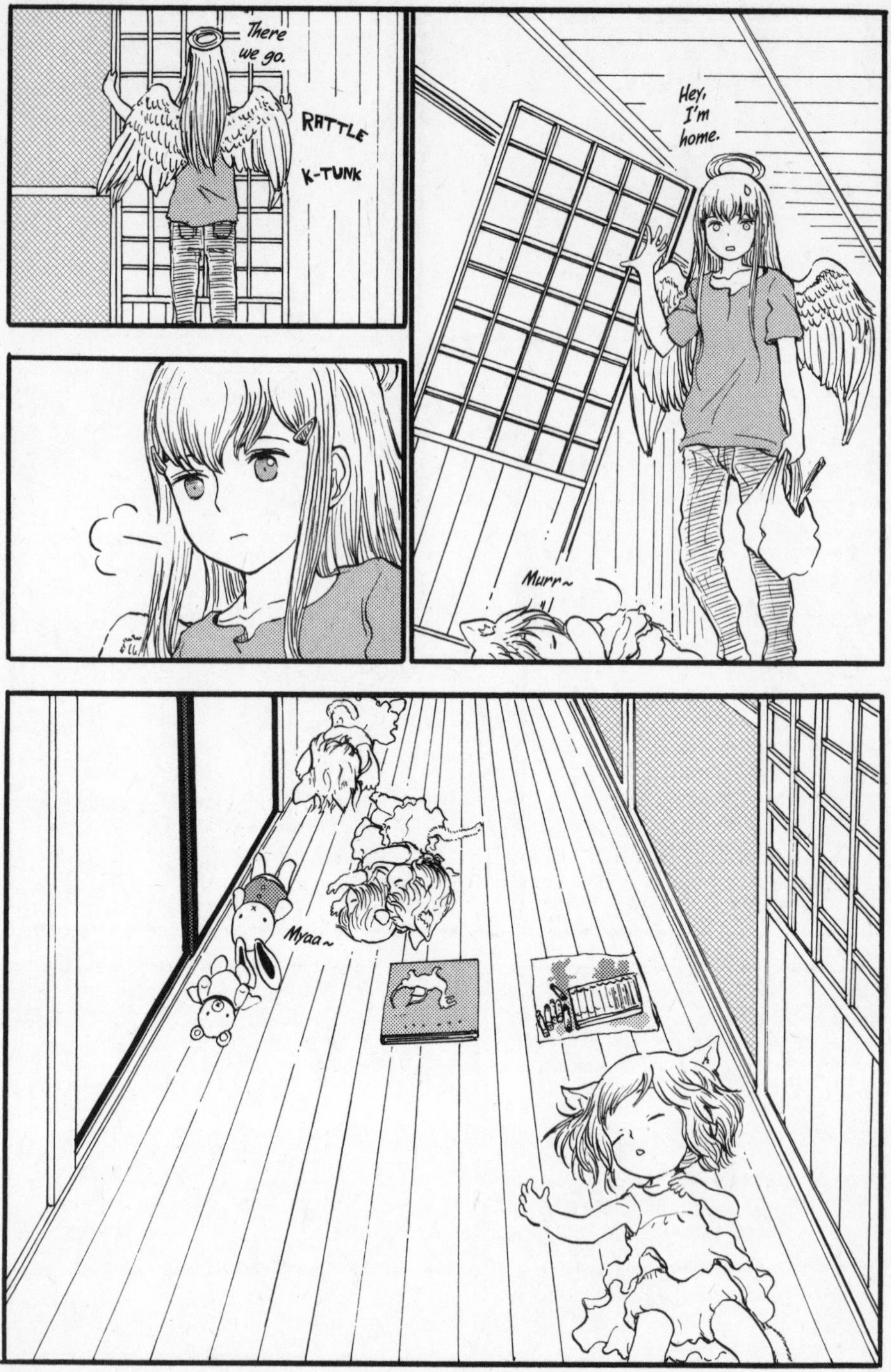
Hey, I'm home.
Murr~
There we go.
RATTLE
K-TUNK
Myaa~

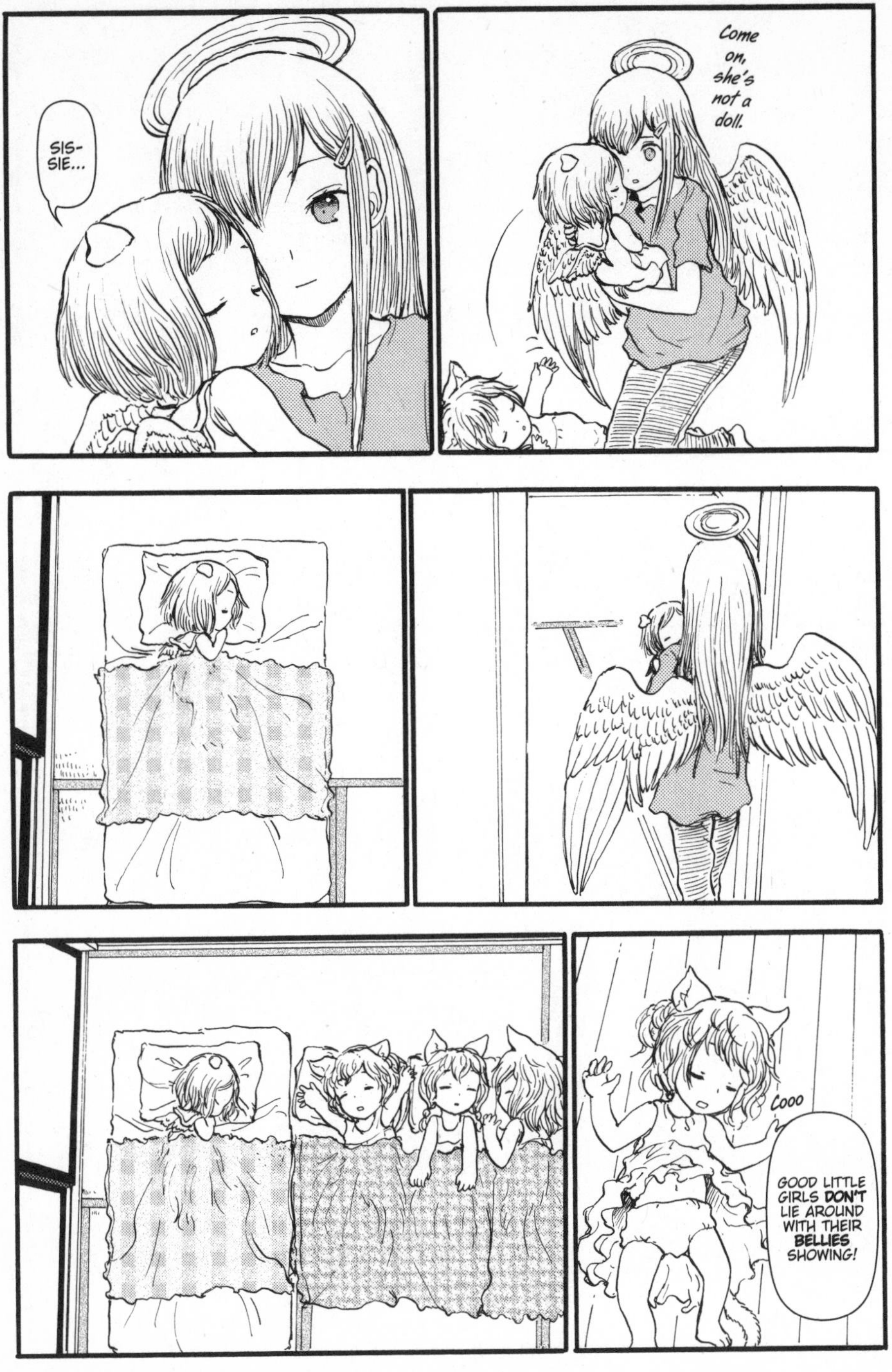
Come on, she's not a doll.
SIS-SIE...
Cooo
GOOD LITTLE GIRLS **DON'T** LIE AROUND WITH THEIR **BELLIES** SHOWING!

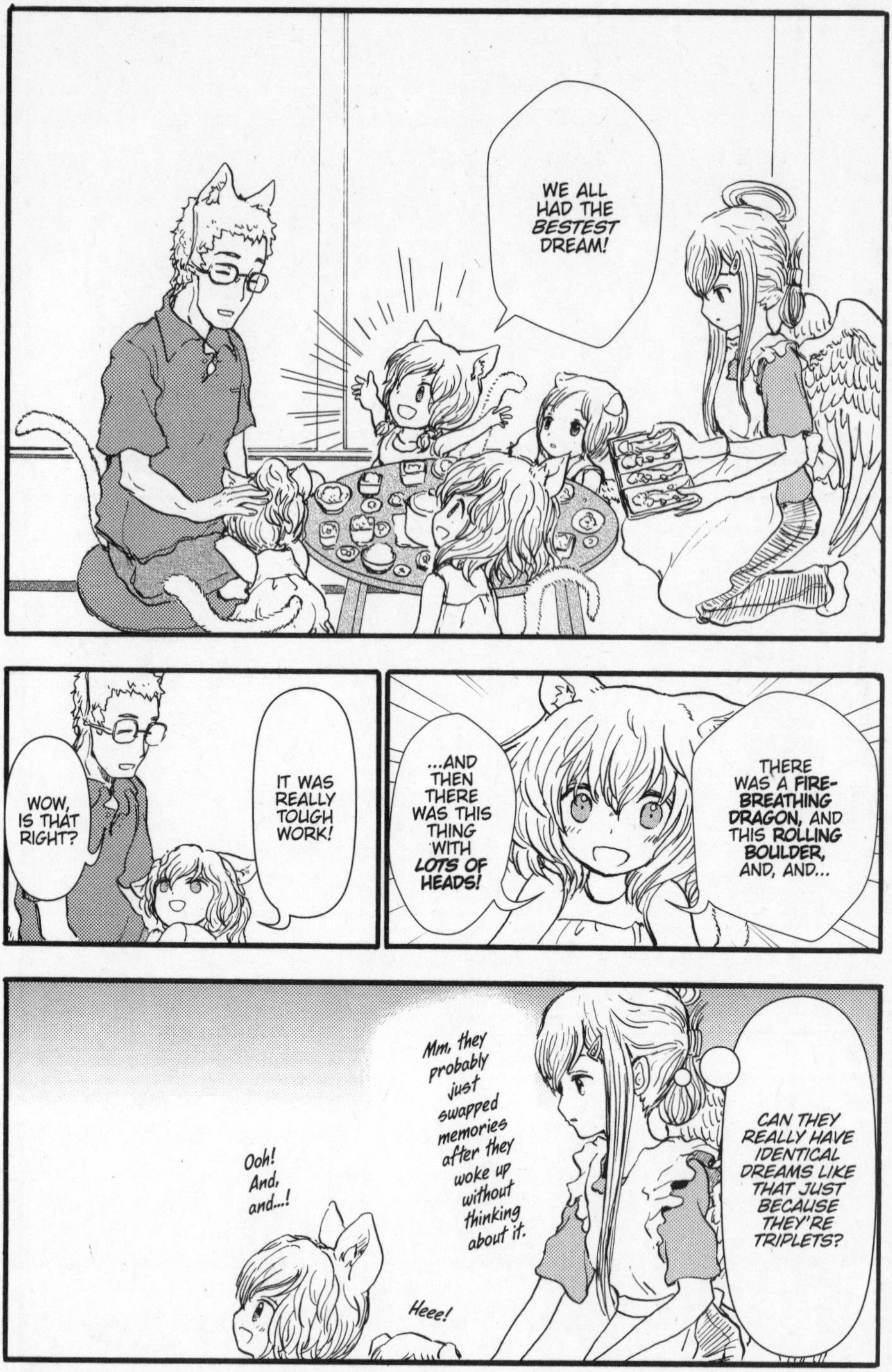
WE ALL HAD THE BESTEST DREAM!
THERE WAS A FIRE-BREATHING DRAGON, AND THIS ROLLING BOULDER, AND, AND...
...AND THEN THERE WAS THIS THING WITH LOTS OF HEADS!
IT WAS REALLY TOUGH WORK!
WOW, IS THAT RIGHT?
CAN THEY REALLY HAVE IDENTICAL DREAMS LIKE THAT JUST BECAUSE THEY'RE TRIPLETS?
Mm, they probably just swapped memories after they woke up without thinking about it.
Heee!
Ooh! And, and...!

A CentaUr's Life

GENETICS MADE EASY: LESSON 7
PROBLEMS ASSOCIATED WITH ATAVISTIC HEREDITY

WHILE SOME SCHOLARS LONG HELD THEORIES ABOUT ATAVISTIC HEREDITY--THAT IS, THE APPEARANCE OF TRAITS NOT ASSOCIATED WITH EITHER PARENT'S RACE--THEY WERE UNABLE TO TEST THESE THEORIES UNTIL THE ADVENT OF GENE-ANALYZING TECHNOLOGY. EVEN TODAY, KNOWLEDGE ON THE MATTER IS HARDLY COMMON. CONSEQUENTLY, IT HAS LONG BEEN A CAUSE OF TROUBLE FOR MANY MARRIED COUPLES. NOW, HOWEVER, IT IS POSSIBLE TO CONFIRM BLOOD RELATION BY MEANS OF MOLECULAR BIOLOGY. CHILD ABUSE IS OF COURSE AN ABHORRENT ACT REGARDLESS OF THE PRESENCE OR ABSENCE OF A BLOOD TIE, BUT THOSE WHO HAVE DOUBT THAT A CHILD IS IN FACT THEIR OWN SHOULD PROMPTLY GET CHECKED AT THE NEAREST MEDICAL CENTER. MEDICAL CENTERS ARE EQUIPPED TO OFFER PSYCHOLOGICAL CARE AND LEGAL SUPPORT IN THE EVENT OF THE UNEXPECTED. ONE SHOULD NEVER RESORT TO HOMEMADE DETERMINING METHODS, OR WORSE STILL, PRACTICES ROOTED IN KOOKY SUPERSTITION. WHILE FALSE DIAGNOSES HAVE STIRRED UP ATTENTION IN THE MASS MEDIA AT TIMES, SUCH PROBLEMS CAN BE AVOIDED BY SIMPLY SEEKING A SECOND OPINION. YOUR KNOWLEDGE AND EXPERIENCE ARE NO MATCH FOR THOSE OF A PAID PROFESSIONAL.

WHILE EXTREMELY RARE, THERE ARE KNOWN CASES OF BABIES OF NON-HYBRID PARENTS BEING BORN WITH TRAITS FROM THREE SEPARATE RACES. THESE CASES ARE PERHAPS THE GREATEST EVIDENCE THAT PEOPLE DO IN FACT POSSESS THE GENES OF ALL OTHER RACES. WHILE THE LIKELIHOOD WOULD BE QUITE LOW, IT IS THEORETICALLY POSSIBLE FOR ALL RACES TO MANIFEST IN A SINGLE ORGANISM.

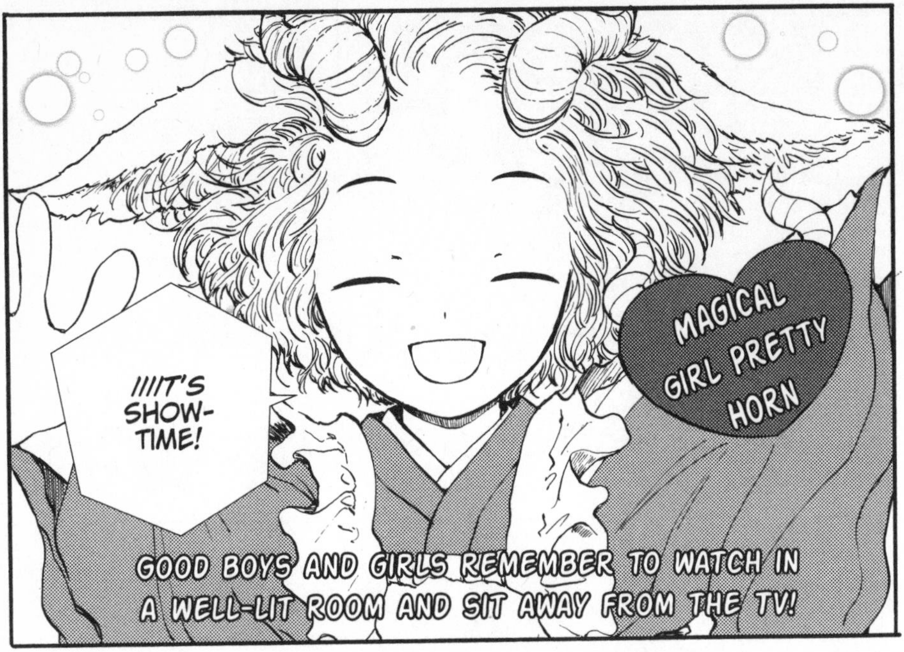
MAGICAL GIRL PRETTY HORN
IIIIT'S SHOW-TIME!
GOOD BOYS AND GIRLS REMEMBER TO WATCH IN A WELL-LIT ROOM AND SIT AWAY FROM THE TV!

CHAPTER 37

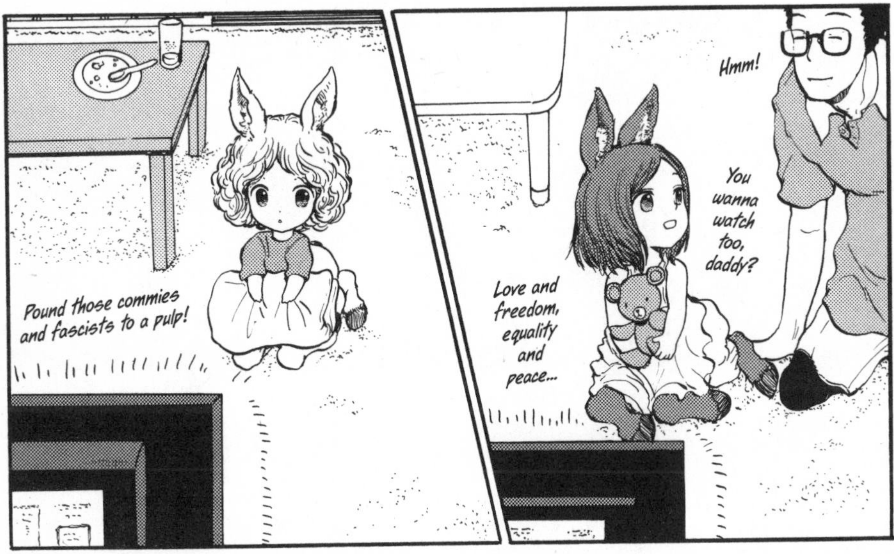
Hmm!
You wanna watch too, daddy?
Love and freedom, equality and peace...
Pound those commies and fascists to a pulp!

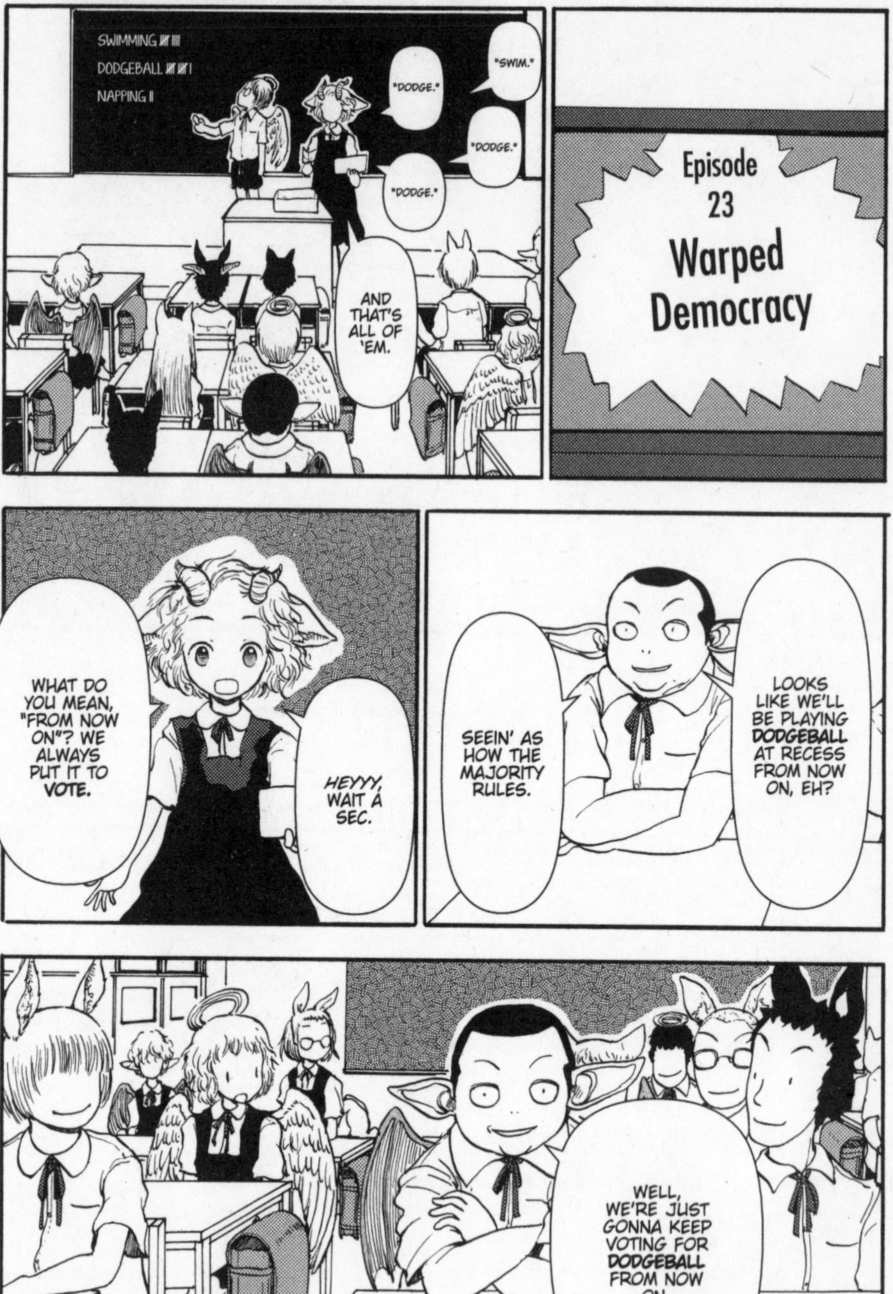
Episode 23
Warped Democracy
SWIMMING
DODGEBALL
NAPPING
"SWIM."
"DODGE."
"DODGE."
"DODGE."
AND THAT'S ALL OF 'EM.
LOOKS LIKE WE'LL BE PLAYING DODGEBALL AT RECESS FROM NOW ON, EH?
SEEIN' AS HOW THE MAJORITY RULES.
HEYYY, WAIT A SEC.
WHAT DO YOU MEAN, "FROM NOW ON"? WE ALWAYS PUT IT TO VOTE.
WELL, WE'RE JUST GONNA KEEP VOTING FOR DODGEBALL FROM NOW ON.

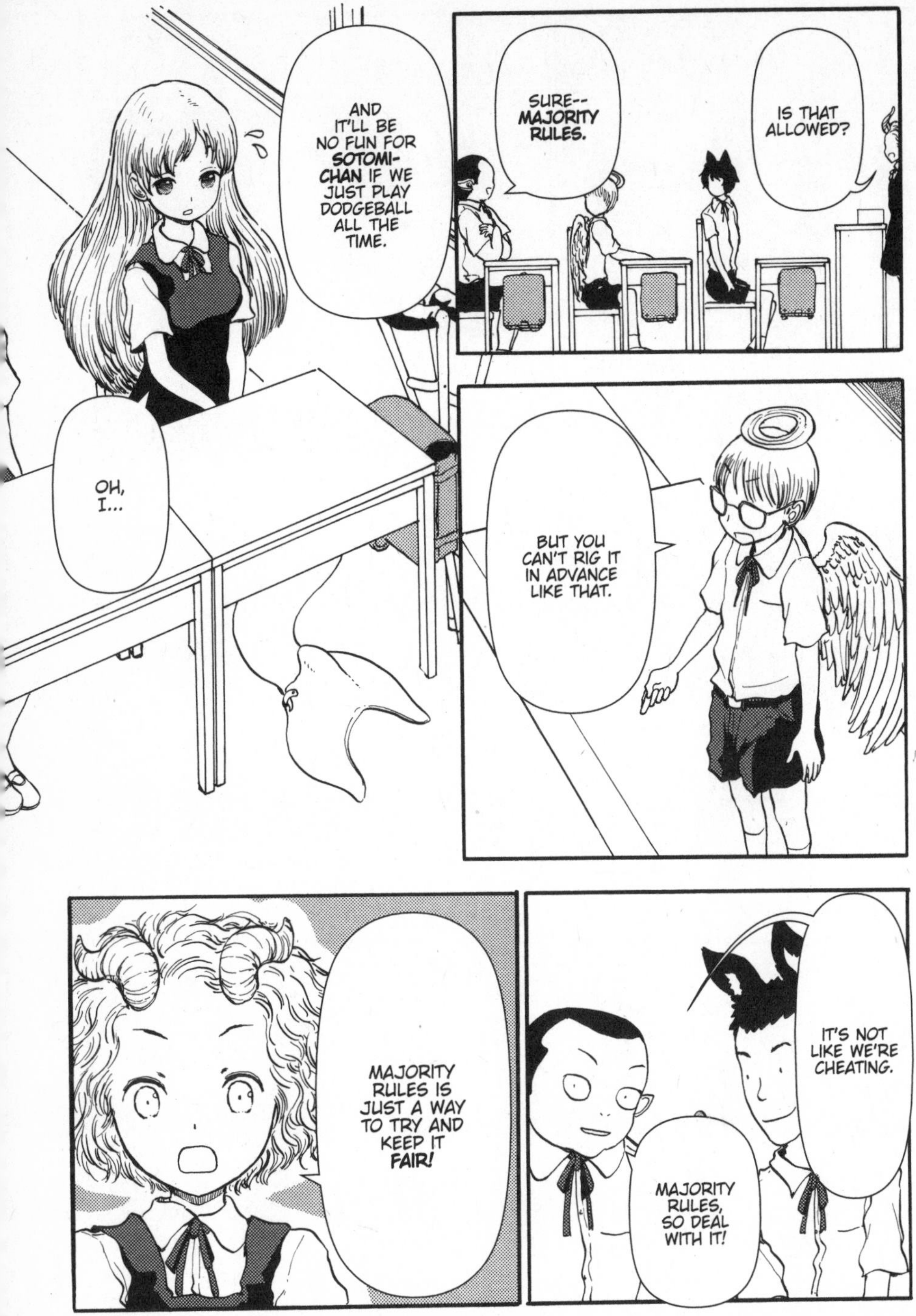
IS THAT ALLOWED?
SURE-- MAJORITY RULES.
BUT YOU CAN'T RIG IT IN ADVANCE LIKE THAT.
AND IT'LL BE NO FUN FOR SOTOMI-CHAN IF WE JUST PLAY DODGEBALL ALL THE TIME.
OH, I...
IT'S NOT LIKE WE'RE CHEATING.
MAJORITY RULES, SO DEAL WITH IT!
MAJORITY RULES IS JUST A WAY TO TRY AND KEEP IT FAIR!

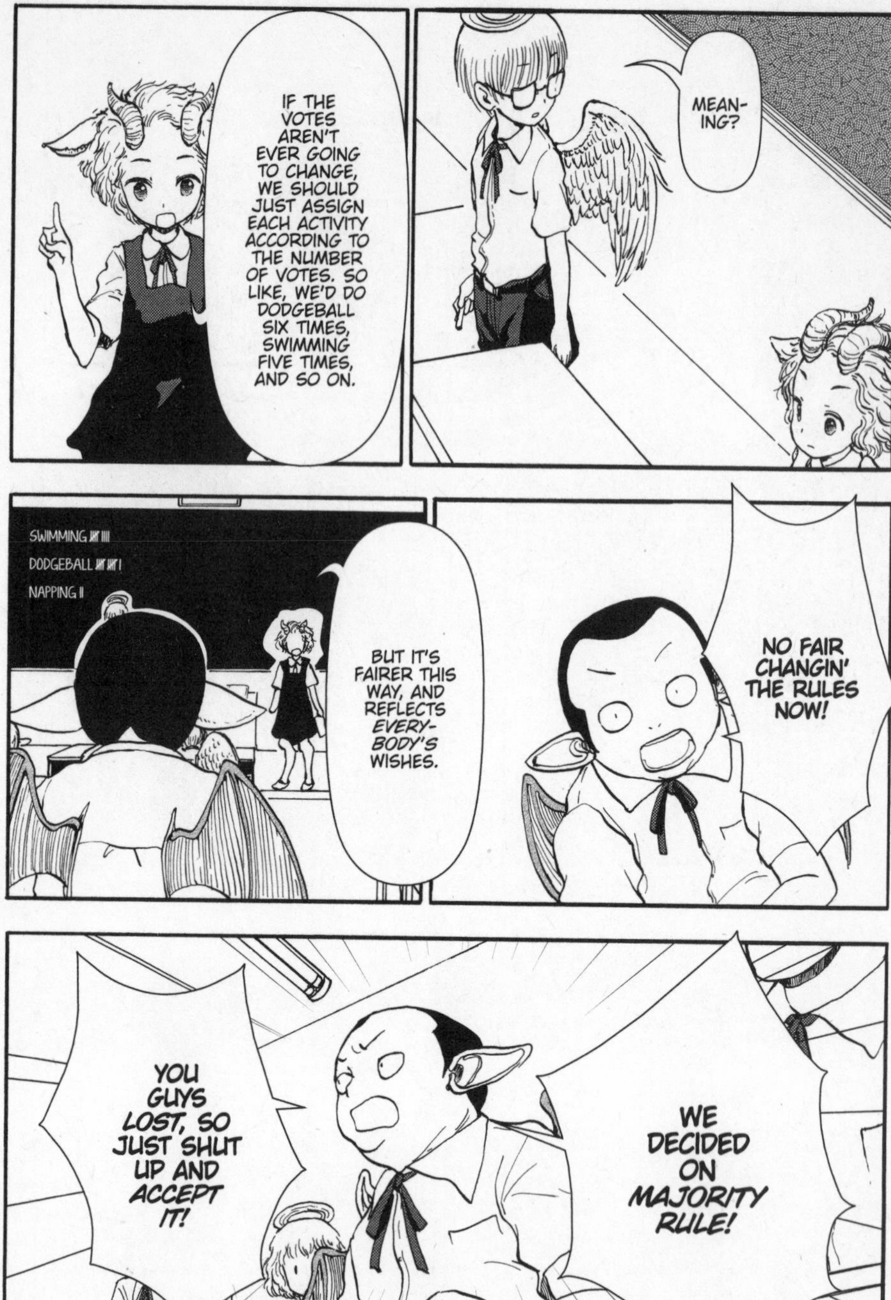
MEAN-ING?
IF THE VOTES AREN'T EVER GOING TO CHANGE, WE SHOULD JUST ASSIGN EACH ACTIVITY ACCORDING TO THE NUMBER OF VOTES. SO LIKE, WE'D DO DODGEBALL SIX TIMES, SWIMMING FIVE TIMES, AND SO ON.
NO FAIR CHANGIN' THE RULES NOW!
SWIMMING
DODGEBALL
NAPPING
BUT IT'S FAIRER THIS WAY, AND REFLECTS *EVERY-BODY'S* WISHES.
WE DECIDED ON *MAJORITY RULE!*
YOU GUYS *LOST,* SO JUST SHUT UP AND *ACCEPT IT!*

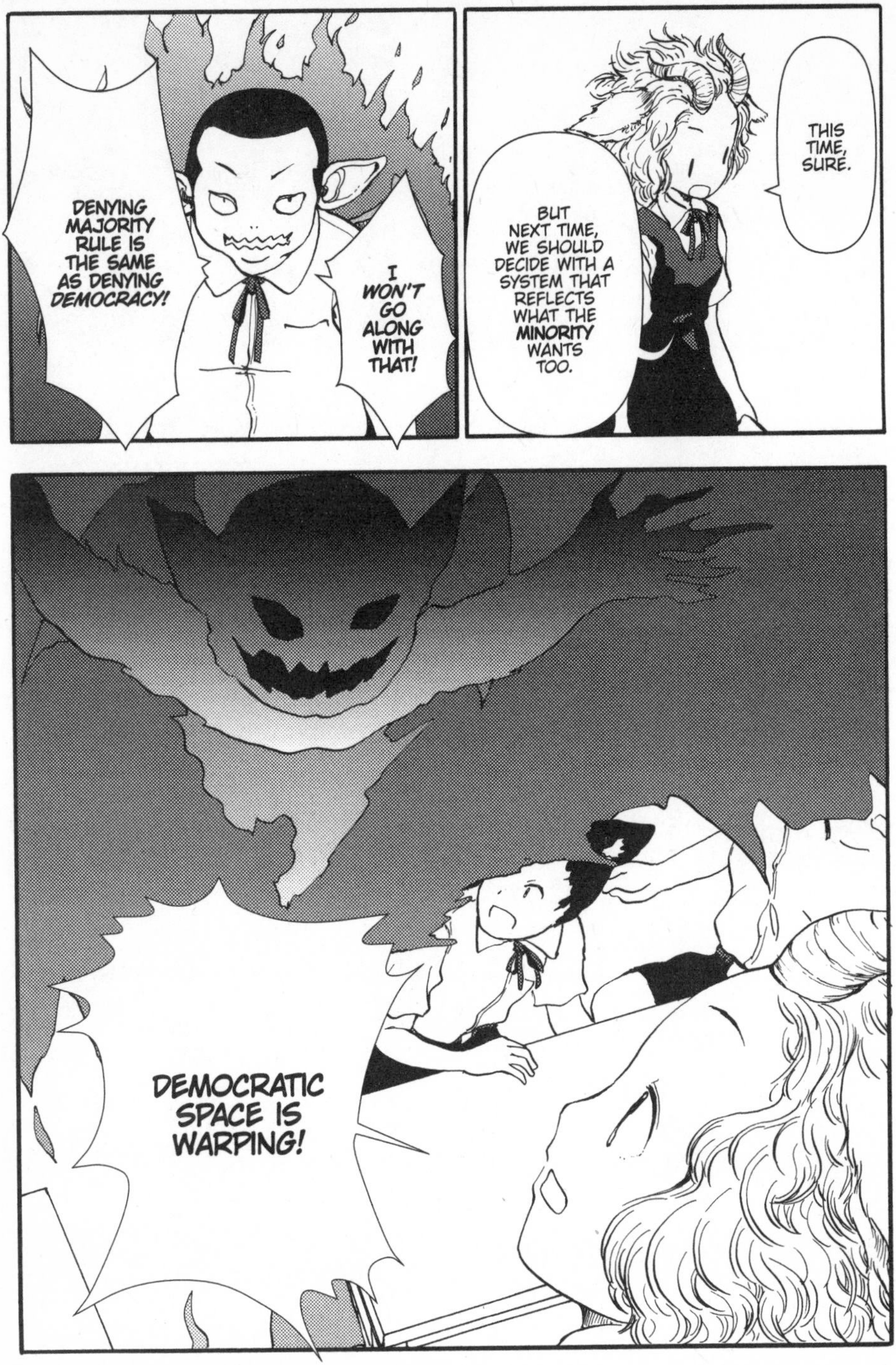
THIS TIME, SURE.
BUT NEXT TIME, WE SHOULD DECIDE WITH A SYSTEM THAT REFLECTS WHAT THE **MINORITY** WANTS TOO.
I *WON'T* GO ALONG WITH THAT!
DENYING MAJORITY RULE IS THE SAME AS DENYING *DEMOCRACY!*
DEMOCRATIC SPACE IS WARPING!

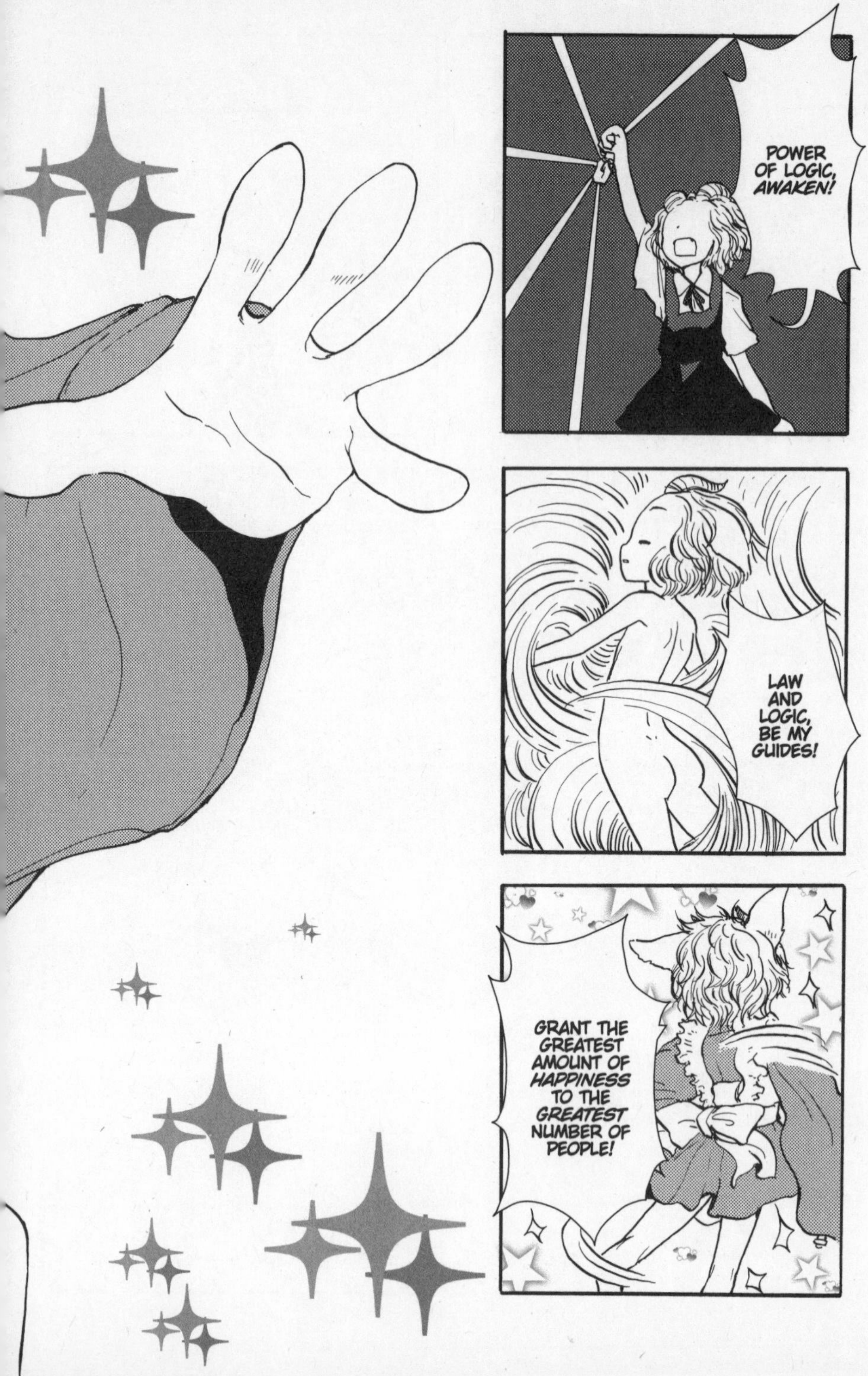
POWER OF LOGIC, AWAKEN!
LAW AND LOGIC, BE MY GUIDES!
GRANT THE GREATEST AMOUNT OF *HAPPINESS* TO THE *GREATEST* NUMBER OF PEOPLE!

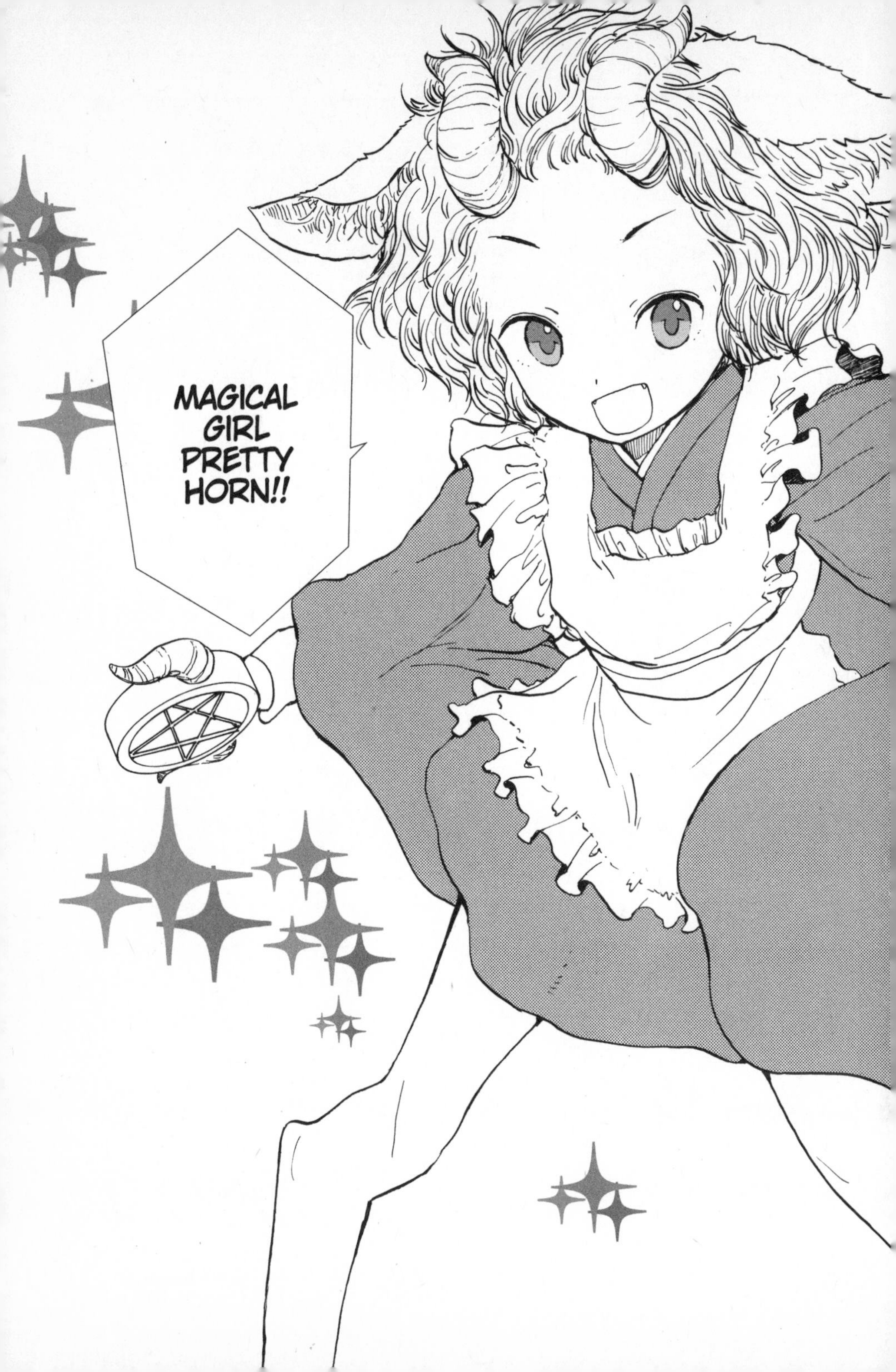
MAGICAL GIRL PRETTY HORN!!

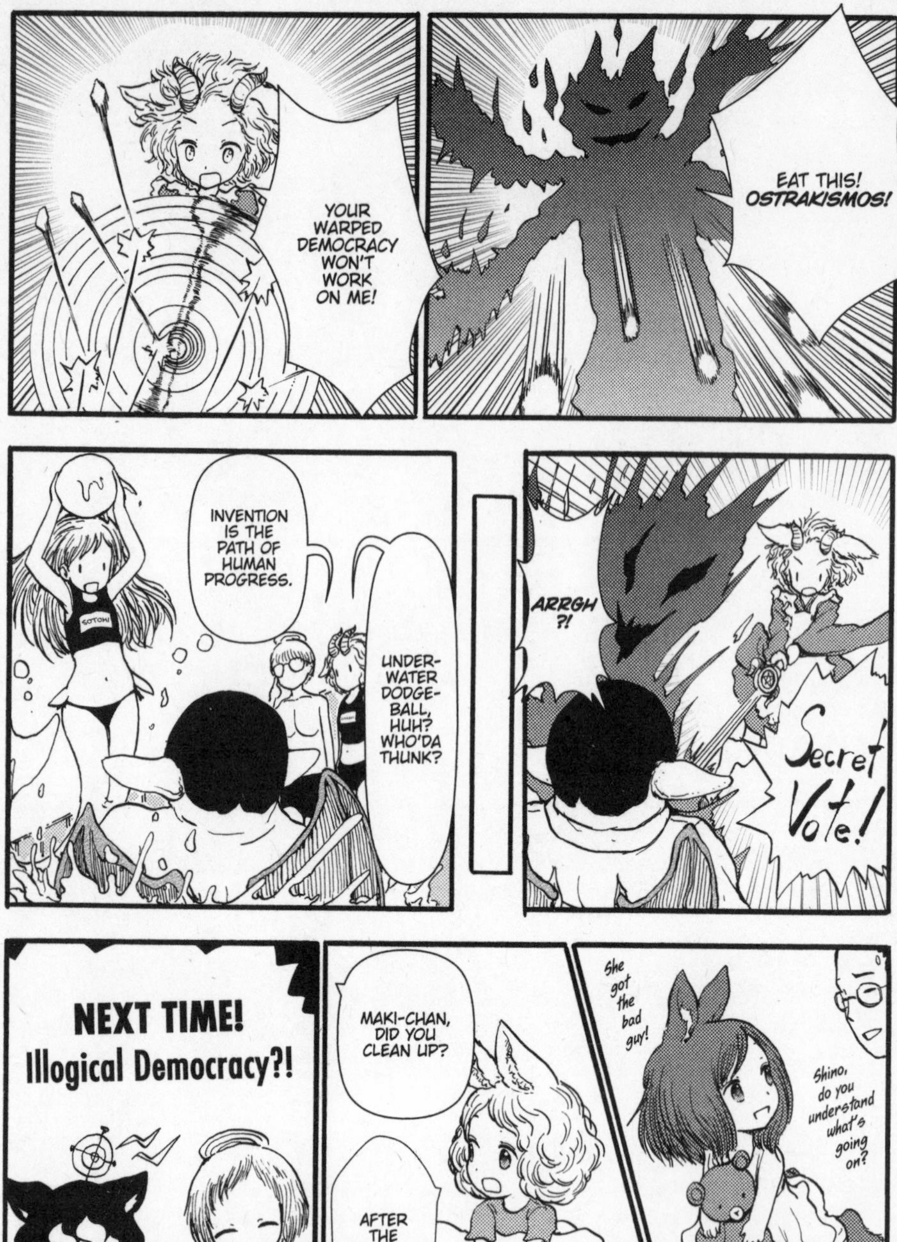
EAT THIS! OSTRAKISMOS!
YOUR WARPED DEMOCRACY WON'T WORK ON ME!
ARRGH?!
Secret Vote!
UNDER-WATER DODGE-BALL, HUH? WHO'DA THUNK?
INVENTION IS THE PATH OF HUMAN PROGRESS.
SOTOMI
She got the bad guy!
Shino, do you understand what's going on?
MAKI-CHAN, DID YOU CLEAN UP?
AFTER THE PREVIEW!
NEXT TIME!
Illogical Democracy?!
Conspiracy Theory
○×
Truth Science Society

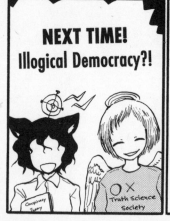

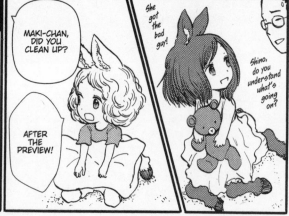

A Centaur's Life

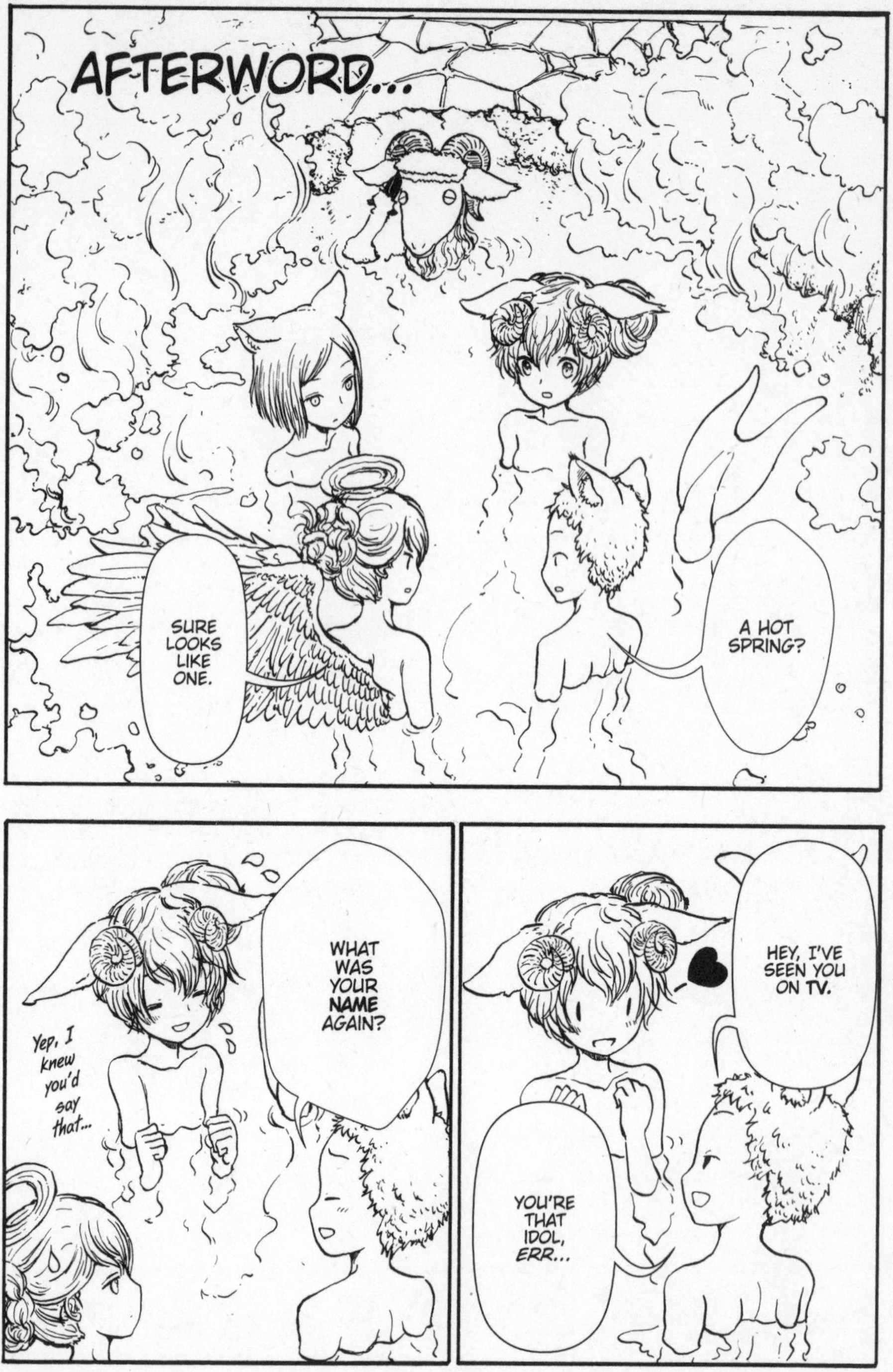
AFTERWORD...
A HOT SPRING?
SURE LOOKS LIKE ONE.
HEY, I'VE SEEN YOU ON TV.
YOU'RE THAT IDOL, ERR...
WHAT WAS YOUR NAME AGAIN?
Yep, I knew you'd say that...

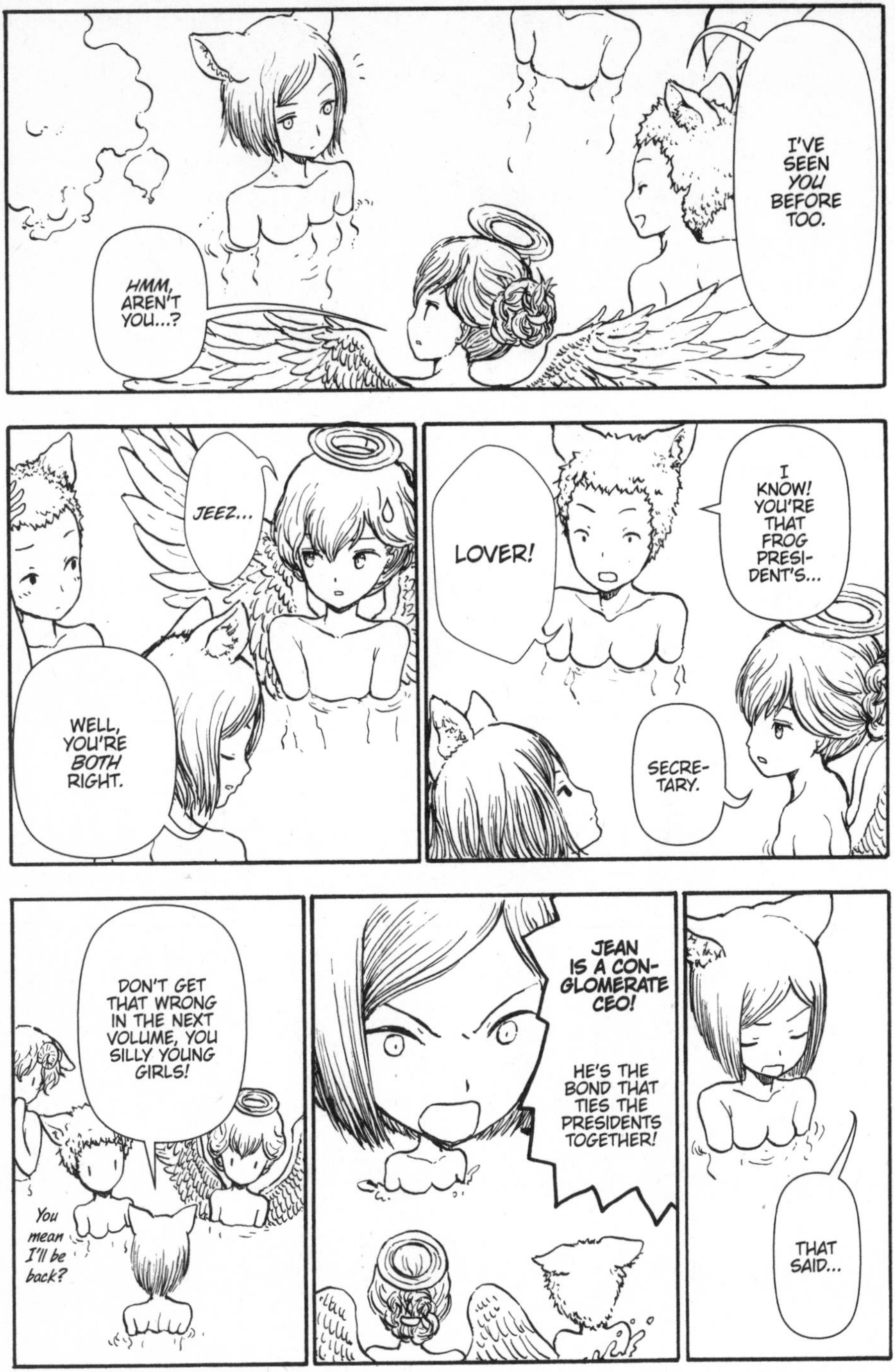
I'VE SEEN *YOU* BEFORE TOO.
HMM, AREN'T YOU...?
I KNOW! YOU'RE THAT FROG PRESIDENT'S...
LOVER!
SECRETARY.
JEEZ...
WELL, YOU'RE *BOTH* RIGHT.
THAT SAID...
JEAN IS A CONGLOMERATE CEO!
HE'S THE BOND THAT TIES THE PRESIDENTS TOGETHER!
DON'T GET THAT WRONG IN THE NEXT VOLUME, YOU SILLY YOUNG GIRLS!
You mean I'll be back?

A Centaur's Life

SEVEN SEAS ENTERTAINMENT PRESENTS

A Centaur's Life

story and art by KEI MURAYAMA   VOLUME 6

TRANSLATION
Greg Moore

ADAPTATION
Holly Kolodziejczak

LETTERING AND LAYOUT
Jennifer Skarupa

LOGO DESIGN
Courtney Williams

COVER DESIGN
Nicky Lim

PROOFREADER
Patrick King
Conner Crooks

ASSISTANT EDITOR
Lissa Pattillo

MANAGING EDITOR
Adam Arnold

PUBLISHER
Jason DeAngelis

CENTAUR NO NAYAMI VOLUME 6
© KEI MURAYAMA 2013
Originally published in Japan in 2013 by TOKUMA SHOTEN PUBLISHING
CO., LTD., Tokyo. English translation rights arranged with TOKUMA SHOTEN
PUBLISHING CO., LTD., Tokyo, through TOHAN CORPORATION, Tokyo.

Seven Seas books may be purchased in bulk for educational, business, or
promotional use. For information on bulk purchases, please contact Macmillan
Corporate & Premium Sales Department at 1-800-221-7945 (ext 5442)
or write specialmarkets@macmillan.com.

Seven Seas and the Seven Seas logo are trademarks of
Seven Seas Entertainment, LLC. All rights reserved.

ISBN: 978-1-626921-35-1

Printed in Canada

First Printing: July 2015

10 9 8 7 6 5 4 3 2 1

FOLLOW US ONLINE: *www.gomanga.com*

READING DIRECTIONS

This book reads from *right to left*, Japanese style. If this is your first time reading manga, you start reading from the top right panel on each page and take it from there. If you get lost, just follow the numbered diagram here. It may seem backwards at first, but you☐ll get the hang of it! Have fun!!

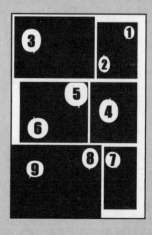